Keeping Children From Harm's Way

*How National Policy Affects
Psychological Development*

Annette U. Rickel
Evvie Becker

AMERICAN PSYCHOLOGICAL ASSOCIATION
Washington, DC

First printing August 1997
Second printing March 1998

Published by
American Psychological Association
750 First Street, NE
Washington, DC 20002

Copies may be ordered from
APA Order Department
P.O. Box 92984
Washington, DC 20090-2984

In the UK and Europe, copies may be ordered from
American Psychological Association
3 Henrietta Street
Covent Garden, London
WC2E 8LU England

Typeset in Palatino by EPS Group Inc., Easton, MD

Cover designer: Minker Design, Bethesda, MD
Printer: Data Reproductions Corp., Auburn Hills, MI
Technical / production editor: Alice Howes

Library of Congress Cataloging-in-Publication Data
Rickel, Annette U., 1941–
    Keeping children from harm's way : how national policy affects
psychological development / Annette U. Rickel, Evvie Becker.
        p.   cm.
    Includes bibliographical references and index.
    ISBN 1-55798-443-3 (acid-free paper)
    1. Socially handicapped children—United States. 2. Socially
handicapped teenagers—United States.   3. Problem children—United
States.   4. Child development—United States.   5. Child welfare—United
States.   6. Children—Government policy—United States.
    I. Becker, Evvie.   II. Title.
    HV741.R54   1997
    362.7'0973—DC21   97-20445
                                                                    CIP

British Library Cataloguing-in-Publication Data
A CIP record is available from the British Library.

Printed in the United States of America

Contents

Introduction

"I wish to have no connection with a ship that does not
sail fast, for I intend to go in harm's way."
—John Paul Jones, 1778

This book grew out of our association and experiences
while working in the United States Senate, as Congressional Science Fellows sponsored by the American Psychological Association. These experiences are described in detail
in the appendix to this book.

In the 103rd Congress, the mood was one of hope. A new
president came into office, one who was believed to be a
strong advocate for children and families. We were engaged
in legislative efforts to put prevention into the national
agenda and to develop a national health care system, and in
the passage of the first Family Leave law in the United States.

We were aware of the massive problems with violence in
our streets, in our homes, and in our media, of homelessness,
substance abuse, and teen pregnancy, but in 1993, the solutions seemed within our society's grasp. Little did we know
how quickly the tide would turn. Today, we scramble to save
the meager prevention efforts remaining, while social problems continue to escalate. Discrimination, lack of opportunity, growing rates of poverty, increasing desperation, widening gaps between rich and poor, a weakening public
education system, rising health care costs, and increasingly
limited access to care, with the attendant public health risks,
all make it easy to fall into despair about the United States'
potential to withstand this internal dissolution.

Outside forces also provide challenges for the next century:
the European Union, the wide distribution of products from
Asia, trade agreements such as the North America Free Trade
Agreement, and other market factors, combined with the
growth of technology and the electronic Internet system, all

require the United States to build a healthy, educated work-force if Americans are to survive and compete. However, the United States is one of only five countries that have not rat-ified the 1989 United Nations treaty on the rights of children.[1]

The expression *in harm's way* came to mind when we viewed the mounting costs of failed social policies and saw that Americans were sending the nation's children directly into harm's way. Thus, we wanted to write a book that would not just chronicle the problems, nor even one that simply offered politically unrealistic "pie-in-the-sky" solutions. We wanted to write a book that would help parents, clinicians, and policy makers understand what can be done in the everyday rearing of children to "inoculate" them against harm. Our intention is to focus on all families, not just so-called dysfunctional families. However, dysfunction is a mat-ter of degree and definition, and under certain economic and social circumstances any family can become impaired.

Discovering the source of the in-harm's-way quotation led us to our title: As Americans "sail" into the 21st century, we suggest thinking like John Paul Jones in the Revolutionary War. This society needs to strengthen families so that they may "sail fast" (i.e., be resilient) and be prepared to "go in harm's way"—into a future that is fraught with potential danger to subsequent generations. Only when families are healthy and strong will they be able to protect their children and keep them from harm's way.

We were also provoked by the commonsense point of view put forth by a Danish pediatrician as she described a parent who was unduly angry and upset over an adolescent son's normal rebelliousness and identity strivings. The pediatrician was incredulous, exclaiming, "She expects a life without problems!" Musing on this statement and the worldview it represents—that of someone whose country knew 5 years of Nazi occupation during World War II and postwar hardships

---

[1]The four other countries are Somalia, United Arab Emirates, Oman, and Switzerland. The treaty has been ratified by 187 countries (Limber & Wil-cox, 1996).

for 2 decades after, but also one whose country is among the most supportive of children and families—led us to consider that post-World War II generations of middle-class and upper-middle-class Americans often harbor a view that life should be problem free. The price that is paid for this view is that when problems arise, people believe they must be doing something wrong. This can lead to the "blame game" of finding someone to hold responsible, to self-recrimination, to anger and frustration, and even to depression.

Imagine that, like the Danish pediatrician, we as a society view problems as an inevitable part of life. We are not surprised or unduly perturbed when problems arise and do not waste energy trying to figure out who is at fault or blaming ourselves and becoming depressed. This leaves us free to focus on problem-solving strategies—a skill that, as it turns out, is a major predictor of resiliency.

This does not mean that people should not examine their behavior in relation to a problem. However, if problems are expected to arise, people may be able to step out of the emotional framework that attends a crisis (or avoid it altogether) in order to take clearheaded action. Instead of recriminations ("What did I do wrong?") and feelings of rage toward a family member who has let them down, people may be able to assess what works and what does not.

Our own research on child-rearing practices and childhood trauma, in designing intervention programs for high-risk children, adolescents, and parents led us to believe that interventions are needed at all developmental stages. Thus, the sequence of this volume reflects interventions throughout the life span. On the basis of these premises, it is clear to us that the following tenets are essential considerations:

1. The earlier intervention is undertaken in the child's life, the better the outcome.

2. Comprehensive approaches are more effective than limited interventions.

3. Services must be easily accessible to individuals, and aggressive outreach may in some cases be required.

4. Staff involvement in and knowledge of the situation are critical.

5. Stable, caring adults, including college student mentors, are important role models who can be a significant source of support for children and for parents.

6. Parental involvement is crucial to success with children.

7. Involvement of the school system is a key element of successful intervention.

8. Highly structured programs are most successful.

Chapter Previews

In chapter 1 we begin by painting a picture of the American family at the crossroad to the next millennium, a family that is increasingly diverse, disturbingly isolated from supportive individuals or structures, and exposed to all manner of stressors, from economic and work-related strains to violent environments. Basic tenets of family dynamics and child rearing are described in this chapter, and the needs of families resulting from today's changing circumstances are discussed, with particular attention to the issue of child care resources. In this first chapter we begin to discuss the implications of these elements of family life today for social policy, a topic to which we return at the end of the book.

Chapter 2 begins with some startling facts about where the United States ranks compared with other countries in regard to child health. Essential risk factors for infants and children are divided into three categories (genetic, prenatal and perinatal, and social–environmental) and are explained in detail. The public health model of prevention (primary, secondary, and tertiary) is presented, followed by descriptions of several exemplary early intervention programs, including Annette U. Rickel's Preschool Mental Health Project.

Chapter 3 delineates various types of traumatic experiences that may occur in childhood, including chronic illness, death and dying, natural disasters, divorce, victimization, and exposure to violence in the home and in the community. Developmental aspects of response to trauma are outlined, along with contextual factors that affect how the various types of trauma are experienced. Implications of the findings from this relatively new line of research inquiry are discussed with regard to prevention, intervention, and policy.

Chapter 4 focuses on adolescent issues, specifically those maladaptive outcomes that become most critical during the teen years: pregnancy, substance abuse, and suicide. Programs directed toward prevention of these negative outcomes are highlighted, including Annette U. Rickel's Detroit Teen Parent Project.

Chapter 5 returns to the discussion begun in the first two chapters of the interactions among family and community environments, parenting problems, and outcomes across generations. The research findings that are presented relate to child-rearing practices, parent–child relationships, and other factors both within and outside the family that affect its functioning. Relationships among all these factors are explained and presented in a broad model designed to aid the understanding of the intergenerational transmission of positive and negative outcomes.

Chapter 6 returns to a broader and more extensive discussion of social policy. The Personal Responsibility and Work Opportunities Reconciliation Act of 1996 is highlighted as representative of the 1990s era of social policy, which denies the reality of today's family needs. Otherwise known as the *welfare reform act*, the Act abolished federal entitlements that have for decades guaranteed a floor of support for children and families in times of need. The initial discussion of the potential destructive effects of this legislation is followed by a review of the history of prevention in this country. Recommendations for work within the current political climate are provided.

We suggest that the findings from research, history, and policy arenas all lead to the same conclusion: Solutions will be found when all systems serving children and families converge to work toward common ends. No one can afford to remain uninvolved and aloof in the face of the multiple crises confronting children and families at this juncture. Although funding has been steadily decreasing for prevention programs, many individuals across this country have taken it upon themselves to start prevention projects. Coalitions of concerned citizens and professionals are attempting make a difference in the lives of children. We urge everyone who reads this book to consider what more they could be doing to contribute to the betterment of children and families. Whether that means starting a prevention program, educating the press, or merely writing a letter to one's congressional representative, everyone can make a difference.

Annette U. Rickel
Evvie Becker

1

Parenting: A Major Commitment

Families are the context in which most children grow and develop. However, in the United States, the make-up of that family has changed dramatically throughout this century. In this first chapter we describe the nature of some of these changes, such as the increasingly isolated nuclear family, the trend toward single-parent homes, and the greater numbers of women in the workforce. The ramifications of these changes for society, for parents, and especially for children reared in today's world are presented. Some basic principles of family functioning, including issues of discipline and child development, also are introduced. Children benefit most from parenting that is authoritative and nurturing, and least from child rearing that is either overly restrictive or too permissive. Parents often need to be supported in order to achieve these child-rearing goals. Whereas some parents may find psychoeducation sufficient (e.g., developmental information), other parents may require more intensive intervention and support to allow them to become effective with their children. Environmental challenges confronting many parents in urban areas add to their dilemma. Finally, we delineate policy implications of our changing society in terms of family needs, with specific attention to the key issue of child care.

The American Family's Changing Face

One major change in American families, which has tended to accompany assimilation for many ethnic groups, is the shift from multigenerational households to individual family units. The movie *Avalon*, for instance, depicts a family of Italian immigrants changing over time from a full, multigenerational household sitting down to a meal at a large table to one in which two parents sit with one child, watching television and eating a meal from TV trays.

The latter scene was set in the 1950s, but it has been repeated across generations in many different ethnic groups. Among families of various ethnic origins, the broad tendency is toward isolation and alienation of the parental family unit from extended family ties. Isolation increases with time spent in America, particularly with social class mobility, and alienation often accompanies poverty. Today, 40 years after the scene depicted in *Avalon*, a further isolated family unit is common: that of a single parent, usually a mother, rearing her children with little support from family or from society. For many families, regardless of their composition, family meals are a thing of the past. In the 1990s, it is not *Father Knows Best*, but *Grace Under Fire*—the sitcom about a single mother struggling to make ends meet, that has popular appeal for American families. One in four children lived in a single-parent family in 1993, a 9% increase from 1985. Most of these households were headed by women (Center for the Study of Social Policy, 1993).

The increase in single-parent families, which often receive little or no support from the absent parent, has been an important factor in the increasing numbers of children living in poverty. According to the U.S. Bureau of the Census (1994), 20% of U.S. children lived below the poverty line in 1993, including 43% of African American children and 38% of Hispanic children.

Growing up in a single-parent household has been shown to affect outcomes for children in a variety of ways: They perform less well in school, drop out more often, and attain lower levels of educational achievement than their counter-

parts from two-parent homes; they have more difficulty finding work; and young girls from single-parent homes are more
likely to begin having children in their teens (McLanahan &
Sandefur, 1994). Many of these negative outcomes are the
direct result of poverty associated with female-headed households or the dramatic decline in income and related family
circumstances (e.g., neighborhood, school quality) following
divorce.

On the other hand, two-parent households have also seen
dramatic economic changes. In 1970, 39% of children had
mothers in the workforce; in 1990, 61% did (National Research Council, 1993). By 1987, only 29% of two-parent
households had one working parent and a full-time home-
maker. On television, Donna Reed had been replaced by
Roseanne, a TV mother working outside the home to make
ends meet. However, many women have entered the workforce by choice, joining the ranks of professionals in the 1980s
and 1990s in record numbers. Yet for large numbers of work-
ing- and middle-class families, two wage earners are a necessity, not an option.

Single parents and two working parents share problems of
adequate child care resources, role strain, increasingly stressful work environments (e.g., corporate downsizing leading
to greater responsibility and demands for the remaining employees; threats of layoffs and demotions hanging over employees where companies are cutting back), rising costs of
housing stretching the family dollar, and lack of supportive
relationships that might ease some of the burdens. The latter
stressor may be the result of a cycle in which work hours
interfere with peer socializing, where friendship bonds could
be formed. Peers all have similarly overstretched schedules,
and the extended family is geographically or emotionally dis-
tant.

Parents depressed by financial circumstances, overburdened by work, lacking in social support, and needing respite from child care activities are likely to have difficulty
attending to their children's needs in an optimal way. Interactions between high-risk infants and their mothers, as well
as between high-risk mothers and their infants, have been

found to be characterized by lack of excitement and responsiveness. This interaction pattern, which has been shown to occur when the mother does not read the infant's signals, has been linked to behavioral and emotional problems when the child reaches school age—problems such as hyperactivity, attentional difficulties, disturbances in peer relations, and childhood depression (Field, 1990).

Fathers—whether present or absent—also play an important role in a child's life. Despite a striking lack of attention by researchers to the father's role in child development, studies suggest that paternal influence on children is similar to maternal influence. Specifically, fathers have been shown to be similar to mothers in studies of attachment patterns, the effects of parental warmth, and the effects of time spent with children (i.e., amount of time vs. how time is spent; Lamb, 1986; Phares, 1992).

In assessing the lack of research on paternal contributions to child development, Phares (1992) noted four possible sources of this bias: (a) an erroneous assumption on the part of researchers, not borne out in actual practice, that fathers are more difficult to recruit as participants in research on children; (b) differential base rates of parental psychopathology that lead to studies of the effects of specific disorders common to men or to women (although depression, more common in women, far exceeds any other disorder in studies of the effects on parenting); (c) reliance on sexist theories (i.e., research is based on unexamined assumptions, usually with same-sex individuals, and then may also be generalized to the other sex without considering differences between them); and (d) research assumptions based on outdated social norms (e.g., investigators assume the model of a two-parent family with the mother staying at home to care for the children while the father works outside the home).

On the other hand, there is a danger in focusing too much attention on father absence or on comparing single-parent families to well-functioning two-parent households. The former denies the reality and viability of the single-parent family today, in which many children are successfully and effectively reared; the latter introduces a bias that does not account for issues of conflict or other dysfunction in two-parent homes, as Sidel (1996) has pointed out. Both approaches may lead to the neglect of policies that address the realities of single-parent families, which, as noted previously, many two-parent families also face: finding adequate child care, affordable housing, and support structures for parents.

The United States is hardly alone in seeing a rise in single-parent families, unmarried parents, and divorce rates, for indeed these same trends are occurring in many industrialized countries, particularly in Europe (Sidel, 1996). However, compared with most of these countries, the United States has a dismal record of response to these issues. We discuss these discrepancies further at the end of this chapter. Before addressing issues of social policy, we present a few basic principles of family dynamics and parenting.

Family Perspective

When clinicians and researchers talk about "dysfunctional families," many people may think they are saying that these families do not function. In fact, all families function. Dysfunction is generally defined as "abnormal" or "impaired" function. These terms are best avoided, because of their pejorative tone. However, when the term *dysfunctional* is used to describe families, the best definition to consider is "impaired functioning," because there is no definition of a "normal" family to contrast with "abnormal," and because "impaired" function suggests that function can be restored or "re-paired."

When we assert that all families function, we mean that all families operate with a set of rules and specific roles played by individual members. Cultural factors influence how these rules and roles are experienced; however, some general principles apply to all families, regardless of cultural differences.

Family rules are spoken or unspoken principles by which members interact with one another. These rules are as diverse and varied as any other characteristic of human beings; no two families have the same rules. A family rule can be as specified as an 8 p.m. bedtime for young children in the home or as nebulous as the unspoken rule that no one talks about grandma's drinking. Nebulous, unspoken rules are the most difficult for individuals entering the family, such as spouses or significant others, to understand. Differences between cultures may also make rules and roles in one family virtually invisible to an individual entering the system from another family or another culture.

As with rules, the roles played by family members may be as specific as who takes out the garbage or as unspoken as who in the family expresses the emotions felt by other members. *Roles* define the functions of each member of the family group. Rules and roles can be rigidly followed, so that changes that come naturally with child development and societal fluctuations create family crises because of the family's inability to adapt. At the other extreme, families may be so flexible and loosely organized that members feel off-balance and in a state of chaos most of the time. In the "healthy middle" is some blend of rigidity and flexibility that allows the family system to adjust to changes, while providing a firm enough structure to give comfort and security to members, particularly to the children.

Families pass these structures on through generations by verbal and nonverbal modes of communication. Sometimes these verbal and nonverbal messages are contradictory, which may lead to a great deal of stress within the family. When a parent verbally encourages exploration by the child while giving signals of anxiety in facial expressions, the child is left with an ambiguous message—"explore at your peril."

Also important to family functioning are the ways in which members manage closeness and distance. Displays of appropriate boundaries between individuals, between an adult caretaking unit and the children in the house, and between the family and outside groups or individuals model for children the ways in which closeness and distance are to be negotiated. Again, culture influences the degree of closeness and distance with which people feel comfortable, so that individuals coming together from different cultures may find differences in their degree of comfort that lead to misunderstandings in their relationship. Interpretations across cultures often are at the heart of such misunderstandings; that is, bringing one's own cultural interpretation to signals from another always carries the risk of misattribution.

Despite differences across individual families and across cultures, some type of family unit provides a structure for the negotiation of life-cycle challenges and transitions. Socialization occurs first for the child within the family unit, and values are transmitted from generation to generation. Throughout human history, children and their families have survived horrendous circumstances from within and without. In some cases, children who have survived deprivation and abuse go on to make great contributions to society (Carnegie Council on Adolescent Development, 1995). Most children survive childhood and manage to get by in life.

Behind prevention and intervention efforts are the goals of improving the quality of life for more people, creating a better society for the future, and giving children the best chances for thriving, not just for survival. When facing the realities of child rearing, however, it is important that caregivers keep in mind that perfect parenting is not a reasonable goal. Rather, many parents need to know that children are remarkably resilient by nature and that there are ways to increase the chances of a good outcome. It is important that they know that most children survive the parenting they receive and that most parents survive the child-rearing experience.

Parenting in Context

Overstressed parents today often turn to psychotherapy for solutions. Whether they come in for individual work or bring in a "problem child," they often harbor feelings of failure. Single parents in particular may believe that "everyone else" must be doing a better job than they are, or they may feel that others are not finding the job as difficult.

Those who come to therapy often lack the social support and connections to other parents that would normalize these feelings. In some cases, parents in the poorest neighborhoods may look around and see few models for effective parenting. These parents may have particularly unrealistic ideals of family life based on media images. Indeed, the stressors endured by impoverished single mothers may be so overwhelming that even the therapists working in public-sector settings begin to feel helpless when confronted by the reality of these women's lives. Providing only emotional support to those who need so much practical help may often feel like trying to put a Band-Aid on a bleeding artery.

One of the most important messages for parents today is that parenting in itself may be the hardest job there is. One mother who had a highly successful management career in industry confessed that her current full-time job at home—parenting her two children under age 5—was the most challenging work she had ever faced. She felt this despite substantial financial resources and a husband who shared in parenting and household tasks when he was not at work. Many two-parent families today would echo these sentiments.

Most parents find parenting challenging at best and a source of despair at worst. This is not to say that it is unrewarding; successful parenting can be one of the most rewarding experiences of life. However, the work of parenting is demanding for two parents, let alone a single parent, who perhaps struggles to make it in the world of work, keep the house relatively clean, and put meals on the table.

Years ago, it was common for two parents to be surrounded by extended family, a model that still survives in small-town America and in many industrialized countries. Not only the grandparents, but aunts, uncles, and cousins may provide everything from a place for the child to go, to affordable housing (e.g., renting of family-owned property).

Of course, this model is not without its problems, as Americans saw in the tragic case of Susan Smith, the South Carolina woman who in 1994 drowned her children in a desperate moment. Her own family history, with parental suicide in her childhood and an alleged molestation in her teens, hardly provided a base to build a supportive environment in which to rear her own children. Indeed, family circumstances such as these often lead individuals to leave their home towns to get as far away from family members as possible.

When grown children in this country strike out on their own, the family support system often declines. Whether young adults from rural and suburban areas head for urban areas to make their fortunes or to escape from family problems, they often end up meeting a partner in their new location, where jobs and other commitments lead them to stay. When a family crisis arrives, distances may prohibit family support even when family members want to help.

By now the African saying "it takes a whole village to raise a child" is a familiar axiom, particularly since the release of Hillary Rodham Clinton's much publicized book on the subject (Clinton, 1996), but the critical truth in the expression remains. Americans are most fortunate to have a first lady who has spent many years advocating for children and families. With her influence the Clinton Administration has sponsored major initiatives to promote optimum growth and development in the young citizens of our country. For example, the 1997 White House Conference on Early Childhood Development and Learning brought together experts who presented neuroscience research that emphasized the importance of human interaction to a child's development in the first year of life.

As the Clintons have often pointed out, in America parents are expected to rear children with little or no support from society. One mother of two used to say she felt that to be an adequate parent, she "needed at least a degree in nursing, psychology, economics, and education." Although degrees do not confer wisdom or even practical knowledge, and certainly not common sense, this mother was really describing her own feelings of inadequacy and lack of preparation for what she had found to be an overwhelming job. America must do a better job of training its citizens to become parents if we are to remain a powerful nation as we move into the 21st century. In the next section we discuss some of the common issues parents must confront.

Parenting With a Problem-Solving Focus

Problems are an inevitable part of child rearing. Parents who understand this are better equipped to face problems when they arise and are less likely to blame themselves, to see their children as the problem, or to engage in blaming school authorities or others around them.

Crucial to a problem-solving approach is a structure for handling whatever difficulties arise. As we described previously, the extended family often served that function in the past. Where society does not provide this structure (because of changing family structure combined with the lack of subsequent societal provisions of support, such as child care systems), exceptional creativity is often required in order to meet the demands of parenting.

From our work in preventive intervention and in clinical practice, we have found that parents often need reassurance that they are adequate. They need a sense of hope, they need to have feelings of frustration validated, and they need a sense of history about family rituals and obligations. Beyond that, there are additional areas that parents often find challenging. The first is in grasping the distinction between discipline and punishment, or the task of teaching versus simply controlling behavior.

Discipline Versus Punishment

Although the terms *discipline* and *punishment* may often be used interchangeably, the primary definition of each is dramatically different. *Discipline* is defined as "training to act in accordance with rules" and "activity, exercise, or a regimen that develops or improves a skill; training" (*Random House Webster's College Dictionary*, 1992, p. 383). *Punish,* on the other hand, means "subject to pain, loss, confinement, or death as a penalty for some offense or fault" (*Random House Webster's*, 1992, p. 1094). The relationship between the two, by dictionary definition, is that punishment can be a form of discipline, albeit a harsh one. In strict behavioral terms, punishment is any applied measure that decreases the likelihood that a behavior will be repeated.

Is it any wonder parents become confused? In general, it is important to increase the effectiveness of discipline; that is, parents must be able to train children to live in society and to optimize their relationships with other human beings. Implementing various types of "activity, exercise, or a regimen" enables parents to carry out this socialization. It is also important for parents to decrease simultaneously their reliance on punitive measures that result in "pain, loss, [and] confinement" and certainly those that could result in the death of a child. Examining the dictionary definition makes the connection between punishment and child abuse readily apparent. It is, however, a matter of debate whether all punishment is, by its nature, abusive. This issue is not addressed in this volume because it seems apparent that whatever the threshold for behavior defined as abusive, the use of punitive measures increases the likelihood of crossing that threshold at some point.

Specific behavioral interventions, without attention to cognitive elements (e.g., an appreciation for the most basic underlying beliefs and how to address them) are not likely to be effective. Simple instructions in the use of "time-out," are often insufficient to produce changes in parent–child relationships. Deeper probing of parental beliefs, experiences, and attitudes related to children and to the caretaking role often reveals the stumbling blocks to successful intervention. For example, parents who have experienced severe physical punishment in their own upbringing may react by repeating the pattern and staunchly defending their behavior by asserting that it was "good enough for me." This pattern is particularly striking in settings in which a parent is in treatment for severe chemical dependency, but does not make any connection between the experience of painful childhood penalties and his or her current need to escape through the use of substances.

Other parents who, as children, felt the sting of punishment are overly reluctant to impose any limits on their children. These parents need help examining their underlying beliefs, which often include hidden fears of losing control. Learning to distinguish discipline from punishment can be an important milestone for these parents, because it opens up the possibility that imposing limits is actually helpful to the child and functions as an important teaching task, rather than merely as a means of forcing one's will on the child. Permissive parents need help understanding that socializing their child is a key task and responsibility of child rearing. Once the underlying attitudes and beliefs are addressed, these parents are often quite amenable to learning behavioral tools and resources to help them better train their offspring.

Punishment by parents is often tied to the belief that control is the primary purpose of parenting. Parents who overcontrol may believe it is their duty to impose their will on the child; some may even have underlying assumptions that a child's will must be "broken," similar to breaking a horse of its wild instincts. In research, this belief has been conceptualized as *restrictiveness* and represents an authoritarian view of child rearing in which the parent attempts to force the child to conform to the parent's standards of behavior, which often extends to forcing conformity of feelings and thoughts as well. In this view, there are acceptable and nonacceptable feelings, thoughts, and behaviors.

Research has found restrictive parenting styles to be associated with a variety of problematic outcomes, which include lower self-esteem (Loeb, Horst, & Horton, 1980), lower levels of empathy (Field, 1981), and weaker social problem-solving skills (Jones, Rickel, & Smith, 1980). A recent study conducted with low-income mother–child dyads in a clinical setting (Prinos, 1996) revealed that mothers who had been substantiated by protective services as abusing or neglecting their children were significantly higher on restrictiveness than mothers with no protective services involvement.

At the same time, studies have repeatedly found that parents who exhibit the quality of nurturance tend to have better adjusted, healthier children (Baumrind, 1971; Hess & Shipman, 1967). Parents high on nurturance are more flexible in their child-rearing practices. Nurturing parents see children as people, listen to them, and share their own feelings and experiences with them, rather than seeing children as needing control. Research has demonstrated that parents can be taught to decrease their restrictiveness and increase their nurturance (Rickel, 1989; see also chapter 2, this volume).

Developmental Issues for Parents

A second area where parents often have difficulty is in understanding a child's developmental abilities and needs. Many studies have linked inadequate or abusive parenting with a lack of understanding of child development (Azar, Robinson, Hekimian, & Twentyman, 1984; Peterson & Urquiza, 1993). Rarely do parents have any education in this area, and usually they rely on what they learned from their own childhood experiences. Thus, intergenerational transmission of negative parenting practices is common in these cases.

Specifically, unrealistic expectations of the child's developmental capabilities have been implicated in abusive parenting (Azar et al., 1984; Azar & Rohrbeck, 1986). Such expectations include beliefs about the child's ability to care for himself or herself, to care for others in the family, to provide help and affection toward the parents, to stay alone, and to behave properly. Parents commonly make mistakes in these areas. For example, they may expect an 8-year-old to be able to get ready for school without assistance or to care for preschool siblings. Likewise, children may be expected to help with chores beyond their capability, to listen to and comfort a distressed parent, and to follow adult rules of behavior. Attributions of malevolent intent are often made by parents with such unrealistic expectations; that is, they believe the child to be willful, defiant, or selfish when the child does not meet these expectations. One tiny 3-year-old in a foster home was made to carry a large watermelon, and when she dropped it, she was hit. This is an example of demanding a developmentally inappropriate task at which the child is doomed to fail, attributing willful rebellion as the cause of the failure, and then punishing the child for that failure.

Early intervention succeeds best when parents are involved, because the child's most influential experiences occur in the parent–child relationship (Mesibov & Johnson, 1982). Education in developmental issues has been employed in several intervention programs as a strategy for improving parenting skills (Reisinger & Lavigne, 1980). These interventions provide parents with age-specific information while increasing their skills in behavior management and enhancing their ability to stimulate their child's intellectual development. Techniques such as role-playing and behavioral rehearsal are used to address real-life situations and to provide potential solutions to parenting problems (Rickel & Dudley, 1983).

Helping parents modify their responses to children's behavior has the potential to alter the parent–child relationship in a permanent and positive way. Working with parents provides the therapist with greater access to the natural environment of children—the home and family. Involving parents in this manner moves them from mere recipients of the therapeutic process to active cotherapists for the child (Berkowitz & Graziano, 1972). Behavior change in the child comes about more quickly when behavioral contingencies in the child's environment are controlled more effectively by the parents (Glogower & Sloop, 1976). As the primary socializing agents for the child, parents are in the best position to effect change in the child (Baumrind, 1978).

Numerous studies have demonstrated the effectiveness of modifying parental responses to children's problem behavior (Johnson & Katz, 1973; O'Dell, 1974; Patterson, 1980). Changing parental behavior has been found effective in eliciting positive changes in children with problems ranging from school phobia and speech dysfunction to immature, oppositional, and antisocial behavior. The importance of the professional's work with the parents to maintain consistent approaches to child management has been emphasized in these studies.

"Children Learn What They Live"

In general, children learn behavior from those around them. Lessons learned in childhood shape the developing adult. Family members are particularly influential; however, the surrounding environment and the peer group can be powerful forces against which families sometimes must valiantly struggle (*Children of War*, 1992; Luthar & Zigler, 1991).

Unfortunately, for children living in many urban neighborhoods, threat to survival may be a very real fact of life. In most dangerous circumstances, it is more difficult to give parents the sense of hope they so badly need. However, hope and reassurance must be found for these parents. Studies from many different arenas have shown that a close relationship with a caretaker or other adult is a strong protective factor for preventing negative outcomes (Emery & Forehand, 1994). Strengthening the parent–child bond is more critical the more risk laden the environment.

Parents in the most impoverished settings often struggle with a sense of despair at the conditions in which they must rear their children. In 1995, ABC's Nightline chronicled life in South Philadelphia and depicted this despair. South Philadelphia, parts of which look like the poorest sections of developing nations, has rapidly deteriorated since the influx of crack cocaine. In a desperate attempt to protect their children, parents there erected a simple wooden barrier between the worst of the drug-infested streets and the street on which their children played. Even so, dealers and users were in full view of the 4- and 5-year-olds, who could also readily see the violence all around them.

Poignantly, parents interviewed on the show spoke of trying to shield their children, only to have 4-year-olds talk about needles in the alleyway. One family had for many years owned a small house on the street and tried hard to keep it painted and livable, and to keep the outside surroundings at bay. But they eventually gave up, abandoned their home, and moved elsewhere. Within no time, the house became run down, was filled with drug users, and began looking like the surrounding area.

In such environments, hopelessness and despair move in early in a child's life, so that by the early teens, many youths cannot imagine a future and, in fact, do not even expect to live to see adulthood (*Children of War*, 1992). For example, one inner-city youth told his counselor: "Drugs are not the problem; drugs are the solution" (Allen, 1995). Use of substances to numb the response to intolerable circumstances, then, is one of the more costly lessons to be discovered in hazardous environments. Throughout history and in diverse human cultures, harsh conditions have often been cushioned by the use of alcohol or drugs, so that such behavior in urban "war zones" should come as no surprise to anyone with a sense of historical perspective.

The importance of a close relationship within the family cannot be overemphasized. Testifying before the Senate Labor Subcommittee on Children, Family, Drugs and Alcoholism in 1993, 15-year-old Liany Arroyo of Bridgeport, Connecticut, spoke dramatically about her experiences with inner-city violence. Liany—an honor student at a magnet school—reported a close relationship with her mother and grandmother, with whom she lived in one of the city's most high-crime sections. She and a few other Bridgeport youth had begun to speak out about the violence they witnessed, testifying first before the state legislature and then before Congress. She did not appear nervous before the U.S. Senate; in her life, fear was a constant she learned to manage:

> I live in a place where I must go through metal detectors and carry an i.d. card before I can enter school. I live in the America where I lie awake some nights listening to semiautomatic Uzis going off and not hear a single police siren come to investigate the matter. How do I know what kind of gun is going off? Easily. After having heard them so many times, I know what kind of gun it is just by hearing it. . . .The youth of the city of Bridgeport have become numb to the violence. We have seen as much death as any child in a war-torn country. This is the America that I know. One where I was once scared of

walking down the streets in broad daylight. Why am I
not scared now? Now I have nothing to lose. My sense
of childhood and all of the security that goes along with
it was lost a long time ago. I mustn't be scared. (*Keeping
Every Child Safe*, 1993, p. 15)

By most criteria, Liany would be considered a resilient teen-
ager. Yet her testimony speaks eloquently to the side-effects
of traumatic experiences that lie close to the surface even in
the most resilient children. She continued her testimony to
speak of the burial of two friends, and the belief that she
may not live past her teen years. She clearly reported symptoms of posttraumatic stress: psychological numbing, despair,
and a sense of a foreshortened future.

One can also see in Liany the factors identified with resiliency, which are reflected in her willingness to join with other
youth to speak out: close ties with caretakers, intelligence,
sociability, internal locus of control, and a problem-solving
orientation (Emery & Forehand, 1994). Liany's response
might also be categorized as a *survivor mission*, as described
by Herman (1992). That is, in response to having thus far
survived her dangerous and traumatic environment and with
an awareness that others have not been so lucky, Liany has
chosen to respond by speaking out, attempting to make a
difference—to have an impact on the course of events. A
well-publicized example of this phenomenon is the "Brady
bill," and the Bradys' work in attempting to halt the flow of
handguns in this country, after the shooting of Jim Brady. It
is one of the most potent forces in the course of human
history—individuals finding meaning in senseless acts of violence and using these acts as a catalyst to action in the
world.

Adult behavior is often a logical extension of the behaviors
learned in childhood, particularly those resulting from traumatic experiences (Briere, 1992). The despair and psychological numbing resulting from trauma can have lasting effects,
but so too do the factors of resiliency, which may propel resilient adults to join with others, to seek help, to solve problems, and to maintain (sometimes despite all signs to the con-

trary) a sense of self-efficacy and the belief that they are in control of their own destiny.

Thus, helping parents teach and nurture traits of resiliency in children can hardly be overemphasized. When children experience maltreatment or other childhood trauma, they learn coping behaviors that are then carried into other relationships in which the behaviors are often inappropriate to the circumstances.

Most maltreated children do not go on to abuse their own children (Kaufman & Zigler, 1987; Gelles, 1987); however, difficulties with interpersonal relationships, including parent–child relationships, may be a pandemic outcome for the adult maltreated as a child (Becker-Lausen & Mallon-Kraft, 1995; Becker-Lausen, Sanders, & Chinsky, 1995). These topics are discussed in greater depth in chapter 4.

Parents Helping Parents

For at least a decade, the importance of social support as a buffer against stress and as a protective health factor has been recognized. In 1988, Dunst, Trivette, and Deal reported that, across studies of different populations with a variety of needs, "informal support from personal network members" has been found to be a powerful factor in the promotion of healthy individuals and families (p. 32). The authors noted that the effects were strong, and they recommended the use of informal support over more formal support structures for families.

In 1987, Surgeon General C. Everett Koop formally recognized parent-to-parent support as an important factor in care for children with special needs (Hartman, Radin, & McConnell, 1992). Cooley (1994) outlined what he termed the "concentric rings of support" for families of children with special needs, which consist of three subsystems: (a) natural support, which includes immediate and extended family, friends, neighbors, churches, and others connected to the family; (b) informal supports, which are primarily other parents of children with similar problems, who may be encountered by chance, through informal networks, or through formal parent-support programs; (c) formal supports, including financial and health insurance resources, respite care, coordination of services, early intervention programs, and other services provided by government and public agencies (p. 118).

Cooley (1994) noted that the more "empty" the first two rings of support, the more dependent families will be on formal structures (p. 118). He also urged the inclusion of families in the planning and development of formal structures.

In recent years, a major reconceptualization has taken place among professionals providing mental health services for children and adolescents. Rather than viewing the family as the source of problems, work has been directed toward including families in the intervention process. Fuller participation of families in treatment planning has led to the development of family support networks, both formal and informal (Kutash & Rivera, 1995).

Family-support models have also been promoted for prevention of child maltreatment and neglect (Cole, 1995; Wolfe, 1993). Groups such as the Children's Defense Fund, the Family Resource Coalition, and the Harvard Family Research Project have been encouraging movement away from "rescuing" children and advocating community-based services that support the well-being of children, strengthen and stabilize families, and increase parental competence (Weiss, 1990).

Formal family-support services have been designed to meet the needs of families so that they are able to remain together and to alleviate some of the stressors that threaten them. Initially, respite services were the primary purpose of such programs. A broad range of services has become more common, including self-help groups, advocacy, education and training, information and referrals, and cash or other assistance to meet basic needs, in addition to respite care (Kutash & Rivera, 1995).

The less formal parent support groups are usually those devoted to self-help and support approaches, although there may be wide variation in membership, formality, and duration of groups (Kutash & Rivera, 1995). Typical groups are made up of between 4 and 20 members who meet regularly to discuss mutual concerns. Emotional support has been most often cited by parents as the primary value of these groups (by 72% of parents in one national sample). Overall, research findings have tended to be positive for the effects of these groups.

Hartman, Radin, and McConnell (1992) outlined a number of reasons that parents are better able to support other parents than professionals may be. Although the authors were specifically addressing the issue of parents of children with special health needs, these factors may be applied to mental health issues as well:

1. Support parents can be consistently available in a way that others cannot be (family members because of their emotional reactions; formal caretakers because of the nature of the relationship); they may have more time available to give.

2. Support parents are usually able to be nonjudgemental; they understand the issues confronting the parents, from their own experiences.

3. Support parents share feelings with the parents; they understand and empathize with the stress the parents are under; they know that support will be needed for the long term.

4. Support parents can provide positive models from their own successes and failures. Membership in a support group helps parents find a new social reference group where their experiences can be normalized.

5. Support groups help parents make more efficient and effective use of professional support. Shared experiences help parents know who, when and where to call, how to inform professionals of their needs and concerns, how to work with providers in carrying out interventions, and how to evaluate professional services.

Professionals can assist families by making referrals early to parent-support groups; by validating parents' feelings and concerns; by including parents in decision making and planning; by providing information about local, state, and national resources; and by empowering families to develop their own competencies, unique coping mechanisms, strengths, and solutions (Hartman, Radin, & McConnell, 1992).

Implications for Families and Society

Changes in U.S. family life, such as those noted at the beginning of the chapter, indicate that most parents are finding it increasingly prohibitive to provide children with sustained, full-time care in the home. Experience with peers and with child care settings early in life has not been found, in general, to interfere with infants' attachment to their parents or primary caregivers. In fact, experience in quality child care settings appears to enhance the child's ability to form multiple attachments and to be a more socially active child. Sociability has been identified as a key factor in resiliency (Gibbs, 1989; Herman, 1992; Luthar & Zigler, 1991).

In most industrialized countries, what cannot be provided in the context of home and family becomes the province of the larger society, particularly when it comes to caring for children. Thus, most of these countries create social systems that support children as families adjust to the changes in work and marriage patterns.

In the United States, the National Research Council's (NRC) 1993 assessment of systems designed to assist children found such systems woefully lacking. The NRC concluded that the major social systems in the United States had not met the needs of young people and often exacerbated the problems they were designed to address.

Sidel (1996) noted that the United States has the lowest level of welfare benefits and the highest rates of poverty compared with six other Western industrialized countries (Canada, France, the former West Germany, The Netherlands, Sweden, and Great Britain) and concluded that, contrary to some politicians' assertions, "generous welfare benefits do not lead to higher rates of poverty" (p. 181).

Specifically, four areas in which many other industrialized countries support children and families to a far greater degree than the United States does were identified (Sidel, 1996): (a) universal cash benefits, in the form of a children's or family allowance that is given to families no matter what their income and is based on the number of children; (b) some form of national health care system; (c) benefits for divorced families that guarantee child support when non-custodial parents fail to pay; and (d) preschool child care, which is free or low cost and thus available to most or all children.

The United States is a long way from providing most of these benefits to any significant degree. The need of working parents for high-quality and affordable child care is a growing problem that affects single- and two-parent families regardless of social class (Kamerman & Kahn, 1995).

Hofferth (1996) reviewed national data from the 1960s through 1995 and reported that the use of early child care programs has continued to increase, with center-based services growing at the fastest rates. Children enrolled in these centers are more likely to be from higher income families and are more likely to be preschool age than to be infants or toddlers. Thus, families with infants and toddlers, low incomes, and work hours other than traditional business hours have the fewest options for child care. Finally, the author found that despite increasing costs for child care, quality of care has declined through the past 3 decades.

A national study of child care centers conducted in 1993 and 1994 found that 86% of the centers provided mediocre- to poor-quality services (Helburn & Howes, 1996). Only 14% were judged adequate to support a child's development, whereas 12% were considered so poor that basic health and safety needs were jeopardized and little or no learning opportunities provided. The remaining 74% were rated mediocre. For the youngest children, care was the worst: 40% of centers serving infants were rated as low quality; only 8% were considered high quality.

Similarly, a study of child care provided by relatives revealed dismal results: 35% of these arrangements were found to provide inadequate care, 56% were judged to be merely adequate, and only 9% were considered good quality (Helburn & Howes, 1996).

In a review of these and other findings on the cost and quality of child care, Helburn and Howes (1996) concluded that despite the low quality of care in general, the cost of child care remains quite high for families. However, they suggest that increasing the quality from mediocre to good would add only about 10% to the present cost of child care. Among the problems associated with poor-quality care are high child-to-staff ratios, poorly educated staff, high turnover of staff, a poor working environment for staff, and ineffective or inexperienced leadership of the center. The authors noted that the findings are indicative of the low priority U.S. society places on children's care.

Cohen (1996) elucidated other factors that have led to a resistance to adequate funding of child care in the United States, including ambivalence toward maternal employment and a belief in parents' right to rear children without interference from the government. At the same time, moves toward gender equity and equality of opportunity have fueled efforts to create child care resources for families. The result over the past 60 years has been a confusing and inconsistent array of funding sources.

Among the proposals to address these child care problems are comprehensive services delivered through the public school system (Zigler & Finn-Stevenson, 1996). For example, Zigler's School of the 21st Century model for this approach is already in place at 400 schools in 13 states. In these systems, funding comes from a mix of local, state, and federal government funds combined with parent fees to provide child care and other social services to children aged 3 and 4. Other proposals include child subsidies for families at or near the poverty level and paid parental leave (Walker, 1996).

Whatever the solution, child care will continue to be a key issue for children and families into the next millennium, because the trends described in this chapter are not likely to be reversed in the foreseeable future.

A Stand for Children

A significant event took place in Washington, DC, on June 1, 1996. The Children's Defense Fund organized a bipartisan rally, Stand for Children, on the steps of the Lincoln Memorial. Over 200,000 people gathered—children, teachers, parents, and pastors—of varied ages, skin colors, and stages in life. In addition, 3,100 national, state, and regional organizations endorsed Stand for Children. There has never been such a massive gathering in America on behalf of children (Loose, 1996).

According to Marian Wright Edelman, president of the Children's Defense Fund, America should do better and put children first. In her 30-minute keynote speech at the rally, she advocated government characterized by justice, not size. She pointed out that a country that can afford to spend large sums on military contracts can afford to take care of its children (Loose, 1996). Among industrialized countries, the United States ranks first in military technology, military exports, and defense expenditures. However, the United States ranks 12th among industrialized countries in mathematics achievement of 13-year-olds, 16th in living standards among our poorest one fifth of children, and 18th in infant mortality (Children's Defense Fund, 1996).

Every day in America, 3 children die from abuse or neglect, 6 commit suicide, 13 are homicide victims, and 15 are killed by firearms (Children's Defense Fund, 1996). In addition, 518 babies are born to mothers who had late or no prenatal care, 1,407 babies are born to teen mothers, and 2,660 babies are born into poverty.

Social policy is influenced by a complex net of interest groups and represents what society wants for itself (Moynihan, 1996). However, policy does not become effective public policy until money is allocated at the local, state, or federal level to implement the policy. Americans are faced today with Congress' dismantling of programs that affect children, youth, and families. For example, programs cited for elimination include prevention and intervention programs to reduce adolescent pregnancy, child abuse, and substance abuse, as well as after-school and summer education and recreation programs. Instead, funding priorities are being directed toward prison construction, stricter sentences, and a wider latitude to prosecute juveniles as adults.

Governments and communities must work together on the problems afflicting America's children and build support for maintaining crucial preventive efforts. Citizens must challenge religious, cultural, business, and government leaders to improve our children's health, safety, school achievement, and quality of life in communities across the United States.

Summary

In this chapter, the changes and challenges faced by American families as they move into the 21st century were described and discussed within a context of basic principles of child rearing and family functioning. The specific challenges of rearing children in urban areas marked by poverty and violence were highlighted; the needs of families within these changing circumstances were noted, with special attention given to the salient issue of child care; and implications for social policy were introduced. We have seen how the United States' failure to implement a prevention agenda and to provide comprehensive support for children and families is reflected globally in comparative statistics. Halting this downward spiral is critical if America is to remain a world leader. In the next few chapters we review some of the concepts and research relevant to children and families, then we will conclude with further discussion of social policy implications in the final chapter.

2

Risk Factors in Infancy and Early Childhood

A lthough many Americans may think of the United States as an advanced society in which health problems are handled in the most sophisticated fashion, the statistics tell another story. In this chapter, we chronicle some of the startling facts about the United States' ranking with regard to child health and provide a broad overview of the essential risk factors affecting infants and children. These factors are divided into three categories: genetic, prenatal and perinatal, and social–environmental. After a brief description of the public health approach to prevention, the latter part of this chapter describes several model programs of preventive intervention. Included are interventions for prevention of postpartum depression, school-based interventions, and preschool intervention programs.

Child Health in the United States

The United States ranks behind a majority of industrialized nations on key indicators of infant and child health. The U.S. infant mortality rate is worse than in 17 other countries, and for Black infants, the U.S. rate is higher than that of 31 other nations. In fact, women who are poor and Black experience the highest rates of infant mortality in the United States— twice the rate for the U.S. population as a whole. Likewise, the rate of U.S. infants with low birthweight is worse than the rates in 30 other nations, and the same rates for Black American infants is higher than 73 other countries, including many developing nations and Eastern European, formerly Communist countries (Center for the Study of Social Policy, 1993; Children's Defense Fund, 1996; U.S. Bureau of the Census, 1994).

Such figures reflect the widening gap between socioeconomic groups in the United States—a gap that threatens cherished images of equal opportunity, while challenging citizens' moral and ethical obligation to "secure the blessings of liberty to . . . our posterity" as promised in the Declaration of Independence. In addition, from a practical, "bottom-line" standpoint, such chasms also threaten the United States' ability to produce a workforce for the 21st century capable of competing with those advanced technological societies ranking above us on these key indicators, that is, those who currently are ensuring that all their children are able to grow, to learn, and to produce.

Furthermore, developmental problems stemming from prenatal and perinatal risk carry their own costs, in human and in fiscal terms. Much progress has been made in identifying risk factors and their causes. Much more could be done to reduce the risks in order to prevent prenatal and perinatal difficulties. More still could be done to intervene once these difficulties occur.

In general, infants are put in danger of developmental problems either because of reproductive or caretaking risks (Field, 1982). A continuum of reproductive risks, first described by Pasamanick and Knobloch (1961), represents a range of prenatal and perinatal hazards, including congenital disorders (such as Down's syndrome), premature birth, and low birthweight. Caretaking risks, which are not necessarily independent of the reproductive continuum, include developmental problems experienced by infants postnatally, resulting from exposure to parents experiencing various emotional or socioeconomic stressors. Examples include malnutrition, physical or sexual abuse, and physical or emotional neglect. Infants at both reproductive and caretaking risks also include those prenatally exposed to HIV infection or to alcohol and other drugs, as well as those born to low-income adolescent mothers. Infants born with physical disabilities may also be at risk of both forms of trauma. This chapter addresses reproductive and caretaking risks as well as model preventive programs designed to ameliorate them.

Reproductive Risks

Risk factors on the reproductive continuum can be divided into three categories: (a) genetic, (b) prenatal and perinatal, and (c) social–environmental.

Genetic factors. An infant's risk for developmental problems is determined by a number of genetic factors. One of these is physical attractiveness, which has been shown to be a fairly predictable quality across cultural norms. That is, symmetrical features generally associated with attractiveness have been shown to be preferred to less symmetrical faces. Physically attractive people, in general, tend to be judged more positively and experience more success in life. However, for women, the relationship is not as clear-cut because there is some evidence that attractive women are only at an advantage for jobs with low levels of responsibility and that attractiveness may even be a liability for them at higher levels of management (Heilman & Stopeck, 1985; Samuels & Ewy, 1985).

Attractiveness, intelligence, coordination, and temperament are initially determined genetically, although the phenotypic expression of all of these qualities is subsequently affected by the environment, including factors such as nutrition and child-rearing practices. Consequently, prevention efforts must take the genetic component into consideration in the design of programs. Prevention programs must be developed to meet individual needs and take into account inherited vulnerabilities. Thus thorough assessment of a child's needs and careful program planning is critical (Field, 1990).

Emotional adjustment is itself affected by genetic predispositions; for example, affective disorders, schizophrenia, attention deficit disorder, and substance abuse appear to have hereditary components (Schuckit, 1994; Szatmari & Nagy, 1990). However, even in the most controlled studies of identical twins reared apart, concordance rates for these disorders reach 35% at most. The 65% who do not express the disorder are often cited as evidence for the still powerful influence the environment has on the outcome for the individual.

Likewise, studies of intelligence indicate that both heredity and environmental factors are significant contributors to level of ability (Neisser et al., 1996). Thus, if Americans want to tap our natural resources as a nation, we must attend both to the wasted brilliance languishing in our most deprived settings, and to the developmentally disabled who can, with proper nurturance, become productive members of society.

In the 1990s, the controversy over racial differences in scores on tests of intelligence has bubbled up again, after 15 to 20 years of relative quiet (Gordon, 1995). The controversy was timed, perhaps not coincidentally, with a conservative takeover of the U.S. House of Representatives. The theory that the difference (an average of 15 points, about one standard deviation, between mean scores for Blacks and Whites) is based on genetic differences between races, as proposed by the authors of *The Bell Curve* (Herrnstein & Murray, 1994), has been roundly criticized.

In response to the controversy resulting from the publication of *The Bell Curve*, the American Psychological Association created a task force to review the issue. The task force issued a report, published in the *American Psychologist* in February 1996 (Neisser et al.). The numerous problems with the debate identified by the Task Force included:

1. Although there are many types of intelligence, such as creativity, social skills, or "wisdom," the range of abilities currently measured by intelligence testing is fairly narrow.

2. Intelligence test scores (IQ scores) show relatively high correlations with school performance and with adult occupational status in the United States; however, this represents something of a "chicken and egg" phenomenon, because grades and test scores act as "gatekeepers" for entry into so many career paths.

3. Intelligence is clearly the result of both heredity and en-

vironment, but the relative contribution of each is often very difficult to measure.

4. Key factors in the environment affecting IQ scores are presence or absence of formal schooling and quality of the schooling; prenatal exposure to alcohol; exposure to lead in the environment; malnutrition; and perinatal complications.

The task force concluded that "because ethnic differences in intelligence reflect complex patterns, no overall generalization about them is appropriate" (Neisser et al., 1996, p. 96). It found that several culturally based explanations of Black–White differences, while plausible, have not yet been demonstrated conclusively with research findings. Finally, the authors noted that "There is certainly no such support for a genetic interpretation" (p. 97), concluding that the test score differences have not yet been explained.

Prenatal and perinatal factors. Maternal illness, malnutrition, and alcohol and other drug use all increase the prenatal and perinatal risk factors to infant development. Prematurity, the most common birth abnormality, results from a variety of pregnancy complications. The relationship between prematurity and later negative developmental outcomes is not necessarily a straightforward correlation, however. Other variables mediate or moderate the relationship, including low birth weight, perinatal complications or trauma, and the home environment (Rose, Feldman, Rose, Wallace, & McCarton, 1992). Prematurity alone, for an infant subsequently reared in a warm, stimulating environment, does not have a significant effect on development beyond the first 2 years. Studies with the Bayley Scales of Infant Development indicate that premature infants generally score at their gestational age for the first 2 years, but score according to their chronological age after that time (Bayley, 1993).

When developmental problems do arise for the premature infant, they may be related to factors that limit the infant's ability to engage in effective, mutually responsive interactions, particularly with a young, inexperienced parent or an emotionally impaired caregiver. For example, the preterm infant often lacks integrated physiologic and motoric functioning, limiting mother–infant responsiveness, but interventions with premature infants in the first weeks of life have been found to enable more responsive interaction with their mothers (Field, 1990). Furthermore, the infant's stay in a neonatal intensive care unit may prevent sufficient opportunity for infant–caregiver interaction, so that the necessary familiarity between infant and caregiver is not established. Field et al. (1986) showed that the length of stay in a neonatal intensive care unit is shortened by the application of daily massage to the premature infant, indicating that human touch is also a factor in development.

Prematurity may result from the mother's lack of adequate prenatal care, from alcohol and other drug use during pregnancy, or from the mother's physical condition. Although frequently preventable, premature birth sometimes occurs despite all efforts to avoid it. Particularly in the latter case, premature delivery may be experienced as a crisis demanding tremendous emotional adjustment by parents (Campbell & Cohen, 1991). Whatever the circumstances surrounding the birth, some women experience postpartum depression sufficient to compromise their ability to care for their infant, and birth complications may serve to exacerbate these problems. Thus, there are many ways in which the future biological, social, and psychological functioning of preterm infants rests not on the specific impairment of the baby, but on factors external to the child.

In fact, the biological impairment measurable at birth is actually a poor predictor of future general functioning of premature infants, whereas the attitudes and child care practices of caregivers show signficant correlations with the child's later adjustment and development. Although the incidence of developmental disorders is higher in preterm infants, prematurity alone does not always lead to developmental delay. Healthy premature infants often have very good developmental outcomes, and size at birth does not predict later performance on developmental tasks. The necessity of continuing developmental assessments to determine the risk status of the premature infant as he or she grows was established long ago and is equally true today with the growing number of infants prenatally exposed to alcohol and other drugs. For the latter, developmental assessments have revealed that the amount of drug exposure, severity of birth complications resulting from the mother's drug use, and gestational age at birth are not clear predictors of later developmental outcome (McCord, 1988). As in the case of prematurity related to other causes, the postnatal environment seems to be an extremely significant factor in the outcome for the child.

Social and environmental conditions. What has been true since humans left tribes and began living as nuclear units, especially since the Industrial Revolution, is still true today: The poorer the family, the riskier the existence, especially for children. This correlation has been long recognized in literature (e.g., Dickens's *A Tale of Two Cities*, 1859/1938; Hugo's *Les Miserables*, 1862/1967). Social scientists throughout this century have cited poverty as a major factor, perhaps the most significant one, in developmental risk, as is reflected in the reproductive casualty continuum (National Research Council, 1993). In addition to the negative birth outcomes described previously, economically disadvantaged children experience environmental hazards such as lead paint and community violence, and they often experience unfavorable emotional outcomes related to the complex interplay of biological and environmental factors.

Many European countries, particularly the Scandinavian nations, have acted on this knowledge and created social supports for children and families that have virtually eliminated poverty as it is known in the United States (i.e., homelessness, ghetto neighborhoods with high crime rates, massive unemployment, inadequate health care, and crumbling public school systems). The result of European social reforms is reflected in the statistics on infant mortality and low birthweight noted at the beginning of this chapter, as well as in low rates of homicide, delinquency, teen pregnancy (despite high rates of sexually active adolescents), and school dropouts.

In the United States, because many ethnic minority groups are overrepresented in the lower socioeconomic classes, ethnicity is also a factor increasing risk from the public health standpoint. For most indicators, however, when social class is controlled for, racial or ethnic differences disappear—from homicide rates (American Psychological Association [APA] Commission on Violence and Youth, 1993) to numerous other outcomes for youth (National Research Council, 1993).

Again, this is not a new finding, but one that has been known for decades. More than a quarter-century ago, Birch and Gussow (1970) wrote:

> The poor woman having a baby may be at risk because of her age, her nutritional status, her probable poor growth, her excessive exposure to infection in the community which she inhabits, her poor housing, and her inadequate medical supervision, as well as because of complex interactions between these and other potentially adverse influences. (p. 175)

Biological outcomes of pregnancy are likely to be less than optimal among individuals who live in disadvantaged environments. In the classic 30-year longitudinal study on the Hawaiian island of Kauai, Werner and Smith (1992) studied the effects of socioeconomic status and perinatal complications on child development. From assessments of infants at birth and through age 30, it was apparent that perinatal complications only led to problems of physical and psychological development when they were combined with consistently poor environmental conditions. That is, birth complications did not necessarily result in developmental consequences except where there was severe damage to the central nervous system. The best predictor of negative developmental outcome following birth complications was exposure to a deprived environment after birth.

Furthermore, access to and use of good prenatal care eliminated socioeconomic differences in the distribution of perinatal complications, emphasizing the importance of such care for mothers and their infants (Werner & Smith, 1992). In the United States, however, large segments of the population do not receive any prenatal care; many receive infrequent, inadequate, or late care. According to the U.S. Department of Health and Human Services Prevention Profile (1991), about 15% of Mexican American mothers receive late (third trimester) prenatal care or none at all, and the same is true for 13% of Native American mothers, and 12% of African American and Central and South American mothers (1989 figures). Recipients of early prenatal care, which is critical because of the fragility of the fetus' development in the first trimester, also differed by ethnicity. Although 86% of Japanese American and 79% of White mothers received early care, only 57% of Mexican American mothers, 58% of Native American mothers, 60% of African American, 61% of Central and South American, and 63% of Puerto Rican women received it.

When Werner, Bierman, and French (1971) assessed the children as 10-year-olds, they found that the correlation between a parent's and his or her child's scores on standard intelligence tests increased during the first 8 years of life, suggesting that as the influence of family and social factors increase, the prenatal and perinatal risk factors decrease in significance. Werner et al. (1971) concluded that the effects of a disadvantaged early environment account for 10 times as many children suffering physical, intellectual, or behavioral problems, compared to the children experiencing problems stemming from perinatal difficulties.

Recent research conducted in the Middle East using the Portage Program developed in Wisconsin in the late 1960s provided further support for the importance of the environment (Roth & Constantine, 1995). At the end of 3 years, developmental scores of the high-risk toddlers receiving the intervention averaged two standard deviations above that of a control group.

The relationship between disadvantaged environments and negative developmental outcomes has been quite firmly established. What is not understood at this juncture is why this understanding has not translated into social policy in the United States. Beyond the moral imperative to care for society's future generations, there is a more prosaic reason for attention to these findings, and that is a fiscal one. Expenses are astronomical for neonatal intensive care, and the long-term costs of poor development translate into tax dollars for continued health care, special education, possible lifelong public dependency, and sometimes even long-term adult care. Humanistic social scientists have often been reluctant to resort to these hard-line points to sell prevention, but perhaps it is time we became willing to state the case in these terms. Cost–benefit analyses such as those of the Perry Preschool Program (Barnett, 1993) are possible considerations for future research.

Future researchers would also do well to study the mechanisms by which research findings make their way into public policy. In pediatric medicine, maternal and child health has long been part of a political agenda for the American Academy of Pediatrics. Likewise, the public health field has focused attention on maternal and child health, although to a lesser degree, understandably, than in pediatrics. Developing a better understanding of public health campaigns and the manner in which public opinion is shaped may be one important area of research for coming generations of professionals interested in prevention. Prevention must be marketed and sold to the voting public.

Socioeconomic status clearly exerts a strong influence on the reproductive risk continuum, as is reflected in differential rates of birth complications, but it is also a major factor for caretaking risks, beginning with the interaction between the prenatal complications and subsequent developmental problems, described previously.

Caretaking Risks

Caretaking risks include detrimental postnatal factors created by early parenting practices. Once a child is born, parents must create a protective and nurturing context in order for healthy growth and development to occur. When parental behavior breaches the minimal requirements for a child's normal, healthy development to proceed, the child becomes at risk for a variety of problems. If the parental breach is severe enough to come to the attention of authorities, the state may step in to remove the child from the environment, often creating yet another risk factor by subjecting the child to broken attachments, potential multiple placements, and sometimes abuse or neglect in the foster care setting.

Child maltreatment has reached epidemic proportions in the United States. Reports of child abuse and neglect increased 50% between 1985 and 1992 (McCurdy & Daro, 1993). Those tempted to believe that this reported increase represents only heightened awareness and subsequent increased reporting should consider this fact: During that same period, child abuse fatalities also increased 49%. Thus, it appears that, in addition to a rise in reporting, child abuse is, in fact, increasing—both in numbers and in severity. In 1992, 84% of those victims were under age 5, and 43% were under 1 year of age. In that same year, in the Chicago area, nearly half of all violent child fatalities were at the hands of caretakers—a fact publicized extensively by the *Chicago Tribune* (Johnson, 1993). In the first half of 1993, the child fatalities had continued in the same pattern, with about half the cases resulting from child abuse (McMahon & Johnson, 1993).

In their survey of 19 states, the National Committee for the Prevention of Child Abuse (McCurdy & Daro, 1993) found that 40% of cases confirmed by child protective services as abused or neglected received no further intervention—an 18% decline in response since 1990. Of the child fatalities resulting from abuse and neglect, 35% were children who were prior or current clients of the child welfare system. Quite simply, child protective services have been completely overwhelmed by this increase.

Primarily as a result of increased cases of child abuse and neglect, numbers of children in foster care have risen 53% since 1987 (McKenzie, 1993); today there are nearly half a million U.S. children in foster homes. A study of the Michigan child welfare system, aptly titled "Raised by the Government," revealed that one third of these children never find a permanent home (Schwartz, 1993). Other studies have found that about 50% of homeless adolescents and 70% of adolescent psychiatric inpatients have a history of foster care placements (Mundy, Robertson, Greenblatt, & Robertson, 1989; Mundy, Robertson, Robertson, & Greenblatt, 1990).

Moreover, a history of child abuse and neglect has been shown to be predictive both of later violent behavior (Widom, 1989b) and of adult victimization (Becker-Lausen, Sanders, & Chinsky, 1995).

In a prospective study of physical abuse and aggression in 309 kindergarten children, Dodge, Bates, and Pettit (1990) found that those who had been physically harmed by parents had significantly higher levels of aggression than nonharmed children. This finding held across teacher, peer, and observer ratings, and it was equally true for girls and boys. Furthermore, Dodge et al. found no correlation between abuse and child temperament or health problems and concluded, "There is no evidence in our data for blaming the victim of abuse" (p. 1682).

Vissing, Straus, Gelles, and Harrop (1991) reported similar findings for verbal abuse in a national sample: Children who experienced frequent verbal aggression from parents had higher rates of physical aggression, delinquency, and other interpersonal problems, compared to those who did not experience verbal abuse. These findings held for all age levels and across both genders, regardless of the presence or absence of physical abuse (although those who experienced both verbal and physical abuse had the highest levels of aggression, delinquency, and interpersonal problems, underscoring the importance of investigating the aggregated effects of different forms of abuse).

However, because Dodge et al. (1990) used the Child Behavior Checklist (CBCL; Achenbach & Edelbrock, 1986), they had teacher ratings of the child's *internalizing behaviors* (the tendency to withdraw and isolate from others), as well as the externalizing aggressive behaviors. When the researchers looked at the ratings of internalizing behaviors, they found that these behaviors were 19% higher in harmed boys and a startling 87% higher in harmed girls, both of which represented statistically significant differences from the nonharmed children. "Even though our study focused on aggression, our findings indicate that abused children, particularly girls, are also at risk for the development of internalizing problems, such as withdrawal and isolation, that have been hypothesized to be precursors of depression," the authors noted (Dodge et al., 1990, p. 1682).

The investigators also found that the cognitive developmental pathways for externalizing and for internalizing behaviors appear to be quite different (Dodge et al., 1990). Harmed children who were aggressive were likely to develop "biased and deficient patterns of processing social information, including a failure to attend to relevant cues, a bias to attribute hostile intentions to others, and a lack of competent behavioral strategies to solve interpersonal problems" (p. 1682). Whereas the results supported the hypothesis that the path between physical harm and externalizing behavior was mediated by the development of this particular cognitive style, this style did not hold as a mediator for internalizing behaviors. Dodge et al. (1990) concluded that internalizing outcomes may be mediated by the development of a different set of patterns, such as self-blame: "Why some children follow a path of hostile attributions and aggression and other children a path of self-blame and depression awaits further inquiry" (p. 1682).

Physical battering, such as shaken baby syndrome, is often the most graphic evidence of parental caretaking casualty. However, sexual abuse, according to many studies (Briere, 1992; Browne & Finkelhor, 1986), may leave the most profound scars on the child victim, and is often exacerbated by the hidden nature of the crime. Substantial evidence suggests that the effects of emotional and physical neglect are also quite profound. Widom (1989a), for example, found those with a history of childhood neglect had nearly as great a likelihood of later violent or criminal behavior as those with a history of physical abuse. We discuss the theoretical implications of these findings in chapter 5.

Failure to thrive is another severe outcome of child neglect, in which a child's physical development is thwarted and sometimes even halted, but there is no medical explanation for the decline. As described 20 years ago by Sameroff and Chandler (1975), failure to thrive represents "gross parental inattention to the needs of their children, abandonment, starvation, and unusual isolation of the child from the community" (p. 225).

Abuse and neglect often coexist. Researchers in recent years have turned to examining the concept of *psychological maltreatment* as a means of understanding the common denominator present in all forms of child maltreatment (Becker-Lausen, Sanders, & Chinsky, 1995; Garbarino & Vondra, 1987; Garrison, 1987; Hart & Brassard, 1987). Disregard of the child's needs in favor of those of the adult, for example, is a common element, as is the violation of trust and boundaries, perpetrated by adults charged with protecting the child (Finkelhor & Browne, 1985). The International Conference on Psychological Abuse of Children and Youth generated the following definition:

> Psychological maltreatment of children and youth consists of acts of omission and commission which are judged on the basis of a combination of community standards and professional expertise to be psychologically damaging. Such acts are committed by individuals, singly or collectively, who by their characteristics (e.g., age, status, knowledge, organizational form) are in a position of differential power that renders a child vulnerable. Such acts damage immediately or ultimately the behavioral, cognitive, affective, or physical functioning of the child. (Brassard, Germain, & Hart, 1987, p. 6)

Although the American Psychological Association identified psychological maltreatment as a research priority some time ago (Garrison, 1987), it has been among the "thorniest" of issues to study, with "a shifting emphasis from one type of maltreatment to another with little energy directed toward integrating findings across maltreatment areas" (Rosenberg, 1987, p. 166).

In an attempt to address this problem, Briere and Runtz (1988a) gave 251 college women a simple questionnaire that separated physical abuse from verbal abuse and maternal from paternal maltreatment. They found that all four types of maltreatment (i.e., physical, verbal, maternal, and paternal) were likely to occur in the same family (and thus, were significantly intercorrelated) and were associated with somatization, anxiety, suicidal ideation, obsessive–compulsive behavior, dissociation, depression, and interpersonal sensitivity in the survivors. The latter three symptoms showed particularly strong statistical associations with abuse history. The authors postulated a postabuse symptom complex and suggested that childhood maltreatment "is associated with substantial psychological difficulties later in life, much in the same ways as have been demonstrated for sexual abuse" (p. 337). Since the Briere and Runtz study, Claussen and Crittenden (1991) have also demonstrated the simultaneous occurrence of different types of maltreatment.

Recently, Finkelhor and Dziuba-Leatherman (1994) reiterated the need for "theory and research that cuts across and integrates the various forms of child victimization," and recommended the examination of "pandemic" victimizations (e.g., corporal punishment), rather than only "the acute and the extraordinary, which have been the main foci in the past" (p. 182).

Life crises often result in an adequately functioning individual responding with disabling emotions to environmental stress. Pregnancy, childbirth, and the postpartum period can be life crises that affect the development of all the members of a family. The popular literature warns new mothers that following the birth of their child, they may experience a moderate depression or the "baby blues." However, if postpartum depression is left untreated, longstanding problems may develop in the mother and her offspring (Beck, 1972; Sweeney, Anderson, & Bailey, 1986). Prevention programs can be designed to build on the available findings of factors that mitigate the devastating effects of postpartum stress, for example, providing opportunities to learn parenting skills and roles. Such an intervention program designed to decrease stress and increase support during the postpartum period is discussed in the following section.

Preventive Intervention: Model Programs

Following the model of public health and its emphasis on prevention as the most effective method of averting disease, the three levels of prevention and illustrative model programs are presented. Primary prevention involves lowering the rate of new cases of mental disorder in a whole population. Although some individuals may become ill, the numbers will be reduced. Secondary prevention again is elevated to the community or population level. It typically reaches large numbers of people and uses paraprofessionals to increase the staff available to address identified problems. Tertiary prevention focuses on the reduction of the prevalence of a disorder (Caplan, 1964).

Intervention programs have been proven beneficial in ameliorating a wide variety of risk factors associated with infancy. Successful programs include hospital-based, home-based, and daycare-center-based efforts using a variety of techniques. This wide range of intervention efforts succeeds because most of the key risk factors for infants are directly or indirectly related to parental attitudes and child-rearing practices.

The common thread in successful intervention strategies is that they provide some form of direct stimulation for the child, and also promote parental change through (a) supportive peer discussion of shared caretaking difficulties with high-risk infants; (b) methods that increase the self-image of parents and their sense of competence in child rearing; (c) education in physical and psychological child development; (d) teaching specific techniques for interacting with their infant to foster social–emotional and cognitive development; and (e) increasing parent's awareness of supportive social services and encouraging their use of these services.

Although many risk factors cannot be avoided or altered, most are preventable. Improved parental attitudes and child care practices can create a context for healthy growth and development in which a child can thrive.

Preventing Postpartum Depression

In the 1980s, an investigation was begun in Detroit with first-time parents whose characteristics placed their children at risk for developmental problems and maladjustment. The Detroit project was designed to determine the stress of giving birth and the incidence of postpartum depression, and focused on the prenatal and postnatal environment.

The investigation was based on several converging lines of research and theory. A study of postpartum depression by Atkinson and Rickel (1984), which demonstrated the effects of social support on postpartum depression, and the research and theoretical underpinnings of Seligman's learned helplessness model (Seligman, 1975) became a major foundation for the intervention. In addition, the Detroit study extended the work of Broussard (1982) in the Pittsburgh First-Born Project.

The study of postpartum depression by Atkinson and Rickel (1984) assessed 78 primiparous couples 8 weeks before and 8 weeks after the birth of their infants. A major focus of the research was the effects of social support and the theoretical underpinnings of Seligman's learned helplessness model. Although the best predictor of postpartum depression for both men and women was prepartum depression, important suppressor effects were found.

Findings indicated that expectancy may play a key role in the development of depression postdelivery. For women, postpartum depression was related to reports of a high level of pleasant events at the prepartum assessment, combined with a reported low level of pleasant events postpartum. For men, postdelivery depression was related to prepartum reports of expectations that their infant would compare favorably to an average baby, combined with postpartum reports that they perceived their infant as comparing less favorably to an average baby. For both mothers and fathers, a change in perception from a positive perception prepartum to a negative perception postpartum was related to higher levels of depression after delivery.

These findings suggested that an intervention could be designed that would reduce the incidence of postpartum depression, in order to enhance the infant's early environment, by helping parents (a) develop more realistic expectations of the events following childbirth, (b) increase parents' sense of mastery over these events, and (c) increase the level of interpersonal support between spouses.

The work of the Pittsburgh First-Born Project, reported by Broussard (1982), focused on the prevention of psychosocial disorders. The lack of a positive maternal perception of the newborn was found to be associated with a high rate of subsequent psychosocial disorder in the child. Consequently, a mother's ratings of her infant on the Neonatal Perception Inventories (NPI), which compares her perception of her baby to her image of the average infant, were used to determine the adaptive potential of the mother–infant unit in the first month of life. High-risk infants were thus identified for participation in the program or for inclusion in a control group. These physically healthy infants were first-born children in their respective families.

The intervention consisted of an initial interview with one or both parents, participation in mother–infant group meetings, and home-based intervention sessions. Seven to eight mother–infant pairs were put into groups that met biweekly from the time the babies were 2 to 4 months until they were $3^1/_2$ years old. Broussard and a coleader conducted meetings, and child development specialists made home visits. The Broussard team actively studied the mother–infant interaction throughout the project, so that they could intervene according to each dyad's needs. Thus, the nature and timing of the interventions was individualized for each dyad. Developmental progress of the infant was continuously monitored, and interventions were directed toward optimizing individual development.

Assessment of development was conducted at 1 and $2^1/_2$ years of age to determine the impact of the intervention. Naive observer–raters scored children on items reflecting (a) the separation–individuation process, (b) confidence, (c) implementation of contacts with the nonhuman environment, (d) aggression, (e) affective balance, (f) investment in the use of language for communication, (g) coping, and (h) play. Results indicated the groups of high-risk children receiving the intervention, as well as a low-risk control group, exhibited superior functioning across all factors, compared to the high-risk group who did not receive the intervention.

School-Based and Preschool Intervention Projects

Primary prevention programs housed in public schools could create classroom environments that promote mental health, rather than addressing behavioral and educational difficulties after they develop. Although this primary prevention approach seems to be slipping further and further from the public consciousness, the possibility still exists for an efficient and effective means of screening, diagnosis, and remediation of early maladjustment, which could be incorporated into the structure of the existing school system.

More than 40 years ago in Rochester, New York, such a landmark school-based secondary prevention program was developed. Cowen's Primary Mental Health Project (PMHP) has served as a model for secondary prevention with children since that time (Cowen et al., 1975; Cowen et al., 1996). The PMHP uses early mass screening of primary-grade children to identify behavioral and academic difficulties. Children who exhibit acting out, withdrawal, or learning problems are given remedial activities that are implemented by carefully selected, specially trained paraprofessional aides. Screening data includes cognitive and personality measures, interviews with mothers, and teacher behavior ratings for targeted children collected by PMHP professionals.

In an initial assignment conference attended by project professionals, teachers and aides, the assessment data are reviewed, children are assigned to specific aides, and working objectives are outlined. The aide then begins to see the child on a regular basis. At midyear, the same team evaluates changes in the children, modifying goals as necessary. At the end of the year, the team meets to determine whether each child should continue in the program.

During the year, the mental health professional acts as a

consultant to teachers and other personnel, providing additional on-the-job training and supervision of aides. Most children are seen individually by aides; however, some are seen in groups. The extended helping team works to bring effective remediation to large numbers of identified children showing signs of early maladjustment, in order to head off the development of more serious difficulties later on.

An important aspect of the PMHP is the successful use of nonprofessional aides. Mental health professionals have often been reluctant to use this valuable source of assistance, but studies have supported the efficacy of their use (Sobey, 1970). As funds for prevention and intervention become ever scarcer, the use of trained nonprofessional aides can contribute significantly to the cost effectiveness of intervention programs.

Initial findings at the end of the school year (Cowen et al., 1975) indicated that the PMHP children improved more than control children, based on teachers' and aides' assessments of academic and interpersonal behavior and teachers' direct comparisons of PMHP and control children. PMHP children also showed significant improvement on all criteria following the intervention, based on teachers' and aides' ratings of treatment group change. Evaluation has continued for the PMHP project (Cowen, Lotyczewski, & Weissberg, 1984) and, in general, PMHP children consistently demonstrated significant improvements compared to control groups.

In a meta-analysis of PMHP studies (Stein & Polyson, 1984), improvement effects of the intervention were found to be only half as large as those observed in studies of psychotherapy with adult populations. However, the comparison to adult psychotherapy studies may be problematic because child development cannot be a factor in adult outcome studies. That is, early intervention may have cumulative effects that cannot be fully appreciated unless one follows the subjects into adulthood. For example, the studies of the Perry Preschool intervention (Barnett, 1993) indicate that the gains throughout the subject's lifetime are quite substantial, but that the initial improvements in school settings do not tell the entire story. The PMHP is a model of secondary prevention with primary school children that has endured the test of time. The program has been disseminated nationally and internationally and is now in more than 700 school districts located in both urban and rural settings (Cowen et al., 1996).

Head Start

Another milestone in the history of secondary prevention was the development of the multifaceted Head Start program of the 1960s, designed for economically disadvantaged children. In the case of Head Start, the intervention occurs early, at the preschool level, rather than in the primary grades. It is a multidimensional program that includes educational, health care, and social services for children and families.

The research of Piaget (1950) and Bruner (1961) demonstrated that the child is an active learner and a participant in the learning process. Furthermore, it was believed that a child's cognitive structure might be accelerated by matching appropriate activities with the child's cognitive level (Piaget 1950). From this, the concept was conceived that Head Start could serve as an intervention for those children who lagged behind their peers in cognitive development (Bruner, 1961). A great many programs emerged that were aimed at enabling disadvantaged children to achieve cognitive parity with their middle-class peers through the help of trained preschool teachers and parents.

In fact, the extensive involvement of parents in the program often changes their lives as well as the lives of their children, as was evident when former Head Start mother Dolores Baynes testified before the U.S. Senate hearing on Head Start reauthorization in 1993 (*New Challenges for Head Start*, 1993, pp. 16–19). Ms. Baynes told the Senators that she had dropped out of school at 14, lived on the streets, given birth at 15, and was in prison by 16. At 18, pregnant again, she was thrown against a cement wall by her boyfriend; the infant lived a few hours before dying of traumatic brain injuries. At 23, after giving birth to a third child, she found the strength to leave this abusive relationship.

Ms. Baynes was alone with two children and living on welfare when she found two women from Head Start at her door, making a visit that was to transform her life and her children's lives. With the help and encouragement of Head Start staff, Ms. Baynes completed high school, obtained a certificate in child development, and became a paid staff member at Head Start. She continues to pursue her own college education, while her son, who was 18 at the time of the hearing and was in the Army Reserves, was about to begin college and planned to become an attorney.

The dramatic story of Dolores Baynes's success is not that unusual; it is what Edward Zigler, the founder of Head Start, calls "the untold story" of the program. However, since its inception in the 1960s, Head Start has stirred controversy over the long-term effectiveness of early intervention programs for the disadvantaged (Zigler & Muenchow, 1992). Nevertheless, Project Head Start has been one of the most influential social experiments in U.S. history and began a new and exciting era in American preschool intervention.

A basic assumption underlying the creation of Head Start was that preschool training in learning readiness skills for high risk, disadvantaged children would increase their chances for success in the formal education system. Such assumptions required that Head Start produce gains in children's intellectual development that persisted over time. The vision of Head Start was the ultimate disruption of the cycle of poverty, which has become manifest in the increased educational and occupational opportunities offered to thousands of disadvantaged children (Weinberg, 1979).

Initial evaluations of Head Start's effectiveness were discouraging (e.g., Westinghouse Learning Corporation, 1969; Wolff & Stein, 1966), and the program was believed to have failed because immediate gains on cognitive and personality measures were not sustained after the first 2 or 3 years of elementary school (Zigler & Muenchow, 1992). The "washout" phenomenon was an indicator that a 1-year Head Start program did not produce positive lasting changes in behavior. However, early evaluations were inadequate because the programs had not been set up for assessment of long-term effects, making accurate evaluations difficult and methodologically flawed (Campbell & Erlebacher, 1970; Smith & Bissell, 1970; Weinberg, 1979; Zigler & Muenchow, 1992).

In measuring the impact of Head Start interventions, researchers encountered several difficulties obtaining accurate information. The Westinghouse Learning Corporation Head Start evaluation is a good example of these difficulties (1969). This early study is a well-known negative finding of an 8-week summer Head Start program showing a detrimental effect on the achievement of preschool children. However, the finding was not totally negative because children were found to benefit from the full-year Head Start programs. Furthermore, subsequent reanalyses of the Westinghouse data concluded that the summer programs were effective for certain groups of individuals (Magidson, 1977). Both the summer and full-year programs were effective for White children from families headed by mothers, but were ineffective for White children from families with two parents. In addition, Black children who participated in the program showed a 5-point gain in IQ when they were assessed in the first grade.

The subsequent reanalyses of the early Westinghouse Learning Corporation study data also corrected some of the methodological errors, revealing more positive outcomes. Later follow-up studies provided evidence that gains produced by Head Start and similar preschool experiences are maintained into high school (Darlington, Royce, Snipper, Murray, & Lazar, 1980). Furthermore, the recent 28-year follow-up to the Perry Preschool program, which was similar to Head Start, has indicated that substantial gains accrue to society, as well as to the individual, and are cumulative into adulthood (Schweinhart, Barnes, & Weikart, 1993).

The early experience with Head Start raised awareness of the need for evaluation components to be built into prevention programs when goals are being established. Nevertheless, even with today's expanded evaluation technology, difficulties still arise in the assessment of preschool mental health programs. Evaluation is essential, however, because the unequivocal demonstration of long-term humane and fiscal benefits encourages the establishment of early intervention programs as a routine procedure.

Preschool Mental Health Project

In the 1970s, the Wayne State University Preschool Mental Health Project was begun in the Detroit Public Schools (Rickel, 1979; Rickel & Smith, 1979). The program was designed to prevent maladjustment in low-income, high-risk children and to promote positive cognitive, social, and emotional growth through early screening, diagnosis, and remediation. It was built, in part, on the pioneering work of Emory Cowen in the Rochester, New York, Public School system (Cowen et al., 1975; Cowen et al., 1996).

The Preschool Mental Health Project uses an approach similar to that of Cowen et al. (1975, 1996), as a means of expanding the delivery of mental health services. The Preschool Project departs from the Cowen model with innovations in three areas: (a) the age at which screening and intervention are attempted, (b) the manner in which the multiplication of the mental health professionals' impact is achieved, and (c) the research design. To illustrate, we describe a single year's activities of the project, as well as a 2-year follow-up built into the program to determine its efficacy.

A basic tenet of the Preschool Project is that the earlier the intervention occurs in the child's development, the more likely it is to be successful (Rickel, Smith, & Sharp, 1979). Maladaptive patterns are less firmly established in younger children, so that they are more amenable to positive and long-lasting change when identified early (Rickel & Smith, 1979). Thus, the project was designed for preschoolers.

The mental health professional's role in the Preschool Project is primarily one of providing diagnostic assessment, training, and supervision. Teachers assist by identifying children who need diagnostic assessment for behavioral or learning difficulties. Specific prescriptive interventions are developed, tailored to each child's identified problem(s). Within the classroom setting, interventions are implemented using college students (senior psychology students from Wayne State University) who have been trained and are under the supervision of mental health professionals.

A carefully planned, well-controlled research design is a

key aspect of the project. The research design included a control group and blind assessment procedure that ensured that treatment effects were not an artifact of the assessor's knowledge of the treatment the child received. All children in the project were enrolled in Title I Preschool Programs in three Region 7 schools of the Detroit Public School system.

The Preschool Mental Health Project used a two-faceted approach: (a) a program of prescribed interventions for high-risk children that took place within the classroom and (b) a parent training program designed to improve the home environment by enhancing the parent's child-rearing techniques. These are explained in more detail below.

The Child Program. Children in the program were assessed in four phases: (a) an initial observation of children's classroom behavior, (b) the identification of high-risk children who were then assigned to treatment conditions, (c) the training of student aides who then implemented prescriptive interventions, and (d) evaluation of the intervention effects (Rickel, Smith, & Sharp, 1979).

In the first 5 weeks of the school year, the children were allowed to become adjusted to the preschool setting while teachers became familiar with each child's behavior and needs. During this period, the children engaged in traditional preschool activities, while teachers worked individually with children and observed each child's interactions with other children.

After the period of initial observation, children were screened for adjustment difficulties, identifying and diagnosing those having the greatest problems. Screening, identification, and diagnosis were based on a developmental history obtained from the child's parents, a standardized achievement measure, and standard social–emotional scales.

Based on these assessments, 64 children were identified as having problems sufficient to be classified as high risk. Specifically, children were judged at high risk if they scored in the top third of the maladjustment range on either achievement or behavioral adjustment inventories (or on both), or if they had physical problems (e.g., speech abnormalities) considered severe enough to interfere with the child's adjustment to school. The 64 children identified as high risk were then randomly assigned to either a prescriptive remediation program or a placebo control group. Random assignment was used irrespective of the school the child attended or the nature of their problems; thus, experimental and control children were in every classroom. The experimental group had 13 aggressive and 19 shy–withdrawn children, and the control group had 10 aggressive and 22 shy–withdrawn preschoolers. All 64 children had some type of learning problem. Teachers were blind to the group assignment of each child and also to the nature of the experimental and control group experiences.

Training and intervention. Senior-level psychology students from Wayne State University received academic credit for their work as intervention aides for the project. Participating students, who were required to have an overall grade point average of 3.0 (B) or better, were screened for their participation through an interview with project staff. All aides received general training, including didactic presentations, reading assignments on normative preschool behavior, and discussions of appropriate techniques for handling various child-management situations.

Half of the aides then were selected by random assignment to work with experimental children; the remaining half worked with control children. Each half received additional training unique to their assignment. During the training, neither group was informed of the experimental or control nature of their assignment.

Aides who were to work with experimental children received supplemental training in prescriptive intervention techniques designed to familiarize aides with behavioral symptoms of the specific problem types represented: the shy–withdrawn child, the hostile or aggressive child, and the child experiencing learning difficulties. Prescriptive techniques are described in full detail in the program training manual (Rickel, 1979).

Aides assigned to control children received supplemental training based on a control training manual, which provided instructions for conducting traditional preschool activities such as singing songs, coloring, and playing with blocks.

The intervention phase of the program began in the third month of the school year (November). Project staff developed a program of prescriptions and activities for each experimental and for each control child. The individualized programs were written in a standardized format, and reviewed with each aide, and referenced specific activities in the aide's training manuals. As the year progressed, project staff made on-site visits once a month to observe each child and that child's aide. Staff also held separate group meetings every 4 weeks with experimental and with control aides where each child's progress was reviewed and the prescriptive program updated by staff as needed.

This intervention phase lasted 8 months (November–June). During this time, each child was scheduled to meet four times a week with an aide, for 15 to 20 minutes per session. Because of illness and weather factors, this schedule was not always maintained, but each child was seen by an aide at least twice a week for approximately 20 minutes each session.

Evaluation of the Classroom Program. Program evaluation was first conducted at the completion of the program and again 2 years after the program's completion.

Results of the first evaluation (Rickel, Smith, & Sharp, 1979), at the end of the intervention year, indicated a definite advantage for treatment children compared to control children based on their scores on achievement and behavioral adjustment scales. (As noted previously, teachers administering the instruments were blind to the treatment status of the children.) Using multivariate analysis of variance and follow-up univariate analyses, treatment children were compared to control children, and shy–withdrawn children were compared to acting-out–aggressive preschoolers. Analyses revealed that treatment had a significant, powerful effect on the outcome for the experimental children, and it was equally effective for both types of child problems.

In general, postprogram analyses suggest that the Preschool Mental Health Project was effective in addressing the problems of high-risk children, facilitating a better adjustment to the classroom environment than was observed in those children who did not receive a prescriptive intervention. To determine the lasting quality of these effects, the children were reevaluated 2 years after they completed the program. For this follow-up evaluation (Rickel & Lampi, 1981), 70 first-grade children were examined, including 42 who were originally diagnosed as high risk and who participated either as experimental or control children in the original intervention. In addition, 28 children who were initially identified as low risk were included in this follow-up as a "normal" comparison for the high-risk groups. This 2-year postprogram multivariate analysis examined the data collected preprogram, at the end of the intervention, and at the 2-year follow-up and compared the children on the criterion measures.

Results of these analyses revealed significantly more maladjustment for high-risk controls than for low-risk controls at each time period. Conversely, the high-risk treatment group showed no significant differences from the low-risk controls at the end of the intervention year and at the 2-year follow-up. An additional finding was that shy treatment children showed greater benefits from the intervention at follow-up than did the aggressive treatment children.

Results of the 2-year postprogram evaluation established the potential for long-term effectiveness of the Preschool Mental Health Project's program of prescriptive interventions. High-risk children receiving the intervention were much more similar to low-risk control children compared to the high-risk control children 2 years after the treatment.

Parent Training Program. In addition to increasing the coping effectiveness of the preschoolers, another major objective of the Preschool Mental Health Project was to extend its influence into the home through a parent-training program. Goals of the Parent Training Program were research-oriented, as well as preventive: (a) the program was designed to explore the relationship between parenting styles and a child's adjustment, and (b) the program was an attempt to determine how best to conduct an effective training program in parenting skills (Atlas & Rickel, 1988; Rickel, Williams, & Loigman, 1988).

To address the first goal, parenting styles were assessed using a modified version of the Block (1965) Child Rearing Practices Report (CRPR; Rickel & Biasetti, 1982). The original Block CRPR contained 91 statements of self-reported child-rearing practices administered in a Q-sort format. The Rickel Modified CRPR consists of 40 of the original 91 items presented in the form of a questionnaire using a 6-point Likert scale. In this modified form, the CRPR yields scores on two subscales, Nurturance and Restrictiveness. The alpha coefficient for the Nurturance subscale is .82, and the alpha for Restrictiveness is also .82.

The Parent Training Program consisted of five weekly sessions and a final follow-up session. Sessions were held at the local school during regular school hours, and lasted about $2^1/_2$ hours each (Rickel, Dudley, & Berman, 1980). Topics for discussion, such as how to handle a child's expression of anger, fighting, or appropriate discipline methods, were introduced by group leaders. Typical and atypical preschool behaviors were explained to parents, along with techniques for dealing with inappropriate child behavior. Parents were provided a notebook for keeping handout sheets that outlined the key points discussed in each session and for their own notes taken in the sessions or at home.

Extensive role playing and modeling were used to present concepts to parents, who then used the majority of the sessions to practice these techniques. Every effort was made to create a safe and comfortable atmosphere for the parents to discuss their thoughts and feelings because for most of them these were new experiences.

At the end of each session a behavioral homework assignment was given that encouraged the parent to try out some aspect of the new techniques at home. Parents were also urged to discuss the concepts with a spouse or other adult with whom they lived. As each session began, parents were invited to share their experiences of trying out the new techniques at home during the prior week.

For the most part, sessions were favorably received by parents participating in the program. Participants reported they felt better about themselves as parents and more confident of their ability to handle specific behavioral problems or situations.

Training program effectiveness was evaluated using a control group format that involved both center-city and suburban parents (Rickel & Dudley, 1983). The placebo control group programs received the same number and length of sessions as parents in the treatment program, but the sessions consisted of nondirective discussions of the participants' parenting experience. Before the program, center-city parents were more restrictive (i.e., expected more conformity to their demands) than suburban parents, as measured by the Rickel Modified CRPR; however, the nurturance of center-city versus the suburban parents did not differ on the CRPR before the intervention. From preprogram to postprogram, experimentally trained parents significantly decreased in their self-reported restrictiveness. Furthermore, center-city parents receiving the training program showed a significantly greater change in their CRPR scores than did suburban parents who received the same training (Jones, Rickel, & Smith, 1980; Rickel, Dudley, & Berman, 1980).

After the extensive project just described, the Detroit Parent Training Project was implemented with adolescent mothers. The teen project provided a comprehensive 6-month program of parent education designed to enrich the teen mother's knowledge of child development, to evaluate and enhance their parent–child interactions, and to help them identify and manage stress more effectively. Small-group training sessions and in-home visits provided the opportunity to disseminate information, discuss shared concerns, and promote social support networks. The Detroit Teen Parent Project is discussed in chapter 4.

Summary and Conclusions

Research has repeatedly demonstrated the relationship between child-rearing practices and all aspects of a child's adjustment, including academic achievement and interpersonal skill development. Ideally, all parents should be educated in optimum child-development and child-management techniques and encouraged to recognize the kinds of models they present to their children. The neighborhood school is an important socializing agent and could be the focus of intervention programs to enhance parenting skills. Such an approach could serve as a preventive function for those children who may develop problems later if parental behaviors are not altered and could serve a remedial purpose for children already exhibiting adjustment difficulties.

In this chapter, we have described the types of risks facing families today, together with some of the interventions that have been found to be successful in preventing negative outcomes. Some negative outcomes may be unavoidable, but with effective preventive strategies, most problems of pregnancy, birth, and childhood can be averted. The tragedy in the United States is that for vast numbers of mothers and children, medical care, nutrition, and even physical safety are compromised to such a degree that negative outcomes are inevitable. Under managed care cutbacks, some of these threats are now beginning to encroach on the security of middle class family life as well. Children are society's investment in the future, and through effective early intervention Americans can make sure that every child acquires the skills necessary to meet that future with the highest level of competence possible.

Chapter

3

Traumatic Experiences of Childhood

The study of psychological trauma has burgeoned in recent years, boosted by the medical recognition and increased detection of child physical abuse, the "rediscovery" of child sexual abuse, and the increasingly sophisticated understanding of posttraumatic stress gained from studies of Vietnam veterans (Briere, 1992; Herman, 1992; Vandeven & Newberger, 1994). Researchers have also explored the response to various other types of trauma, such as natural disasters (McNally, 1993). Divorce, illness, or the loss of a caretaker may also be traumatic for the developing child.

In this chapter we describe the effects of traumatic experience on children, delineating the different types of trauma children are likely to encounter, including chronic illness, death and dying, natural disasters, divorce, victimization, and exposure to family and community violence. Implications for preventive interventions are also discussed.

Effects of Trauma

Psychological trauma is generally defined as a life event or experience that overwhelms one's ability to cope and, in childhood, has been linked to changes in cognitive, affective, behavioral, and physiological systems (Armsworth & Holaday, 1993; Briere, 1992; Eth & Pynoos, 1985; Herman, 1992;

Van der Kolk, 1987). Traumatic effects appear to be dependent, in part, on the developmental level of the child at the time of the experience, on individual characteristics of the child, and on the social context in which the trauma occurs. The latter factor includes such elements as caretaker availability (physical and psychological), reaction of significant others to the child's trauma, and the cumulative effects of other forms of risk in the child's life (Finkelhor, 1995; Newberger & DeVos, 1988).

Psychosocial sequelae documented in traumatized children include such diverse symptoms as depression, sadness, guilt, shame, helplessness, anxiety, low self-esteem, phobias, aggression, cruelty to animals, self-destruction, substance abuse, delinquency, violence, lack of trust, withdrawal, isolation, regression, sleep disorders, fatigue, failure to thrive, hyperarousal, language disorders, lowered scores on intelligence tests, and a variety of somatic complaints (Armsworth & Holaday, 1993; Briere, 1992; Cicchetti & Carlson, 1989; Johnson, 1989; Vandeven & Newberger, 1994).

Adolescents and adults who have experienced traumatic events in childhood may exhibit a wide range of psychiatric symptoms, which can lead to a variety of diagnostic labels, including dissociative disorders, affective disorders, anxiety disorders, eating disorders, substance abuse, and personality disorders. However, recognition of the etiology of these symptoms leads to a conceptualization of these behaviors as learned in (and useful within) the context of the traumatic experience and, subsequently, overgeneralized to situations where they are no longer useful or helpful to the individual (Becker-Lausen, Sanders, & Chinsky, 1995; Briere, 1992; Sanders & Becker-Lausen, in press).

The tension between this behavioral approach to symptomatology and the medical model of psychiatric disorders results in some substantial problems of differential diagnoses. The appeal of a disorder that has the potential for treatment is compelling, compared with the (often ineffective) attempts of mental health professionals to intervene in the lives of children who are victims of overwhelmingly tragic social circumstances. For example, the tendency to overdiagnose attention deficit disorder (ADD) in traumatized children is striking. Recently, an informal review of an inpatient psychiatric unit for children indicated that, despite the presence of documented abuse, neglect, deprivation, family violence, and familial substance abuse, all of the children had been given an ADD label.

Nevertheless, as practitioners we must be ever mindful of the need to determine the degree to which fear, anxiety, hypervigilence, dissociation, depression, or simply the distraction of living day-to-day with trauma (or its aftermath) is affecting a child's ability to attend to, concentrate on, and learn from his or her surroundings.

Types of Trauma

Researchers have attempted to differentiate among types of traumatic experiences in order to better understand variations in outcome. Terr (1991) distinguished between Type I and Type II traumatic experiences. *Type I* events are single instances or acute traumatic experiences. *Type II* represents the chronic, prolonged, repeated experience of trauma. Type II events are more likely to result in denial, psychic numbing, self-hypnosis, dissociation, and emotional lability. Type II trauma best fits Selye's (1956) description of the *general adaptation syndrome*, identified as the consequence of this chronic exposure to stress. More recent work on trauma has extended these findings, but the basic principles of human reaction still apply: When exposed to stress, humans respond first with alarm, then with resistance (a time where the individual appears to be coping, but internal, maladaptive physiological responses continue), and, ultimately, with physical exhaustion and illness.

On the other hand, Finkelhor (1995) has argued for a distinction in outcomes based on developmental effects, which does not fit neatly into the Type I and Type II categories. He suggests that, although Type II events are more likely to result in developmental effects, Type I events may also affect the child's development, especially when they occur at a crucial developmental transition. These developmental effects are subdivided by Finkelhor into three areas of concern: (a) the developmentally critical period of the child at the time of the trauma, (b) the developmentally specific cognitive abilities that affect the child's appraisal of the experience, and (c) the forms of symptom expression available to the child as a result of her or his stage of development.

Victimization may also be distinguished as a special case of childhood trauma (Finkelhor, 1995), compared to other types, such as natural disasters, poverty, bereavement, divorce, and illness. When a child is victimized, "the agency of harm is very identifiably human and personal, as opposed to the more physical, biological, or remote social forces that lie behind other stressors" (p. 188). Furthermore, harm is often directed at a specific, targeted individual, rather than family or community. Finally, there exists a system of intervention and social policy surrounding victimization that does not accompany other stressors such as illness, divorce, or disasters; that is, the intervention of police, protective service workers, courts, judges, or district attorneys dramatically affects the child's experience. For many or all of these reasons, victimization often results in a more serious impact on the child than other types of traumatic experiences.

Herman (1992) explained the special case of victimization this way:

> To study psychological trauma is to come face to face both with human vulnerability in the natural world and with the capacity for evil in human nature. To study psychological trauma means bearing witness to horrible events. When the events are natural disasters or "acts of God," those who bear witness sympathize readily with the victim. But when the traumatic events are of human design, those who bear witness are caught in the conflict between victim and perpetrator. It is morally impossible to remain neutral in this conflict. The bystander is forced to take sides. It is very tempting to take the side of the perpetrator. All the perpetrator asks is that the bystander do nothing. He appeals to the universal desire to see, hear, and speak no evil. The victim, on the con-

trary, asks the bystander to share the burden of pain. The victim demands action, engagement, and remembering. (pp. 7–8)

In the sections that follow, we discuss examples of traumatic experiences of childhood, including illness, death, natural disasters, and divorce. We conclude with a section on the special case of victimization, with particular focus on violence within the child's family environment.

Chronic Illness

Judith Rossner eloquently described the character Theresa in *Looking for Mr. Goodbar* (1975) as someone whose early experience with chronic illness leads her to use fantasy and repression to deal with the pain and discomfort of multiple medical procedures and prolonged hospitalization:

> There were innumerable examinations and tests before she could enter the hospital for surgery. The first so bad that after that it almost didn't matter—she felt little. Or she felt a great deal but dimly, as though it were happening to someone else .... For years she drifted into fantasy as she lay in bed at night or sat quietly looking at a book without reading it. Now her fantasies began to serve a more urgent purpose. It was much more bearable to be a princess getting tortured in a dungeon than a crooked little girl being tortured by doctors .... (pp. 27–28)

Theresa was first hospitalized when she had polio at age 4, but later complications of the polio led to a year-long hospitalization from age 11 to 12. We begin to get a glimpse of the painful emotions that drive Theresa to bars, searching for sexual experiences without any strings attached. At one point, when she talks about the year in the hospital, the painful feelings begin to emerge:

> "I was in the hospital for a year."
> "That must have been ghastly."
> She shrugged. "I guess. I don't remember too much of it. Anyway, I don't know why I'm talking about it .... I never should have been there in the first place," she went

on compulsively. "If they'd caught it in time I would've had maybe a brace for a while. But my older brother was killed in the service . . . my mother was in a . . . she was depressed . . . they were both depressed and . . . preoccupied. Nobody noticed what was happening."

Oh, God, it was like yesterday! Fifteen years and she was flooded with it. With wanting to tell them how badly it hurt and not being able to because they walked around the house with their eyes on the floor and she knew, anyway, that it was something she'd done that had brought this retribution on all of them. Not just on her. The pain was in some way directed even more at them; what would they do when they found out? So that every time she felt she finally must make them see her pain this other feeling got in the way and she would complain without ever making them *know*.

She stood up. "This is ridiculous. I don't want to get into all that . . . . Maybe we should call it a night." (pp. 205–206)[1]

So it is that Theresa flees this confrontation with traumatic memories of childhood, leaving her to continue her compulsive bar crawling, until eventually she takes home a man who murders her. Thus, Rossner created a portrait of cumulative traumatic childhood experiences, none of which involves intentional abuse or neglect: Theresa endured painful and invasive medical procedures, the separation and isolation of prolonged hospitalization, and sibling loss resulting in parental depression and neglect of her physical and emotional needs.

Rossner's portrait of the psychological effect on Theresa is brilliantly and realistically presented, with Theresa's dysfunction becoming increasingly apparent as she matures and as she becomes intimately involved with men. The reader is slowly provided the information that is key to understanding why this bright, attractive young woman behaves in ways that are so detrimental to her well-being.

---

[1] Reprinted with the permission of Pocket Books, a division of Simon & Schuster from LOOKING FOR MR. GOODBAR by Judith Rossner. Copyright © 1975 by Judith Rossner.

Fortunately, chronic illness does not necessarily lead to such tragic outcomes. Most of the estimated 10% of all children who experience one or more long-term medical conditions by age 16 probably do not face so many multiple stressors simultaneously as Rossner's character endured. The most common physical disorders among children are asthma, eczema, and epilepsy. Such illnesses often involve pain, discomfort, anxiety, embarrassment, isolation, and stigma. These conditions may dramatically affect the child's interpersonal relationships, especially with peers. Adults may alter their behavior toward the child, and siblings may resent the attention to the ill child (Garralda, 1994; Pless, Cripps, Davies, & Wadsworth, 1989).

Recently, researchers have stressed that most children with chronic illness cope well with their medical conditions, are psychologically adjusted, and demonstrate considerable resiliency (Midence, 1994). Like most experiences of childhood, the link between chronic illness and negative outcomes is neither simple nor direct, but rather is influenced by numerous other factors in the child's environment.

Although studies have demonstrated some relationship between chronic illness and psychological adjustment, moderated by severity of the medical condition, longitudinal research shows that the majority of children with chronic medical conditions are as well adjusted as their peers at midlife (Garralda, 1994; Pless et al. 1989). On the other hand, those from families with low socioeconomic status were less well adjusted than their peers from higher status families. Factors affecting adjustment include characteristics of the illness, of the child, and of the family (e.g., coping style and social environment; Midence, 1994).

Programs to prepare children for the hospital have been developed in response to research on the effects of medical encounters on children. Providing information, encouraging the child to express emotions, establishing a trusting relationship with medical personnel, preparing parents for the experience, and actively teaching coping strategies to the child all have been used in pediatric settings (Spirito, Stark, & Tye, 1994). As research continues to explore specific factors that affect the child's adjustment, interventions with children in medical settings will become increasingly sophisticated.

Death and Dying

For parents and for children, death and dying are among the most stressful experiences encountered. Studies of children facing death have suggested that open communication between adult caregivers and the afflicted child helps the child cope. Dealing with the child with a life-threatening illness requires special skills. Preschool children may not ask if they are going to die, but they can take their cues from the hospital staff and from parents who often inform them that their situation is serious. Researchers generally agree that by the age of 10 a fatally ill child is able to conceptualize her or his own death regardless of whether anyone has informed them about the severity of their illness (e.g., Pettle & Britten, 1995; Speece & Brent, 1992). Siblings of dying children may also need to have the opportunity to give voice to their fears, concerns, and emotional reactions.

Children afflicted with human immunodeficiency virus (HIV) often face multiple family problems, including parental incarceration, addiction, illness, abandonment, hospitalization, or homelessness, as well as protective services involvement and multiple out-of-home placements. These children need interventions at many levels from multiple systems, as do their noninfected siblings (Dubik-Unruh, 1989; Gyulay, 1989; Siegel & Gorey, 1994).

Parental death. An estimated 5% (or about 1.5 million) of U.S. children lose a parent by the time they are 15 years of age. Although childhood bereavement has been linked theoretically to adult depression for decades (Bowlby, 1980; Freud, 1917/1957), inconsistent research findings suggest that the relationship between them is neither direct nor inevitable (Mireault & Bond, 1992; Saler & Skolnick, 1992).

As with the experience of chronic medical conditions, with bereaved children there appear to be numerous factors that either facilitate resiliency or increase vulnerability to harmful outcomes. The role of the surviving parent, as well as the family environment, has been shown to be significant to the child's adjustment. Provision of physical and emotional support, open lines of communication between child and parent, stability, consistency, empathy, and warmth have all been linked to better outcomes for the bereaved child (Saler & Skolnick, 1992).

Recent studies have compared types of loss (death vs. separation; e.g. Kendler, Neale, Kessler, Heath, & Eaves, 1992) or, in some cases, types of childhood stressors (bereavement vs. divorce vs. childhood illness or parental mental illness; e.g. Sandler, Reynolds, Kliewer, & Ramiriz, 1992; Landerman, George, & Blazer, 1991). In general, such studies support the hypothesis that specific types of stressors are more likely to be linked to certain specific outcomes. For example, a study of twin adult women indicated the relationship between loss and adult psychopathology varied by type of loss, by which parent was lost, and by type of psychopathology (Kendler, Neale, Kessler, Heath, & Eaves, 1992). Depression and anxiety were related to separation, regardless of parent lost, but not to death; panic disorder was associated with death of either parent, but with separation only from the mother; and phobia was related to parental death, but not to separation.

The relationship between particular stressors and specific childhood disorders has also been studied with children aged 8 through 16 who had experienced either the death of a parent, divorce, or childhood asthma (Sandler, Reynolds, Kliewer, & Ramirez, 1992). The strongest findings for a specificity hypothesis were for bereaved children; that is, for these children, conflict stressors were more likely to be related to conduct disorder, and separation events were more strongly related to depression.

Furthermore, stressful events in adults' lives were also found to interact with specific types of traumatic experiences in childhood (Landerman, George, & Blazer, 1991). Parental mental illness was found to increase the likelihood that stressful events would result in depression for adults, whereas parental divorce increased the chances that stress would lead to alcohol abuse and various psychiatric disorders. Parental death, however, did not appear to interact with stressful events in any way that would increase risk of psychiatric problems.

Disasters

Floods, earthquakes, hurricanes, avalanches, and other disasters have all become the province in the past decade of researchers seeking to understand the effects of such traumatic experiences on children. Earthquakes in California, hurricanes in Florida, and floods in the Midwest have added to our knowledge of trauma reactions. Disasters such as the explosion of the Space Shuttle Challenger in 1986, which occurred while school children around the country watched the launch of the first teacher into space, or the 1995 federal building bombing in Oklahoma City, in which 168 people died, have also increased researchers' and clinicians' awareness of the reactions to extreme events.

In general, researchers have found what they sought: Symptoms of posttraumatic stress disorder (PTSD) have been documented in response to a wide range of natural catastrophes. In an attempt to determine prevalence of traumatic experiences, Norris (1992) studied 1,000 adults in the southern United States. In a year's time, 2.4% of households in the study had experienced disaster or damage. Over their lifetime, 13% of the participants were exposed to disaster. By comparison, 21% of the same group of subjects had experienced some type of traumatic stressor, with a lifetime prevalence rate for all trauma of 69%.

Among the major findings in this area of trauma research are those from longitudinal studies of survivors of the Buffalo Creek flood, which occurred after a dam collapsed in 1972. A 14-year follow-up of 121 victims, 32% of the original sample ($N = 381$), indicated that 44% of the sample had PTSD symptoms in 1974 whereas 28% had such symptoms in 1986 (Grace, Green, Lindy, & Leonard, 1993). However, those who refused to participate in the long-term follow-up had significantly higher levels of bereavement at the earlier evaluation, compared to those who did take part in the follow-up. This discrepancy illuminates one of the problems with this type of research: Those who are most traumatized may also be the least likely to want to take part in studies that bring them face-to-face once more with their memories of the traumatic experiences.

As with other childhood stressors, however, the symptoms vary for individual children and appear to be mitigated by other factors in the environment (Bradburn, 1991; Shannon, Lonigan, Finch, & Taylor, 1994). Characteristics of the disaster itself, severity of exposure to the disaster, and the degree of harm to the child's immediate environment (e.g., destruction of the home), have all been found to be related to symptomatology. Likewise, individual characteristics of age, race, and gender also have been related to symptom development, with younger children, females, and Black children reporting more symptoms diagnostic of PTSD, and male children reporting more symptoms of cognitive and behavioral disturbances. These and other findings have led to the design of early intervention programs for children in response to natural disasters, as well as to human-caused disasters such as the Oklahoma City bombing.

Schools are important in the prevention of traumatic responses to disasters. Because any class is likely to experience one or more critical incidents in a year, school staff should be trained and ready to intervene with their students when a potentially traumatic event occurs (Johnson, 1989). Staff should be aware and understand the possible reactions to trauma, watch students for their reactions, and provide supportive responses to them.

Johnson (1989) suggested that school professionals be prepared to intervene through individual conferences or with entire classes during a period of crisis; that they provide coordination and follow-up with students, parents, and other staff; and that they team up with school or outside mental health professionals to provide the most effective, wide-ranging, and supportive services to students. As the knowledge base on trauma has improved, such interventions have become increasingly sophisticated and are being implemented in a variety of traumatic situations by a number of different organizations (Pynoos, Steinberg, & Goenjian, 1996).

Divorce

Perhaps the most common, potentially traumatic experience to which American children are exposed today is the permanent separation of their parents from one another. If the parents are married, divorce involves dissolution of the marriage through the court system, often with legal representation on both sides. Unfortunately, this system is often adversarial, contentious, and expensive.

In the United States, 50% of all marriages end in divorce (U.S. Bureau of the Census, 1994). Countless other parental relationships break up with less legal entanglement than those that began in marriage, but these break ups still may be contentious or even violent. Children, therefore, are frequently left to deal not only with loss and separation, but also with ongoing conflictual relationships, diminished financial resources, and overstressed caregivers.

Long-term outcomes for children include, as might be expected, effects on their own marital patterns (Rickel & Langner, 1985; Tasker & Richards, 1994). Some grow up to view marriage with distrust, particularly where there was considerable parental conflict and where the parent–child relationship was not adequately sustained. However, sometimes the accompanying social outcomes of divorce, including diminished resources, lowered socioeconomic status, and decreased educational opportunities lead adolescents and young adults to enter into early heterosexual relationships (Rickel & Langner, 1985). Girls are more likely to make these early commitments, but both genders may be likely to do so when they live in low-income households, they have witnessed parental conflict, their relationship with a parent has deteriorated, or the residential parent has remarried (Tasker & Richards, 1994).

A longitudinal, multimethod milestone study (Chase-Lansdale, Cherlin, & Kiernan, 1995) examined the long-term psychological effects of parental divorce on all children born in Great Britain during 1 week in 1958 ($N = 17,414$). Children were examined at birth and at ages 7, 11, 16, and 23 by means of maternal and child interviews and by psychological, school, and medical assessments. Controlling for economic status, children's emotional problems, and school performance preceding marital dissolution, parental divorce had a moderate, long-term negative impact on adult mental health. The relative risk of serious emotional disorders increased in the aftermath of divorce, but the large majority of individuals did not exhibit such risks. Only a small subgroup is seriously affected, but this subgroup does produce a large proportional increase in the size of the young adult population that may require clinical intervention.

Conflict: A key factor. Despite the negative consequences, research has shown that where considerable conflict exists, children actually fare better when parents divorce than when they stay married. For example, in a 12-year longitudinal study (Amato, Loomis, & Booth, 1995), adult children from high-conflict parents who divorced had higher levels of well being than adult children whose high-conflict parents stayed together. However, where conflict between parents was low, the opposite was true: Adult children were healthier when low-conflict parents stayed married than when they divorced.

Children may also be affected after divorce by the amount of ongoing contact between parents, the subsequent amount of continued conflict, and the quality of the parent–child relationships. Again, conflict appears to be the primary moderator of outcomes for the child. In one large, national survey (Amato & Rezac, 1994), the outcome was particularly noteworthy for boys: Where there was ongoing conflict between parents, boys with a great deal of contact with the nonresident parent had more behavior problems; where there was little or no conflict between parents, boys in frequent contact with the nonresident parent had fewer behavior problems. For girls, there was no such relationship among these variables.

However, youth in divorced households are no more likely to experience ongoing conflict than those from intact families (Forehand & Thomas, 1992). In fact, after the first year, post-divorce families may actually be less conflictual than intact families.

Implications for child custody disputes. The long-standing finding that conflict is the key factor in divorce outcomes for children (Hetherington, Cox, & Cox, 1982), which has now been replicated numerous times, has important implications for child custody arrangements. Ongoing contact with both parents appears to be the best arrangement only when conflict between parents is low. In fact, one study found that "feeling caught" between parents was a common experience for adolescents whose parents were high in conflict and low in cooperation, that this experience was worse for youth in dual residence, and that such a feeling was associated with negative outcomes for these youth (Buchanan, Maccoby, & Dornbusch, 1991).

Divorce mediation is often sought in place of litigation and was created in an attempt to mitigate the effects of conflict and to diminish the adversarial nature of the divorce process. However, mediation alone does not ensure improved outcomes for the children. In fact, comparisons of mediation and litigation families indicated no differences in child outcomes, and it appears that, once again, the key factor for child outcome is the level of conflict between the parents, regardless of which method they choose for marriage dissolution (Kitzmann & Emery, 1994). These and other findings of the pervasiveness of conflict as problematic suggest that early teaching of conflict resolution in school settings may be important for the long-term health of our society as a whole.

Victimization Experiences of Childhood

Violence in this country is pandemic and cuts across race, class, and gender, although women, children, and youth are most often its victims. For example, although it is well publicized that homicide is the leading cause of death for young Black men, the fact that it is also the leading cause of death for young Black women is less widely recognized (APA Commission on Violence and Youth, 1993). Family violence also cuts across race, class, and gender.

Family violence. According to the Report of the APA Presidential Task Force on Violence and the Family (1996), family violence and abuse includes "acts of physical abuse, sexual abuse, and psychological maltreatment; chronic situations in which one person controls or intends to control another person's behavior; and misuse of power that may result in injury or harm to the psychological, social, economic, sexual, or physical well-being of family members" (p. 3).

The report defined *family* in broad terms, so that it includes extended family, stepfamilies, intimate partners (whether or not they are legally married), and gay or lesbian families.

Child abuse and neglect fatalities increased by 49% between 1985 and 1992, according to the National Committee for Prevention of Child Abuse, and reports of abuse and neglect rose 50% during the same period (McCurdy & Daro, 1993).

According to the U.S. Advisory Board on Child Abuse and Neglect (1995), about 5 children die each day from abuse and neglect—2,000 each year in the United States—the vast majority of whom are under 4 years of age. This rate, the highest in 40 years, is probably a gross underestimate of the actual death rate. The U.S. Advisory Board estimated that 85% of child abuse and neglect deaths are misidentified as unintentional deaths (e.g., sudden infant death syndrome). But even with this potential underestimate, the death rate for abuse and neglect is twice that of the next leading cause of death for children, motor vehicles. According to the U.S. Advisory Board report, in the 34 years since C. Henry Kempe first described the battered child syndrome, more children have died from abuse and neglect than from urban gang wars, AIDS, polio, or measles.

Each year, abuse and neglect further causes 18,000 serious disabilities (e.g., brain damage from shaken baby syndrome) and 141,700 serious injuries. The incidence of abuse and neglect is substantiated in 992,617 cases annually, and 1.9 million children are reported (2.9 million reports filed) to protective services. Children continue to be exposed to all forms of risk, with little shielding provided by U.S. society. In 1993, an estimated 500,000 to 650,000 parents and children were living in the streets, either temporarily or permanently, and 11 million parents with children were abusing drugs or alcohol. Somewhere between 3.3 million and 10 million households include a violent man with a history of domestic abuse.

Ninety-five percent of adult victims of intimate violence— 2 to 4 million each year—are women (Sugg & Inui, 1992). Researchers and policy makers have, in recent years, begun to make the connection between the assault of women and the abuse of children. The APA Task Force on Violence and the Family (1996) noted, "If one form of violence is present in a relationship, the likelihood increases that other forms of violence are going on as well" (p. 3).

Although figures vary depending on the population studied, Browne (1987) estimated that in about 50% of cases where a woman is a victim of violence from a male partner, children are also being physically abused by the same man. One study, however, found that 70% of children of battered women in a Dallas shelter had been abused or neglected (DeLange, 1988). In some of these cases, the child was also being sexually assaulted. Schechter and Mihaly (1992) reported that between January and April 1992, 22 women in Massachusetts were murdered by partners, some of whom then turned their violence on the children, leaving five children dead and two wounded.

Effects of family violence on children. Witnessing the abuse of a parent may be as harmful as being a victim of abusive behavior (Widom, 1989a). Even if the child is not being assaulted or neglected, she or he may develop sleep disorders, eating disorders, nightmares, respiratory distress, and other symptoms of anxiety and depression. In general, the long-term effects on children of witnessing violence are essentially the same as experiencing abuse directly: depression, dissociation, aggression, anxiety, vulnerability to revictimization, developmental delays, substance abuse, and, in some cases, violence and other criminal behavior (Becker-Lausen, Sanders, & Chinsky, 1995; Briere, 1992; Browne, 1987; Kolko, 1992; Sanders & Giolas, 1991; Widom, 1989b).

Exposure to violence as a child also may be a factor in the perpetuation of abusive patterns across generations. According to one early study of family violence (Straus, Gelles, & Steinmetz, 1980), men who had witnessed their fathers hitting their mothers were three times more likely to hit their wives than were those who did not witness partner violence in childhood (35% compared to 11%). Subsequent research indicated that the only variable that predicted men's use of violence against female partners was the witnessing of parental violence in their childhood home (Hotaling & Sugarman, 1986). Although there may be numerous mechanisms through which perpetuation of violence within the family occurs across generations, some research suggests that one path may be through the damage done to members' relationships with one another. As violence increases in the family, members' perceptions of family strength are decreased, and adults report less satisfaction with marriage and with parenting (Meredith, Abbott, & Adams, 1986).

Regardless of the type of family violence experienced, psychological trauma and its symptoms are similar for the victims (APA Presidential Task Force on Violence and the Family, 1996). The effects of violence on children is consistent with the literature on divorce and family conflict. As described previously in this chapter, the finding that children have more behavioral, emotional, and social problems in high-conflict families, especially when parents continue to argue in front of the children after a divorce, is a longstanding one (Hetherington, Cox, & Cox, 1982; Santrock & Sitterle, 1987). A number of studies have also documented that conflictual intact families are more detrimental to a child's well being than a stable single-parent family or stepparent family (Block, Block, & Gjerde, 1986; Demo & Acock, 1988). Despite these profound and well-documented consequences for the child, few states have laws that allow courts to consider domestic violence history in making visitation and custody decisions.

Effects of violence on female caretakers.   Effects of battering on female caretakers have profound consequences for their relationship with their children (Koss et al., 1994). These effects are not only physical, but are emotional also. In addition to all the possible ways a woman can be assaulted, she also may, as a result, experience strokes, miscarriages, depression, suicide attempts, headaches, sleep disorders, substance abuse (Health Care and Family Violence Field Project, 1992), and what Lenore Walker (1993) has called a *punch drunk syndrome* (a term taken from boxing that refers to a dazed state resulting from repeated blows to the head). This constant exposure to trauma leads women to emotional and physical exhaustion in the manner previously described for the general adaptation syndrome (Selye, 1956).

The traumatic response is further complicated by the effects of dealing with the well-known dilemmas of *approach–avoidance* conflicts (Dollard & Miller, 1950). Anyone considering leaving a spouse or partner is likely to experience the stress of deciding between the multiple reasons to end a relationship and the multiple reasons to remain in it. Depending on the circumstances, this dilemma may be an *approach–approach* (leaving and staying have equally attractive characteristics), or an *avoidance–avoidance* (both have equally negative consequences) conflict. Leaving an abusive relationship is likely to fall into the latter category: Staying means continuing to be battered, but leaving may have numerous negative consequences (e.g., poverty, threat of death).

Practitioners often see women in these various stages of coping with the trauma of exposure to a violent partner. Frequently, women who have separated or divorced violent partners are forced to interact with these men around child visitation and custody issues.

Women experiencing violence in the home often have a long history of exposure to medical professionals who have not asked about the possibility of abuse, despite bruises and other visible signs, despite repeated trips to the emergency room in the middle of the night, or despite symptoms of depression and anxiety or evidence of substance abuse.

More disturbing still, many professionals not only neglect to ask, but do not believe the woman when she finally does disclose abuse. Like the rape victim, the battered woman is often blamed for abuse and discredited. Furthermore, the traumatic response displayed by the woman is often considered evidence that she is unstable, is unreliable, or suffers from borderline personality disorder. The very nature of the traumatic response may lead battered women to be seen as "hysterical." The batterer, on the other hand, may appear calm, clear-headed, and in control—as, of course, he often is.

This "blaming the victim" is predicted by a very basic principle of social psychology: the *fundamental attribution error*. Simply put, humans tend to assign dispositional causes to the behavior of others, consistently underestimating the role that a particular situation or set of circumstances plays in an individual's behavior (Heider, 1958; Ross, 1977). In light of this fundamental bias on the part of observers, the frequently asked question "why doesn't she just leave?" becomes more understandable, as does the underlying assumption that if a battered woman does not leave her abuser, there must be some internal flaw in her character. Add to this fundamental error the complexity of the dynamic issues (e.g., the fact that a woman is often in the most danger when she does leave), and it is easy to see why many professionals simply do not grasp the enormous power of the psychological situation. One group of researchers has attempted to apply hostage theory to child abuse victims (Goddard & Stanley, 1994), suggesting that similarities exist, as delineated in the literature, between child abusers and hostage captors, as well as between abusers and terrorists. For example, captors seek to create an environment in which the victim experiences isolation and powerlessness. In response to this environment, the victim may feel love and attachment toward the captor/ abuser. This phenomenon has been described in the hostage literature as "Stockholm syndrome" (Wardlaw, 1982), and in the child abuse literature as "child sexual abuse accommodation syndrome" (Summit, 1983). Several other parallels are described by Goddard and Stanley. The formulation may also be applied to the dynamics of adult battering relationships.

In addition to the fundamental attribution error to which people are all prone when they judge the behavior of others, most people also have a self-serving bias: They believe their own actions to be situationally determined when their consequences are negative, but dispositionally determined when the consequences are positive (Miller & Ross, 1975). That is, they take credit for their successes and blame their failures on external factors. However, when individuals are depressed or have low self-esteem, the self-serving bias tends to disappear, leaving them prone to blame failure on internal flaws and to believe success to be luck or a fluke (Seligman & Rosenhan, 1984; Sweeney, Anderson, & Bailey, 1986). Because one of the more common responses to trauma is depression, battered women are especially vulnerable not only to being blamed for their abuse, but also to believing they are to blame.

Furthermore, since the wearing down of the victim's self-esteem is essential to the process of power and control in a battering relationship, the abuser is usually all too ready to encourage the victim's belief that she is at fault. Men who have been violent toward women often present with a litany of complaints about all of the failings of their female partners. The battered partner, on the other hand, is more likely to ask, "Do you think I'm a bad mother?" reflecting her own self-doubt and the negative self-image she has come to accept.

Schechter and Mihaly (1992) provide a quote from a woman who describes the terrorizing tactics often seen in these cases:

> He yelled at me to keep the kids quiet and when the baby kept crying, he swatted her. He left her black and blue . . . he told me that if I called DSS, he'd swear to the worker that I did it. I was terrified that they would blame me and take my baby away. I was terrified of him, too. My husband just laughed at me. I was too scared to do anything, and he knew he had us trapped. (p. 2)

When the effects of a patriarchal system that may render a woman helpless are added to the attribution errors and power-and-control dynamics, the result is a complete failure of society to provide women with support, protection from harm and empowerment (Becker-Lausen, Barkan, & Newberger, 1994).

Physicians are often the first professionals to have an opportunity to recognize that violence is occurring in a family. Victims frequently must seek medical attention, putting physicians in the position to be significant gatekeepers. In fact, battering is the single most common cause of injury to women patients (Stark & Flitcraft, 1988), more common than automobile accidents, rapes, and muggings combined. It accounts for one third of all women's emergency room visits. However, studies have raised concerns that health care professionals, particularly physicians, lack sufficient knowledge to ask even the most rudimentary questions, let alone make appropriate responses and referrals (e.g., Stark & Flitcraft, 1988; Sugg & Inui, 1992; Trute, Sarsfield, & Mackenzie, 1988). Although the American Medical Association has developed guidelines for physician response to domestic violence, the programs that train physicians lag far behind in educating these medical professionals about the issues.

Moreover, a 1992 study of five diverse communities conducted by a team at Boston Children's Hospital with the Education Development Center, Inc., revealed that even when family violence was recognized as important by a community's health care system, health care professionals failed to play a significant role in addressing the problem (Health Care and Family Violence Field Project, 1992). Furthermore, although there has been increased awareness of child abuse and neglect among physicians, few have received any formal training in this area; many lack information concerning their most basic role as a mandated reporter. Few medical schools provide training, and residency programs vary widely in the attention they pay to these issues. This lack of training often results in class and race biases in recognition, intervention, and response to suspected child abuse.

Knowledge of violence against women lags even further behind awareness of child maltreatment. Research into physician awareness and response to battered women is very sparse, compared to research on physicians' awareness of child abuse. One study in Canada found that younger physicians and female physicians were more likely to be aware of and to respond to wife abuse (Trute, Sarsfield, & Mackenzie, 1988). The study concluded that much more education was needed for Canadian physicians to be able to recognize and respond to battered women. A study of Seattle physicians (Sugg & Inui, 1992) found that physicians were reluctant to broach the subject of family violence with their patients, for reasons that included class and racial biases, time constraints, and fears that they would be opening a "Pandora's box." Some also admitted they might not believe the patient if the patient revealed they were being battered, even in response to the physician's questioning.

Additional studies of U.S. physicians need to be conducted to assess the level of awareness and the gaps in physicians' training. Educational courses can then be designed to address these gaps. Knowledge of battering and child abuse should become requirements for all health professionals' licensing exams.

California now has a law that all health care professionals working in a medical setting are mandated to report a patient who has been battered. This approach is highly controversial because of fears that it may infantilize women caught in abusive situations, put them at risk of greater harm, and increase their already great reluctance to tell anyone they are being beaten. One can only hope this law, together with recent sensational court cases involving battery covered widely by mass media, will at least help raise awareness of these issues.

Other mandated reporting laws in California have led to requirements for training hours for licensing exams (e.g. child abuse reporting), and perhaps this law will also raise awareness. Other states should consider requiring training hours in family violence for licensing of medical and mental health care professionals. Mental health and social science professionals with knowledge of these areas can play an important role in designing and carrying out the research, as well as in providing the training.

Intergenerational transmission. Kaufman and Zigler (1987) raised the question, "Do abused children become abusive parents?" They suggested that a better question is "Under what conditions is the transmission of abuse most likely to occur?" and concluded that about 30% (plus or minus 5%)

of parents with a childhood history of abuse become perpe-trators of child abuse. This rate is six times higher than the base rate for abuse in the general population (5%). Similarly, Gelles (1987) estimated that about 39% of child abuse victims go on to become abusers of their own children. Furthermore, as noted previously in this chapter, studies have suggested that men who witness parental battering are more likely as adults to use violence against female partners (Hotaling & Sugarman, 1986; Straus, Gelles, & Steinmetz, 1980).

Researchers are attempting to identify mediator and mod-erator variables in the intergenerational transmission of abuse, as Kaufman and Zigler (1987) recommended. As tools for the measurement of childhood trauma and its effects be-come more sophisticated (Briere & Runtz, 1993; Gold, Milan, Mayall, & Johnson, 1994; Sanders & Becker-Lausen, 1995), the intervening variables continue to be identified.

Adult outcomes. Severe punishment may be passed to the next generation through the legitimization or normalization of violence by parents, increasing the chances that a child will adopt similarly harsh techniques. Kelder, McNamara, Carlson, and Lynn (1991) found that individuals who re-ported experiencing more severe discipline in childhood and adolescence considered physical punishment more appropri-ate than subjects less severely disciplined. Those reporting the most abusive experiences in childhood considered pun-ishment less appropriate than those without these experi-ences, however. On the other hand, even severe or abusive punishment, when it was believed by victims to be deserved, was related to a belief that physical punishment is appropri-ate. Those who saw their punishment as undeserved did not believe physical punishment is appropriate. Male partici-pants in this study were more likely than female participants to consider the use of physical punishment appropriate. The authors speculated that the parents' attitude toward their own use of punishment (and what they tell the child about it) may affect the child's belief about culpability.

Developmentally inappropriate expectations of children have also been implicated in child abuse. Inappropriate ex-pectations involve a lack of knowledge of developmental capabilities (e.g., for self-care, responsibility for others, help and affection toward parents, staying alone, proper behavior, and punishment). Unrealistic expectations were found to distinguish a group of maltreating mothers from a group of demographically matched control mothers with no known abuse in their homes (Azar, Robinson, Hekimian, & Twentyman, 1984). To control for the possibility that abuse in the home may affect other variables, Azar and Rohrbeck (1986) compared child abusing mothers to mothers whose partners abused their children. Abusing mothers had significantly greater unrealistic expectations of their children than did the control mothers, and these expectations correctly classified 83% of subjects in a discriminant function analysis.

Child characteristics, such as difficult temperament, attachment problems, developmental abnormalities, and behavioral and emotional difficulties, may contribute to risk, at least for physical abuse (Kolko, Kazdin, Thomas, & Day, 1993); however, child behavior has been found to be an insufficient explanation for child abuse (Ammerman, 1991; Pianta, Egeland, & Erickson, 1989). As was previously mentioned, all of these characteristics may be the result of either witnessing or being a victim of family violence.

Inconsistent, negative, or aggressive child-rearing practices; constricted positive affect; limited social behavior; cognitive-attributional biases (i.e., unrealistic expectations, lack of acceptance, lack of positive attributions); depression; and physical symptoms are parental characteristics that have been associated with potential for child physical abuse (Kolko et al., 1993). More coercive interactions, heightened conflict, and decreased cohesion were found in abusive families, and these families appear to experience greater numbers of stressful life events.

The Kolko et al. (1993) study compared mothers at high risk for abuse to low- and moderate-risk mothers. For these mothers, psychological dysfunction had the strongest relationship with abuse potential. Neither reported parenting practices nor reports of family violence differentiated groups of mothers. On the other hand, the high-risk mothers did report more stressful life events and family problems and their children showed more antisocial behavior, depression, and self-injury. Subsequent research (Becker-Lausen, Sanders, & Chinsky, 1995) has further demonstrated a relationship between reports of maltreatment in childhood by college students and greater numbers of stressful life events, greater negative impact of stressful life events, and increased depression.

As Phares (1992) has pointed out, the absence of data on fathers has been a major problem in research on parenting. Too often, men are included in studies for the purpose of understanding victims or perpetrators, but not in relation to parenting. One such study of father perpetrators of incest found that fathers with a child sexual abuse history reported significantly more chaotic, dysfunctional families of origin than nonabused perpetrators (Hanson, Lipovsky, & Saunders, 1994). However, abused perpetrators were no different from nonabused perpetrators on personality profiles, nor did they differ in psychological symptoms. Both groups reported more dysfunctional families of origin and more psychological symptoms, compared to normative data.

Assessing psychosocial maladjustment in men and women sexually molested as children, Hunter (1991) found that the association between childhood sexual abuse and adult psychosocial dysfunction was as true for men as it was for women, with both sexes showing significantly more dysfunction than controls on a number of psychosocial variables.

Increased psychopathology has been shown to be associated with increased levels of various types of maltreatment in childhood. Studies have demonstrated that child abuse victims exhibit a variety of symptoms, including posttraumatic stress disorder, a damaged self-image and low self-esteem, depression, anxiety, dissociation, and impaired self-reference (Becker-Lausen, Sanders, & Chinsky, 1995; Briere, 1992; Chu & Dill, 1990; Sanders & Giolas, 1991; Sanders, McRoberts, & Tollefson, 1989).

Becker-Lausen and Rickel (1995) reported that for female college students, dissociation was significantly related to reports of becoming pregnant and reports of having an abortion during high school. For these young women, a history of childhood maltreatment alone was not associated with these events, although dissociation was found more generally to be a significant mediator between child abuse history and negative life outcomes. For male college students, however, child abuse history was the only variable significantly related to reports of a girlfriend's becoming pregnant and reports of a girlfriend's having an abortion in high school.

The APA Presidential Task Force on Violence and the Family (1996) concluded, "The best way to promote violence-free families is to stop the development of abusive behavior, especially in boys and men; to strengthen and empower potential victims to resist or avoid victimization; and to change the environment that promotes the use of violence" (p. viii).

The negative effects of childhood sexual abuse, and even its very existence, were dismissed or diminished for numerous years. In part because of this history, many researchers have tended to overemphasize the relationship between child sexual abuse history and mental health difficulties. As childhood trauma, including all the various forms of family violence, becomes an accepted focus of study related to child psychopathology, "abuse clinicians and researchers are more comfortable investigating the other possible contributors to negative adult outcomes" (Berliner, 1993, p. 429).

Community Violence

Violence is pervasive in American communities. Following are the words of a middle-class mother from suburban Virginia who testified before the U.S. Senate Labor Subcommittee on Children:

> [T]his is my son . . . . He was 17 years old when he was murdered. He was the boy next door . . . . He never gave me any trouble. He was an excellent student [and] in 3 weeks, he would have been bound for Virginia Tech. He was killed by a classmate who was 18 years old—an Eagle Scout. He had never been in trouble. There was no alcohol, there was no drugs. They didn't even smoke . . . .

There was never any physical violence. They graduated [and] the killer, found out where Scott was . . . working . . . came on the job and began working . . . made Scott think he was his friend. He took him deep into the woods, and he shot him with an AK-47 assault weapon. The first shot was in the back. It severed the spinal cord and immobilized him. The other shots hit vital organs, and the last was an execution shot to the head . . . . I always had the misconception . . . that everything is drug related, but it isn't. It can happen to your son just like it happened to mine. (*Keeping Every Child Safe*, 1993, pp. 19–20)

Violence in the larger community has been a primary focus of attention recently, as rates of violent crime have increased, primarily among youth. In fact, the United States has the shameful distinction of ranking number one among industrialized nations for its homicide rate (APA Commission on Violence and Youth, 1993). As noted previously, for young Black males and females, homicide is the leading cause of death (Centers for Disease Control, 1992), and homicide rates for children and youth have doubled since the early 1960s (Novello, 1992). As we discussed, too many violent deaths happen within the family, at the hands of those entrusted with the care of a child, or to women murdered by their male partners.

Although it is often exacerbated by stresses associated with poverty, family violence occurs at all socioeconomic levels. "Street violence," on the other hand, disproportionately harms the poorest of our children and youth, those trapped by poverty and segregation in decaying inner-city environments, and those with the least opportunities for education and upward mobility. Nevertheless, as the mother just quoted reveals, the pervasiveness of violence in American culture suggests that sooner or later violence can touch everyone.

Violence has been allowed to flourish in this country, fed by media images of violent heroes; by political leaders who advocate and extol the glories of "kicking butt" (e.g., during the Gulf War); by the proliferation of guns; and by toys which simulate all of these violent icons. The combination of this culture of violence and the existence of increasingly disparate economic circumstances and opportunities creates an explosive situation.

Poverty has been identified as the single greatest risk factor for youth by several panels of experts in varying contexts (e.g., see the APA Commission on Violence and Youth, 1993; National Research Council, 1993). Poverty has greatly increased in the past two decades, even during the periods of national economic expansion in the 1980s, according to the National Research Council (1993) report, that led to increasingly large gaps between the highest and lowest income groups and to a nearly one third decline in the real income of young families.

The APA Commission on Violence and Youth (1993) reported that higher rates of violence among ethnic minority groups largely result from the greater poverty and deprivation among ethnic minorities. When socioeconomic status is controlled for, few differences are found among ethnic groups in rates of violence.

Deprivation, segregation, lack of opportunity, and other conditions to which children of poverty are exposed, particularly in inner cities, breed violent behavior. Posttraumatic stress disorder has been documented in children living in environments in which these conditions flourish. Studying children trapped in the "war zones" of our inner cities, James Garbarino (*Children of War*, 1992) found such children living with a deep sense of hopelessness and despair. When he asked many of these children "What do you expect to be when you're 30?" they answered, "dead," Garbarino reported.

Children so alienated and hopeless feel they have nothing to lose by engaging in violence. Exposing children to these conditions constitutes a form of child maltreatment perpetrated by the larger society. Several authors have suggested that social discrimination, racism, sexism, and war (including inner city "wars") are "culturally supported child maltreatment" (Briere, 1992, p. 15).

For example, in 1993, an estimated 500,000 to 650,000 parents and children were homeless either temporarily or permanently (U.S. Advisory Board on Child Abuse and Neglect,

1995). These children are being reared in cardboard boxes, cars, abandoned buildings, public parks, and occasionally shelters—conditions hardly conducive to basic health needs, let alone educational goals such as reading readiness.

"We live in difficult and dangerous times, in a country deeply divided by class, race, and social philosophy," Lillian Rubin (1994, p. 247) tells readers in her eloquent book documenting the working class family's view of U.S. society. As Rubin and other social scientists have suggested, it has been politically useful for some leaders to create a climate in which the working class blames the underclass for the ills of society (Edsall & Edsall, 1991). This is, as Rubin suggests, a dangerous stance for a democratic nation.

Commissioned panels, such as those of the National Research Council (1993) and the American Psychological Association (1993), repeatedly come to the same conclusions: Compared with every other industrialized country, the United States is seriously lacking in prevention and early intervention efforts with children and families. However, the situation continues to worsen.

Deborah Prothrow-Stith, a violence-prevention policy expert at Harvard University, expressed her frustrations with the American social service system in testimony before Congress:

> We wait. We see these children at risk, and we wait. They may not be able to afford the eyeglasses that they need. They certainly don't have an after-school program. If they need special tutoring, special help, or even a sports program, we can't afford it.
>
> But you let them shoot somebody, or get shot, and we spend money transfusing, operating—we will spend $80,000 a day in intensive care costs. We will spend money arresting, prosecuting, defending, incarcerating, hopefully some rehabilitating. But we spend money on this problem. Our "low-down-dirty-hang-your-head-in-shame" is that we wait. We wait until these children are convicted of a violent offense before we spend any money. (*Keeping Every Child Safe*, 1993, p. 34)

If a fundamental shift in the attitude of the American public is to come about, mental health professionals must join ranks with other interested groups, such as pediatricians, public health officials, and other social scientists, to better communicate the critical importance of prevention and early intervention to the alleviation of childhood trauma and its outcomes.

Summary

In this chapter we have delineated how traumatic experiences can affect a child's development, adjustment, and psychiatric symptomatology. Some forms of trauma, such as chronic illness, death and dying, and natural disasters, may often be unavoidable. For these experiences, minimizing the traumatic effects and ameliorating the consequences of these events may be the best that can be done. However, many traumatic experiences are preventable, such as divorce, experiences of victimization, and exposure to poverty or violence—yet too little is being done in the United States to prevent children's exposure to these negative events. Many professionals in different fields have begun to speak out about the need for prevention. We suggest it is time professionals come together across disciplines to develop strategies to address the multiple problems Americans face. Professionals must learn to speak with one voice if we are to convince the public of the value of prevention.

4

Adolescent Risk Factors and Outcomes

A dolescence is a period of major life transition and perhaps is one of the most complex periods of physical and
psychological growth and development. Every aspect of the
adolescent's life—social, emotional, and biological—is in
flux (Carnegie Council on Adolescent Development, 1995). In
the past, researchers and practitioners focusing on adolescents have emphasized damage to adolescents resulting primarily from biologically based disorders. However, in the
last generation, the rates of morbidity and mortality from
these disorders have fallen dramatically, and a new group of
dangers termed the *new morbidity* have emerged. The new
morbidity is a group of health-related conditions with social
rather than purely biological causes, and include unprotected
sexual behavior, teenage pregnancy, and substance abuse.

Although these problems may not be as debilitating as
physical health threats, they have serious implications for
youth and often lead to increased physical and mental health
risks and lowered opportunities for successful employment,
economic success, and overall productive lives. The new
morbidity disorders can in some situations even result in
shortening the adolescent's life span (Millstein, 1993). For example, AIDS has reached epidemic proportions among high-
risk populations with a predicted increase in prevalence
among the general public. This trend is particularly alarming
because predictions indicate that adolescents will be one of

the highest risk groups by the year 2000. A substantial body of research demonstrates that despite high levels of knowledge with respect to AIDS transmission, adolescents continue to engage in a variety of sexual risk-taking behaviors. Therefore, it is imperative that programs be developed to reduce the frequency of these risk-taking behaviors among adolescents and to promote healthy sexual attitudes and behaviors.

Although the turbulence of adolescence, with its hormonal changes, the maturation of sex organs, and the acquisition of sex-role identity, is widely recognized, there is an insufficient scientific knowledge base concerning the pathways to these "disorders" of new morbidity. This chapter presents the critical damaging disorders or maladaptive outcomes of adolescence, that is, teenage pregnancy, substance abuse, and suicide, as well as exemplary programs to prevent these developmental outcomes.

Teenage Pregnancy

Teenage pregnancy in America is a problem of growing proportions, with 1 out of 10 sexually active teens becoming pregnant every year, and more than half of all pregnant teenagers keeping and attempting to raise their babies. The consequences for teen mothers include dropping out of school, limited employment opportunities, and lower wages. Well-documented risks also exist for the offspring of teenage mothers, including a high incidence of illness and mortality, decreased cognitive capabilities and academic success, and emotional difficulties (Thomas & Rickel, 1995).

The rates of teenage pregnancy, childbearing, and induced abortion are higher in the United States than in most industrialized nations, including France, The Netherlands, Canada, England, Wales, and Sweden (Alan Guttmacher Institute, 1986). Estimates indicate that there are similar rates of sexual activity among teenagers in those countries, but sex education and contraceptives are more widely available to youth in these nations than in the United States. Presumably, these measures have had a significant influence on lowering rates of teenage pregnancy and induced abortion as well as sexually transmitted diseases. Furthermore, the American public views teen pregnancy as a problem primarily for Black teens, but as former Planned Parenthood director Faye Wattleton pointed out, that is not the case (1989). Compared to their European counterparts, White American teens also have a high pregnancy rate: They become pregnant twice as often as their British peers, and six times more often than their Dutch peers.

Researchers have been studying teenage sexuality for some time in an effort to curb the rising incidence of youthful parenting. Several variables have been identified as influencing early sexuality and experimentation: puberty and maturational factors, psychological variables, socioeconomic status, changing moral climate, religion, education, abuse of alcohol or drugs, and lack of sexual knowledge (Rickel, 1989).

Teens often do not initiate effective contraceptive behaviors until as much as 1 year after the onset of sexual activity. The consistent use of contraceptives and the use of more effective methods increase with age during adolescence. However, despite a nationwide increase in contraceptive use by teens during the last few years, pregnancy rates have not decreased. This is possibly due to both a move away from the most effective methods (oral contraceptives and the intrauterine device [IUD]) and the decreasing age of onset of sexual activity, which thereby increases the risk period when adolescents are least likely to use contraceptives effectively.

The educational aspirations of adolescent girls and their families also appear to be powerful predictors of teen pregnancy, as is the presence of a nonmarital pregnancy by either the mother or an older sister (Rickel, 1989). Furthermore, teen pregnancy commonly co-occurs with educational termination, although the direction of the causal linkage is unclear. These findings, while fairly broad, focus primarily on the sociological and demographic factors of teenage pregnancy. Insufficient research attention has been devoted to the psychological and motivational dimensions of teenage pregnancy as predictors of either pregnancy or its consequences. An obvious need exists for longitudinal research focusing on the psychological, social, and economic determinants of pregnancy. In addition, intervention-based research is necessary which focuses on reducing the incidence of teen pregnancy and on minimizing negative consequences for the mother and child when it does occur.

The Detroit Teen Parent Project

The Detroit Teen Parent Project is a collaborative research and intervention effort between an urban university and urban school systems which began in 1987 (Rickel, 1989). It was designed to identify personality, situational, and attitudinal factors associated with early pregnancy and parenting and to enhance parenting competencies. The intervention program was developed in collaboration with school personnel and aimed to intervene as early as possible in the lives of teen mothers to buffer the stresses of pregnancy and promote positive nurturing attitudes and behaviors.

The intervention program was based on a peer advocacy model whereby college students were paired with young mothers for an academic year. Various studies have shown that adolescents are more likely to disclose personal concerns to friends and peers rather than to school personnel or adults (Carr, 1981; McIntyre, Thomas, & Borgen, 1982). Furthermore, McIntyre et al., (1982) found that a peer model of intervention facilitates communication within the context of a trusting relationship because the peer often assumes many roles (e.g., confidante, tutor, big sister), which results in increased social and emotional adjustment for the adolescent.

Participants were recruited from Detroit City and Wayne County Public School alternative education sites that have special programs for pregnant and parenting teens. In the first phase of the project, base rates for adolescent maladjustment were determined by interviewing teenage mothers from alternative education programs as well as nonpregnant and nonparenting teens from schools that feed the alternative education facilities. A total of 450 participants were involved in the two-part study. Initially, 200 teenage mothers from two alternative education facilities participated in this first phase of the study. Among the instruments used were the Minnesota Multiphasic Personality Inventory (MMPI), the Rickel-Modified Child Rearing Practices Report (R-CRPR), the Psychiatric Epidemiological Research Inventory (PERI) Life Events Scale, and a detailed demographic questionnaire (Thomas & Rickel, 1995).

Following computer scoring of the MMPI, teens were placed into categories based on their 2-point code type and using a cutoff score of 65T. The following code types and subgroups were used in the analysis (Lachar, 1974):

1. *Normal.* Scales 1–4, 6–0 less than 65T;

2. *Neurotic.* Clinical elevations on Scales 1, 2, 3, 7, 1–2/2–1, 1–3/3–1, 1–7/7–1, 2–3/3–2, or 2–7/7–2;

3. *Characterological.* Clinical elevations on Scales 4, 9, 1–4/4–1, 2–4/4–2, 3–4/4–3, 4–6/6–4, 4–7/7–4, 4–8/8–4, or 4–9/9–4;

4. *Socially Alienated.* Clinical elevations on Scales 6, 8, 1–8/8–1, 2–8/8–2, 3–8/8–3, 6–8/8–6, 6–9/9–6, or 7–8/8–7; and

5. *Unclassified.* Clinical elevations on Scales 1–6/6–1, 1–9/9–1, 2–6/6–2, 2–9/9–2, 2–0/0–2, 3–9/9–3, 6–7/7–6.

Unexpectedly, only 20% of the sample scored in the normal range. Teens were fairly evenly distributed in the other MMPI subgroups. Furthermore, significant differences were found between the subgroups relative to their self-reported parenting attitudes as measured by the R-CRPR. Teens in the neurotic and characterological subgroups were found to significantly differ from one another on the variable of nurturance, with teens in the neurotic subgroup reporting significantly lower nurturant values than those with characterological profiles. For the variable of restrictiveness, girls with profiles depicting social alienation differed significantly from those in the neurotic subgroup, with socially alienated teens espousing greater restrictive–authoritarian values than those in the neurotic subgroup. Interestingly, teens in the neurotic subgroup were low on both restrictive and nurturing parenting attitudes as measured by the Rickel Modified-CRPR, which may indicate they do little parenting.

These results were surprising, particularly with reference to the small percentage of teens scoring in the normal category of personality adjustment as measured by the MMPI. Recent studies of pregnant and parenting teens seem to suggest that adolescents choosing to bear and raise children are not psychologically maladjusted and in fact are less distressed by their circumstances than once believed (Barth, Schinke, & Maxwell, 1983). Because longitudinal data were not yet available on these teens in the Detroit parenting study, it was impossible to ascertain whether participants' MMPI profiles had changed as a result of pregnancy, or if their maladjustment had predisposed them to sexual experimentation and risk taking (Thomas & Rickel, 1995). Thus a comparison study was undertaken.

Looking to the feeder schools of the two alternative education facilities, 250 nonpregnant and nonparenting teens were solicited to participate in a follow-up study of adolescent personality characteristics and parenting attitudes. A similar format of data collection was used with slight modifications of the questionnaire to exclude items specific to pregnancy and childbirth. The results confirmed that pregnant and parenting teens report more maladjustment on the MMPI than their nonpregnant and nonparenting counterparts. Likewise, a similar finding emerged with regard to personality subgroups and self-reported restrictiveness and nurturance as measured by the R-CRPR. Characterological and neurotic teens demonstrated less restrictive parenting attitudes than those in the socially alienated group. On the dimension of nurturance, teens in the neurotic subgroup tended to be lowest on self-reported nurturance whereas those in the characterological group scored highest.

Many school districts in the United States provide alternative education facilities for youthful mothers to attend while they are pregnant and for a time after giving birth. Such a setting provides a rich opportunity for intervention targeted at enhancing parenting competence. Because there appears to be a link between socially alienated personality types and self-reported restrictive parental attitudes, a simple screening using the Rickel-Modified CRPR could identify those mothers who appear overly restrictive. A parenting intervention could be specifically developed with a goal of moderating parental restrictiveness while taking into account the special treatment needs of the socially alienated adolescent.

The finding of personality differences between groups of parenting adolescents and their nonpregnant counterparts suggests that very real differences that discriminate between groups do exist. However, the personality cluster confirmed by the Detroit teen parenting study to be correlated with early parenting is not always readily apparent to the untrained observer (Thomas & Rickel, 1995). It is neither feasible nor sensible to administer the MMPI to all adolescent females to prescreen for increased risk of pregnancy. Nevertheless, intervention programs are already in place in many school districts that might easily lend themselves to initial screening for high-risk females. For example, many districts have programs that target young people at risk for a variety of maladaptive behaviors such as school drop out, substance abuse, delinquency, depression, child abuse, and suicide. A brief screening of referred females using the MMPI might separate those teens most at risk for early pregnancy and parenting.

As mentioned earlier, a model intervention program was designed and developed for the Detroit Teen Parent Project and was based on a peer advocacy model (Rickel, 1989). Each peer advocate (a university senior-level psychology student) was screened and trained by school and project staff. They were then paired with an expectant or recently delivered mother in the educational facility. Every effort was made to match advocate and teen on demographic variables and personal interests. The initial meetings between the girls and their advocates, whom the girls dubbed their "big sister," were characterized by shyness as well as eagerness. An entry from the journal of one of the advocates illustrates this point:

> It was very enlightening to be greeted at the door by an eager face inquiring as to whether or not I was going to be her "big sister." The thought brought back memories of growing up with my big sister at home and how today

we are even closer as I grow a little older and a little wiser. I realize how important my sister has been at various transition periods in my life, and I know how valuable these kinds of exchanges can be. (Rickel, 1989, p. 89)

The first step in the intervention process was building rapport and a trusting, caring relationship between the advocate and the adolescent. A social support focus was used in the first month, and involved taking the teens on field trips, to movies, and shopping malls with the goal of getting to know one another. Weekly meetings were held by project staff for the peer advocates to facilitate relationship building with their teen mothers. Occasionally the staff met with resistance from the teens' parents who objected to what they called "charity" from the university. The following journal entry from an advocate exemplifies this case:

> I called Donna to ask her if she wanted to go out to Belle Isle for a little stroll. I wanted to talk to her and get to know her a bit, and most of all get her to talk to me. Her mom came out of the bedroom, I said hello and she just walked past me with a stone face. Then she and Donna went to the kitchen and started yelling. I overheard her mom describing what I'm doing with her as charity. Donna came out of the kitchen trying not to cry, and told me she couldn't go with me today. (Rickel, 1989, p. 105)

These issues were discussed candidly in the advocates' sessions with program directors. In such instances, project staff and school personnel invited the teen's parents to meet with them to gain a greater understanding of the goals of the program.

Education was the focus of Phase 2 of the intervention. Specifically, we sought to broaden the young mothers' awareness of the resources available to them within their own communities and how to access them. Advocates met during their weekly sessions on the university campus with various service providers from the community who shared their expertise. This format proved especially useful because the teens appeared to be more receptive to information received from their peer advocates than they were to professional adults in the educational settings. In this way, it was possible to further educate the girls on such issues as contraceptives, medical and psychological services, day care, affordable recreation, infant stimulation, and effective discipline. Peer advocates often accompanied the teens to their childbirth classes and helped them to prepare for the baby's arrival. Furthermore, many of the advocates brought their teen mother to the college campus where they received tips on how to apply to college, as well as for financial aid or a scholarship. The following journal description of the struggles of a teen mother highlight the difficulties of finishing an education:

> Glenda is finding it hard to care for her baby daughter and attend school at the same time. She finds little time for herself and for friends. Glenda says that the baby keeps her up all night and it's hard to get up in the morning to get ready for school. Nevertheless her priority is to finish high school and get her diploma because she is a year behind. Glenda is then planning to find a job and start a college fund. She says that everything will work out if she sticks with it and doesn't give up. (Rickel, 1989, pp. 91–92)

The intervention was highly successful from the point of view of peer advocates and teens who genuinely appeared to enjoy the experience. Often the advocate was invited to the hospital as the adolescent labored and gave birth. The close-knit friendships that emerged were satisfying to all involved. Postpartum, the advocates helped ease the transition into motherhood by offering first-hand assistance, encouragement, support, and advice. Although many of the peer advocates continued to meet with their teens after the intervention period had formally ended, the final sessions of the weekly supervision meetings were spent preparing the advocates for a gentle withdrawal of their influence in the teens' lives.

This collaborative relationship between a university and the public school system has spanned many years. The peer advocate preventive intervention program with adolescent mothers demonstrates a paradigm that can be applied to many settings, urban and suburban. The program has shown how a university with private funding and student resources can provide support and assistance to local schools at basically no cost to the system. The success of such a model is also facilitated by a sensitivity to the goals and needs of the collaborating agency.

Teens at risk for pregnancy might best be served by specific intervention programs that focus on sexuality and contraceptive issues in a candid, fact-based manner. Such a preventive technique might prove far more effective than a group setting with a global goal of enhancing self-esteem or academic survival. Although these issues might not be the primary focus of the intervention, it is possible that ancillary gains might be made in these and other areas as a result of such an intervention program.

In a more primary preventive mode many communities across the country are initiating abstinence programs that target youth ages 9 through 14 years. These programs are based on the premise that premature sexual activity among youth is not only a prevailing health concern, but also a moral and social dilemma that the community as a whole must address. Leaders from the medical, business, church, and school communities are using the mass media to communicate the message that "sex can wait" and following up with programs that equip youth with the refusal skills necessary to reject sexual advances.

Fathers of Babies Born to Teen-Age Mothers

A recent New York Times article (Navarro, 1996) reported that studies have shown most babies born to teenage mothers are fathered by adults. In two out of three births to teen-age mothers, the father is at least 20 years old. In response to such statistics, many states are looking to these older fathers as an unaddressed problem and are enforcing statutory rape laws that prohibit sex between adults and minors.

As a result of state efforts, teenage girls who were often viewed as promiscuous or as abusers of the welfare system are now being considered victims of child abuse. For example, Florida passed a stricter statutory rape law that specifies unacceptable age gaps and creates new reporting requirements regarding child abuse. Any relationship between a man 21 years old or older and a girl under age 16 resulting in pregnancy is defined as reportable. In addition, Georgia approved a bill lengthening some minimum prison sentences for statutory rape from 1 to 10 years. Other states, including California, Delaware, and Massachusetts, are either enforcing old laws or forming special units. California has designated $8.4 million to prosecute men who are over 21 years of age and who have sex with girls 15 years of age or younger resulting in pregnancy. The men usually face prison, or probation which mandates child support to make the fathers financially responsible.

AIDS

More than one million people in the United States are infected with HIV. Although current figures indicate that adolescents comprise a relatively small proportion of reported cases, this group is at risk. Conditions are ripe for the spread of the AIDS virus among adolescents for a variety of reasons. Behavioral factors that predispose adolescents to risk of infection include the high rate of unprotected sexual activity, the fact that many teenagers have multiple sexual partners, and experimentation with drugs. Among the African American and Hispanic adolescent community, a large percentage of AIDS cases are the result of intravenous drug use and sharing of contaminated needles. These behavioral risks are heightened for all groups by widespread confusion and lack of knowledge about the cause and transmission of AIDS (Centers for Disease Control, 1991).

Although research has yielded ambiguous and often conflicting data regarding the degree to which adolescents are knowledgeable about AIDS prevention, studies consistently describe gaps in knowledge and persistence of unfounded myths. Further, some studies have shown that, despite high levels of knowledge with respect to AIDS transmission, adolescents continue to engage in a variety of risk-taking behaviors (Anderson et al., 1990).

Numerous authors have documented relatively high levels of knowledge among adolescents with regard to the cause and transmission of AIDS (Bruce, Shrum, Trefethen, & Slovik, 1990; Roscoe & Kruger, 1990). Overwhelmingly, adolescents perceive AIDS to be a serious disease and express concern over the increased incidence among the heterosexual population. However, despite the generally well-informed status of adolescents, any optimistic conclusions would be premature. Although AIDS education is increasing in schools and the vast majority of high school students are aware of the main modes of AIDS transmission, many erroneous beliefs persist, and confusion regarding susceptibility is apparent.

A large portion of teenagers inaccurately perceive blood donations, exposure to insect bites, and use of public toilets to be potential causes of HIV infection (Bell, Feraios, & Bryan, 1990). More important, however, a sizable minority of students continue to hold views that may actually put them at risk. For example, some state their belief that birth control pills provide some protection against infection. Others state that it is possible to tell whether people have AIDS by looking at them. Racial differences in AIDS-related beliefs were also noted by Bell et al. Black and Hispanic students were about twice as likely as White students to have misconceptions about the modes of transmission of AIDS and to engage in higher rates of unsafe sexual practices.

Educationally based AIDS prevention programs have been advocated by numerous AIDS intervention experts (Coates, 1990; Eiser, Eiser, & Lang, 1990; Gilchrist, 1990) and have been mandated by many states. Although the content varies, a recent national survey showed that since 1985, 87% of school districts provide some AIDS education (Anderson et al., 1990). Typical topics include risks of intercourse, abstinence as the best method of prevention, and the use of condoms to prevent AIDS.

Few evaluative studies have been undertaken to assess the effectiveness of the existing programs. Brown, Fritz, and Barone (1989) described mixed results from a Rhode Island program for 7th- and 10th-grade students. Higher knowledge, increased tolerance of AIDS patients, and more reluctance to engage in high-risk behaviors were reported. One of the difficulties in interpreting the results of this program is that the students demonstrated high knowledge levels prior to participation. More disturbing results were reported with regard to attitudes, with 42% stating that they would not touch someone with AIDS and 28% asserting that persons with AIDS should not be allowed to attend school.

An evaluation of a school-based program in three middle and three high schools in a San Francisco school district revealed that students who participated in AIDS instruction classes demonstrated significantly greater knowledge and changes in attitudes (DiClemente et al., 1989). Similar findings were reported by Ruder et al. (1990), who evaluated the effectiveness of an AIDS-education program in high schools in Westchester County, New York. As was the case in the San Francisco program, the evaluation of this program was compromised because of relatively high pretest scores on AIDS knowledge.

One of the problems in interpreting the existing programs is that they contain several methodological weaknesses that merit consideration. Forst, Moore, and Jang (1990) raised important concerns in their evaluation of the AIDS education programs in the California public schools. According to these authors, the California program lacked a pre–post design, did not use standardized testing procedures, had no long-term follow-up, and stressed only cognitive knowledge, with little consideration given to changes in attitude or behavior. These researchers concur that it is unlikely that simply being well informed will be enough to prevent teens from engaging in high-risk behaviors.

The lack of a behavioral assessment makes it difficult to ascertain whether observed increases in knowledge will in fact contribute to changes in behavior. Thus, the extent to which enhanced understanding affects behavior remains unclear. Consequently, whether the knowledge gained is retained and translated into safer sexual behaviors or whether AIDS will ultimately be prevented in this population cannot be determined.

Several leading researchers have recommended that future efforts aimed at adolescents use cognitive–social learning theory as a basis for prevention programs (Coates, 1990; McCoy et al., 1990). These researchers have suggested that AIDS prevention curricula be modeled after antismoking and teen pregnancy programs that have used the cognitive–social learning theoretical framework. They further recommend that programs include detailed explanations of HIV and AIDS, discussions about adolescents' personal susceptibility to infection, the use of peers as educators and models, reinforcement of positive sexual behaviors, and communication and contraceptive skills.

Many authors have described the benefits of using peers as educators. Often adolescents are able to identify much more closely with peers than with adults, leading them to be more attentive to the message. According to Bruhn (1990), "Part of the message is the information, the other part is the communicator . . ." (p. 65).

Adolescents are a risk group whose vulnerability to HIV infection is growing rapidly, and aggressive intervention efforts are essential. Programs must be developed that incorporate practical skills, peer-led stress management techniques, and efforts that promote self-esteem and foster communication. These strategies would give adolescents the tools necessary to make changes in their lifestyle and behavior and to deal with the pressures that are likely to lead to unsafe choices.

Substance Abuse

Substance abuse remains of central concern to those working with adolescents because of both the potential short-term physiological effects and long-standing consequences. The long-standing consequences may involve the development of physiological difficulties, behavioral patterns surrounding substance abuse, and psychological dependency (Shedler & Block, 1990). The misuse of alcohol and other drugs can adversely affect job and academic performance, personal safety, and interpersonal relationships, as well as emotional and physical health and well being. Long-term, frequent use of alcohol and other drugs can cause a general deterioration of health, impair the immune system, and thereby increase susceptibility to a variety of illnesses. Alcohol and other drug use can lead to medical complications and a vulnerability to numerous ailments, including cardiovascular disease, liver diseases (such as cirrhosis or hepatitis), gastrointestinal problems, respiratory disorders, malnutrition, high blood pressure, depression, suicide, and sexually transmitted diseases, including HIV infection.

Impairment of judgment, reasoning, communication, and perception caused by alcohol and other drugs puts youth (especially females) at risk for sexual exploitation, unwanted pregnancy, and increased risk of sexually transmitted diseases. Sharing of needles among injected drug users (and injected steroid users) increases the risk of being infected with HIV. Drunk driving is also a major risk for youth; it is the number one killer of teens.

However, there has been much less research in and clinical attention to adolescent alcohol and drug abuse compared to adult addiction. Norman (1994) reviewed the research findings on personal attributes related to risk of substance misuse in adolescence. Problematic childhood temperament (e.g., irritability or withdrawal), childhood emotional distress (e.g., depression), behavior problems (e.g., hyperactivity, aggression, impulsivity), antisocial behavior (e.g., theft), and academic failure all were found to be factors increasing risk of substance abuse. In addition, affiliating with drug-using peers and feeling alienated from the dominant culture also puts teens at risk with regard to substances. Specific guidelines for the treatment of substance abuse in adolescence must be developed so that proper care can be given to the young people who are addicted. The substances discussed here are cigarette smoking, alcohol, and drug abuse.

On the other hand, no one pattern of risk factors has been shown to predict substance misuse (Bry, 1996). On the contrary, several studies have shown that, over time, the heaviest users of substances have uniquely individual combinations of risk factors. This has been found to be true regardless of race, ethnicity, or social class, and in both rural and urban settings.

Resisting the use of substances, however, has been found to be associated with close, lasting ties with family members and friends who disapprove of drug use (Bry, 1996). Trusting, accepting relationships appear to be a strong deterrent, with even at-risk teens reporting they were most likely to turn down drugs when they thought their parents would learn of it.

In these various ways, the use of substances is like so many other risky behaviors: those most vulnerable have multiple stressors, few supports, and a paucity of resources available to them (Rickel & Becker-Lausen, 1994). These facts provide another example of the necessity for active efforts to support families, provide early childhood interventions, and set up prevention programs with parent involvement in the schools.

Cigarette Smoking

Cigarette smoking among adolescents rose steadily during the early 1970s, particularly among young women and girls. Although some evidence suggests a decline in recent decades, the problem still continues and may be understated (Carnegie Council on Adolescent Development, 1995). Health teachers in the United States had focused their efforts on the health risks involved in smoking tobacco, motivated by the belief that youth provided with information on the health risks of smoking will be less likely to smoke. However, there is little evidence to support the effectiveness of this approach, which relies on adolescents' level of cognitive development. Their level of cognitive development may limit their internalization of health information regarding smoking because they do not yet perceive themselves as "smokers." Thus, adolescents do not expect to experience the health consequences of smoking (Burnham, 1993).

Recently, school curricula have concentrated on the social influences that motivate smoking and on the short-term physiological consequences of smoking. Studies have shown that same-age peer leaders teaching specific skills to resist social pressures to begin smoking and presenting the physiological consequences of smoking were more effective than adult leaders in deterring adolescent smoking (Strasburger, 1995). Other preventive efforts have occurred through legal controls on cigarettes, media campaigns, public service announcements, family interventions, and community educational activities. The more successful programs have attended to broader areas, such as emotional and behavioral components, which focus more closely on the adolescent's motivations, needs, and level of cognitive development.

Alcohol

The most frequently used substance by adolescents is alcohol. According to Klitzner, Fisher, Stewart, & Gilbert (1993), adolescents view its use negatively between the ages of 6 to 10 years, but by 12 years of age they are beginning to view drinking more positively, and by age 15 adolescents report intense peer pressure to drink. Data suggest that more adolescents are drinking every year. In a 1991 survey of high school seniors, 54% said they had used alcohol in the past month, and 30% reported they had consumed more than five drinks in a row in the past 2 weeks. A broader survey involving students in 7th through 12th grade revealed that 8 million of these students drink weekly, and more than 5 million students report having binged (Office of the Inspector General, 1991). Perhaps of greatest concern were reports from those who drank that 31% drink alone, 41% drink to feel better when upset, and 25% drink because they are bored.

Drinking is a major problem on college campuses. The typical student spends more on alcohol than on textbooks; students spend a total of $4.2 billion each year on alcoholic beverages, despite the fact that most are under the legal age for drinking (Office of Substance Abuse Prevention, 1991). Alcohol has been found to be a source of 40% of academic problems and 28% of college dropouts. Sixty percent of college women with sexually transmitted diseases (including AIDS) report they were under the influence of alcohol at the time they had high-risk sexual intercourse. Deaths from alcohol-related causes among college students are equal to the number of students who go on to obtain master's and doctoral degrees combined.

Alcohol consumption has become pandemic in American culture, with two thirds of all adults reporting occasional drinking (Cloninger, Dinwiddie, & Reich, 1989). Over a lifetime of usage, about 13% of the population becomes dependent on alcohol. Men appear to be more susceptible to alcohol dependence than women.

Among adolescents today, as with many adults, polydrug use is quite common among substance abusers. Heavy alcohol use combined with other drugs is all too frequently seen in clinical settings (Babor et al., 1991). A thorough assessment of the nature of the problem, of the underlying issues, and of the need for other services has been found to be effective in improving outcomes of intervention and treatment.

When Babor et al. (1991) examined the presenting issues of adolescents with substance abuse problems, they found that 26.7% of male participants and 37.3% of female participants reported physical abuse, and 41.2% of female participants reported sexual abuse. In terms of symptomatology, 18.5% of male and 29.4% of female participants indicated potential for suicide; 29.4% of female participants reported symptoms of eating disorders; and 18.5% of male and 23.5% of female participants showed the potential to overdose.

Drugs

Drug use among adolescents is related to environmental, cultural, and adaptational issues such as peer pressure and family influence. The National Household Survey on Drug Abuse (National Institute on Drug Abuse, 1991) found that among youth aged 12 to 17, 16.8% used an illicit drug within the past year, and 9.2% had used an illicit drug at least once in the past month. For the next age group of older youth (18 to 20), the rates were about twice those of the younger cohort (30.3% in the past year; 18.9% in the past month). Nevertheless, although many adolescents experiment with drugs of one type or another, the majority do not end up with serious problems (Shedler & Block, 1990).

Among illicit drugs, marijuana is the most commonly used, and it is second only to alcohol in its prevalence. About 41% of high school seniors in 1990 reported having tried marijuana, compared to about 9% who had tried cocaine, 2.8% who admitted to having used phencyclidine (PCP), and the 1.3% who said they had ever used heroin (Johnston, O'Malley, & Bachman, 1991).

However, although many teens experiment with one or more types of drugs, most do not abuse drugs, nor do many become addicted (Shedler & Block, 1990). *High-risk users* may be defined as those who use the most dangerous drugs (e.g., cocaine, inhalants); those who begin using them at the earliest ages (i.e., preteen years); those who use them in the most inappropriate settings or circumstances (e.g., while driving); and those who begin to show signs of tolerance, dependence, or withdrawal.

Taken together, four factors of high-risk drug use show a pattern of recklessness with regard to the youth's physical and mental well being that indicates a lack of concern for self and others. The link between antisocial behavior and substance misuse has been recognized for some time. One study found that, depending on the city, male youth arrested or detained for criminal activity had rates of positive urine tests for a variety of drugs (National Institute of Justice, 1993). Rates ranged from 10% in St. Louis to 44% in Washington, DC. Other studies have indicated that antisocial behavior develops prior to substance abuse, rather than the other way around (Rickel & Becker-Lausen, 1994).

Early intervention efforts are not economically feasible or necessary for the large numbers of youth who may try drugs or alcohol because most adolescent substance users reduce or discontinue use in adulthood without experiencing clinically significant problems. Nevertheless, targeted early-intervention strategies are estimated to be needed for about 1 adolescent in 15 or 20 (Klitzner et al., 1993). However, many young people do not perceive their substance abuse as a problem because they are in the early stages of use. Likewise, numerous factors or barriers make it difficult for adolescents to commit themselves to drug or alcohol treatment programs.

Agencies and institutions in this country have not been very successful in attracting and holding adolescent substance abusers in treatment. Typical treatment modalities often do not have the range and types of services needed by adolescents. Treatment should involve the entire family, but young substance abusers are likely to be confused and at odds with their family as well as in denial that they have a serious problem. Furthermore, many counselors view adolescent substance abusers as difficult to treat and do not have the resources required to work with the family. Comprehensive, integrated, and systemic services should be available so that a specific treatment approach can be tailored to the needs of each youth.

Types of Treatment

Interventions typically involve a carefully rehearsed and controlled meeting in which the client is confronted by significant others, usually with a professional in attendance (Schonberg, 1993). During these meetings an adolescent listens to information about their use of chemicals along with the concerns and feelings of the significant others present. The goals of an intervention are to convince the adolescent to submit to a formal screening and assessment by professionals, who will also present a plan for entering treatment, if appropriate. In some cases, interventions may include the use of social or institutional leverage—the courts, probation officers, and schools—to encourage the individual to seek treatment.

Detoxification. Detoxification may be required as part of the treatment for the adolescent. Whether detoxification is done on an outpatient or inpatient basis, it should be monitored by appropriately trained personnel under the direction of a physician with expertise in the management of withdrawal. Because adolescents are usually in the early stages of substance addiction, it is rare for them to develop a potentially fatal withdrawal syndrome. In addition, many substances popular with adolescents do not have a significant withdrawal effect.

Treatment communities. Only a small number of structured residential programs specialize in treating adolescents. Most of these programs are highly structured, nonpermissive, and substance-free settings. However, despite a long history of treating substance abusing adolescents, the treatment community is not for everyone. The daily regimen is intense, often including encounter groups or group therapy, individual counseling, family therapy, tutorial and formal education classes, recreational therapy, and occupational training. According to one evaluation study, less than 15% of all those admitted graduate from treatment, and more than half leave treatment before 30 days (DeLeon, 1984).

Aftercare. The issue of aftercare and the return to the primary family is especially important for the adolescent. Adult graduates of treatment communities are encouraged to live independently, but the unemancipated adolescent usually must continue to be a part of his or her family. Family members must be competent mediators of the positive gains in treatment and need to be prepared to facilitate the adolescent's recovery. Through the provision of outpatient services and the development of family networks, the treatment community's basic self-help perspective can continue to influence the aftercare phase of treatment.

Day treatment. The most intensive form of outpatient treatment is the structured day-treatment program, which allows the adolescent to return home in the evenings. Frequently used as an aftercare option following a residential or inpatient stay, it provides evaluation and treatment as well as a specialized school on the premises. Although the primary client is the adolescent, a family-based approach is used. Parents usually are told that the program recognizes their responsibility and authority and supports them in their parenting role. In return the parents are asked to support the day-treatment community's efforts.

Suicide

Prior to the teen years suicide is rare, but it rises rapidly during adolescence and adulthood (McDowell & Stillian, 1994). Some 32,000 Americans commit suicide each year. Among 15- to 24-year-olds, it is the third leading cause of death, and successful suicides are disproportionately far more likely for male suicide attempters than for female attempters. Attempted suicides or parasuicides are also atypical prior to adolescence and then show a dramatic increase between ages 15 to 19. Parasuicides are quite common among adolescents, particularly with young female adolescents. Suicide happens in the so-called "finest of families" with no one social stratum exempt or at less risk than another (Carnegie Council on Adolescent Development, 1995). A case in point is Gloria Vanderbilt (1996), whose son's suicide is painfully described in her book *A Mother's Story*.

The American Suicide Foundation (ASF), a national nonprofit organization, is dedicated to funding research, education, and treatment programs for depression and suicide prevention. The ASF is trying to educate the public that suicide is not a disease, but behind many suicides is a disease called *depression*. Scientists have been able to pinpoint differences in the brain tissue and neurotransmitters of some people who are suicidal, and although this research is in its early stages, it could lead to more effective methods of identification and treatment. Other keys to suicide prevention lie in trends that demographers have predicted. For example, they point out that whenever any large group of people come of age, the competition for everything is harder. This has been the case with the baby boom generation. Life is harder for these baby boomers, and as a result there is among them more divorce, more substance abuse, and more suicide.

Suicides often follow acute stressful life events, with several risk factors being identified as increasing the likelihood of suicide in young people. These risk factors include psychiatric disturbances in parents, abusive treatment by parents, parental separation or divorce, social or financial stress for the family, and another family member who has previously attempted or completed a suicide. Furthermore, adolescent suicide frequently occurs in the climate of a disruptive, chaotic family where the adolescent may have been identified as the cause of the family conflict. Just as suicide can run in families, it can also run in communities. The "copycat" phenomenon has been documented for years by social psychologists. Therefore, when an idol of the current Generation X commits suicide, there is real cause for alarm.

In attempting to prevent adolescent suicide, it is necessary to separate normal fantasies from serious intent to end one's life. Suicidal thoughts are common in the adolescent's development and rather than viewing suicide as a final self-destructive act, most young people merely fantasize about suicide as a solution to the frustrations of daily living. Wellman (1984) listed the following danger signs indicative of suicidal intent: prolonged sadness, concentration difficulties, behavioral problems, disturbed sleeping or eating patterns, poor academic performance, expressed feelings of worthlessness or hopelessness, collecting harmful devices or pharmaceuticals, and giving away treasured possessions. In addition, before a suicide attempt, adolescents frequently complain of strained relationships with parents (often the father), difficulties in school relationships, or a breakup with a boyfriend or girlfriend. Ladame and Jeanneret (1982) have described other indicators, which include social isolation of the adolescent, diagnosed depression, and acute anxiety that builds up to an intolerable level days or hours prior to the suicide attempt.

Several suggestions have been made regarding the prevention of adolescent suicide, but few have been evaluated for effectiveness. These suggestions include the use of the mass media to better inform the public about suicide, education in the schools, social support to dysfunctional families, and courses for allied health professionals to increase their awareness of adolescent problems in order to identify those youth who are at risk for suicide. Also, caution should be exercised by physicians when prescribing psychotropic medication to adolescents because of the potential for overdosing. Bipolar tests have proven effective in measuring life and death attraction and repulsion and in targeting those individuals who may be at risk for suicide.

Preventive interventions for suicide attempts should, whenever possible, involve admittance to a hospital for assessment. Particular attention should be paid to the degree of premeditation of the attempt, whether or not the adolescent planned to be found, and if the young person's behavior preceding the attempt was designed to conceal the suicidal intent. If the attempt does not warrant an admission, a full social and psychiatric assessment should be made and aftercare plans given to the family. Outpatient therapy is the treatment of choice for most suicide attempters and involves individual or family therapy.

Help is also available for the family survivors of suicide. Iris Bolton, a mental health professional in Atlanta, Georgia, founded Survivors of Suicide (SOS) after her 20-year-old son, who suffered from depression, committed suicide. SOS is a national support group that instructs survivors to do four things: (a) tell the story of the suicide until you believe it and cannot deny it, (b) express the emotions of anger or guilt so they do not cause injury to yourself, (c) try to make meaning out of the tragedy even if it is to be a support to someone else, and (d) make a transition from the physical presence of the person to a different kind of relationship (i.e., instead of letting go, incorporate a spiritual or symbolic relationship).

Summary

The group of dangers to adolescents termed the *new morbidity* have been presented in this chapter. These dangers have been described as a group of health-related conditions with social rather than purely biological causes and include unprotected sexual behavior, teenage pregnancy, substance abuse, and suicide. A significant portion of adolescents experience more than one of these problems simultaneously.

At the present time, many financing mechanisms, both public and private, limit the provision of preventive interventions to reach and help troubled youth. Some managed care plans have exacerbated the problem by only providing intervention services for the most severe pathology-focused diagnoses. Adolescents, whose concerns are often given lip service by many politicians, in reality have little support in the policy arena because they cannot vote. Social scientists and clinicians must take a proactive approach to ensure that preventive services are provided for youth in order to avoid maladaptive developmental outcomes as they move into adulthood.

5

Intergenerational Transmission of Positive and Negative Development

We continue the discussion begun in chapters 1 and 2 regarding the relationships among family and community environment, problems of parenting, and intergenerational outcomes. Here we further explicate restrictiveness and nurturance as constructs related to child rearing practices and review some of the research findings for these constructs. Next, we describe research on broader aspects of family environment, including parent–child relationships, other family factors, and factors outside the family that influence its functioning. Teen pregnancy is discussed in terms of its role as both an outcome and a factor in the perpetuation of the cycle of poverty. The relationship of adolescent pregnancy to maladjustment, as well as proposed associations among childhood trauma, psychopathology, and high-risk sexual behavior are presented. Finally, we propose a broad model for the intergenerational transmission of positive and negative outcomes.

Psychopathology has been the focus of clinical psychology and psychiatry throughout the history of these disciplines. Freud's work was focused on psychotic and neurotic behavior (Freud, 1917/1957). He did not have much to say about healthy human behavior, except for his remarkable statement that the healthy person is one who is able "to love and to work" (Partington, 1996, p. 294). Alfred Adler paid more attention to health and well being, suggesting the concept of prosocial behavior—or what he labeled the development of *social interest*—as a criterion for psychological well being (Adler, 1929).

Attention to what constitutes healthy behavior has been a more recent phenomenon. In addition to Freud's and Adler's criteria, among today's characteristics of the "normal" person are realistic (i.e., nondistorted) perceptions, self-awareness, voluntary control of one's behavior, a sense of self-worth, and a feeling of acceptance by others. Currently, research in trauma emphasizes that some "abnormal" behavior may be an appropriate (or at least expected) response to extreme circumstances, such as child abuse, war, and other traumatic experiences, but then becomes overgeneralized to situations where it is no longer appropriate.

Similarly, studies of psychological resiliency have helped focus attention on the factors that enable children to thrive despite difficult or traumatic environments. Werner's 30-year study of infants at risk suggests that autonomy and a positive social orientation may provide some protection for children from negative outcomes (Werner, 1988). Werner found, as did other researchers, that resilient children usually have an established bond with at least one caregiver (see Anthony & Cohler, 1987; Farber & Egeland, 1987; Felsman & Vaillent, 1987; Field, 1990). However, the effects of the family cannot be examined adequately without consideration of the social context in which the family exists. Certainly, there is little doubt that relationships with institutions and organizations influence the family unit, particularly where such issues as racism, sexism, and other forms of oppression impact individual members. The dynamics within the family, in turn, affect individual members, modifying the relationships they encounter outside the home (Parke & Kellam, 1994).

Family Environment: The Intergenerational Starting Point

Understanding the relationship between childhood experiences and later adult behavior, including parenting behaviors, helps guide preventive mental health efforts. Research demonstrates how developmental patterns operate within families and how they are transmitted from generation to generation.

In a discussion of Robert Fulghum's (1993) book, *All I Really Needed to Know, I Learned in Kindergarten*, Forehand, Armistead, and Klein (1995) noted

> Fulghum's primary point is that the important things in life are learned on a simple level in our early years. In contrast to his emphasis on nursery school and kindergarten, our view is that the most important early beginnings to knowledge originate in the home and are then built on in the school setting. The skills learned in the home environment prepare a child to play appropriately in the sandbox at the nursery school, to learn simple skills in kindergarten, and to set out on life's journey. However . . . holding hands and sticking together is important for our development and our learning. Unfortunately, holding hands and sticking together does not occur in increasing numbers of families in our society. . . . (p. 251)

In the following sections we examine some of the findings of research from two perspectives. We review studies that specifically examine parent–child and family factors, as well as those that consider the influence of outside factors on family functioning, particularly those assessing the effects of economic pressure.

Preventing Detrimental Outcomes

Societal changes outlined in chapter 1 indicate that many families are no longer able to provide children with full-time care in the home. More often today, families must rely on child care arrangements outside the home. Studies of child care settings indicate that experience with peers and with day care early in life does not interfere with infants' primary attachments (Zigler & Gordon, 1982). The child's ability to form multiple attachments may, in fact, be enhanced, increasing the chances that the child will be more socially interactive.

Because support for child care is woefully lacking in the United States, any discussion of intergenerational influences on children must address the implications of that lack for social policy. Discussion of welfare reform, such as workfare, must address the critical issue of who cares for the children. Inadequate pay, low status of child care workers, and quality concerns are among numerous issues that have yet to be adequately addressed by policy makers.

Although there have been significant advances this century in reducing risk factors for infants and young children, an abundance of dangerous conditions still exist, particularly for poor and ethnic minority children. The cost to society of these developmental difficulties, in terms of both lost human potential and of fiscal resources, is staggering. Much has already been done to identify risk factors, their nature and cause. Although infants and children sometimes face unavoidable risks from negative reproductive outcomes, such as heredity or genetic predispositions, many prenatal and perinatal factors as well as socioeconomic and environmental aspects for the child are largely preventable.

In particular, the home environment has been shown to play an important role in determining the quality of parent–child relations. Poverty, financial stress, marital dissatisfaction, a parent's childhood history of abuse, gender differences in child rearing, the use of alcohol and other drugs by family members, and family and community violence are among the factors significant to the child-rearing atmosphere. As described in chapter 2, Rickel (1989) and others have found a relationship between self-reported parenting styles and many of these factors. Using the Rickel Modified Child Rearing Practices Report, research studies have documented a number of these relationships.

Intrafamilial Factors

Parenting styles: Documentary studies with the Rickel Modified Child Rearing Practices Report. The Child Rearing

Practices Report (CRPR) developed by Block (1965) for the Berkeley Child Development Study is a direct measure of parenting attitudes. However, there were two drawbacks to the CRPR: a 91-item Q-sort format that was cumbersome and time consuming to administer and a scoring procedure of 28–32 factors that resulted in more scales than were desirable. Therefore, the CRPR was modified to reduce administration time and to derive a more meaningful scoring strategy based on a smaller number of factors. This version was called the Rickel Modified Child Rearing Practices Report (Rickel & Biasatti, 1982).

The Rickel Modified Child Rearing Practices Report yields scores on two subscale factors: restrictiveness and nurturance. The Restrictiveness Factor 1 represents an authoritarian control-related view of childrearing and includes how a child should behave and how he or she should feel. The Nurturance Factor 2 represents greater warmth and flexibility in childrearing attitudes and practices, and also reflects parents' willingness to listen to their children and to share feelings and experiences with them (Rickel & Biasatti, 1982).

The Nurturance and Restrictiveness items had high internal consistency and reliability that held up across different samples. Samples included parents from the center city, parents from a middle-to-upper income community, and college students from a large urban university. Evidence of the construct validity of these factors was demonstrated in a study by Jones, Rickel, and Smith (1980). The responses of children to social problem-solving tasks were related to parents' scores on the factors measured by the Rickel Modified Child Rearing Practices Report. Parents with high scores on Nurturance had children who were less likely to turn to an authority figure to resolve interpersonal problems. On the other hand, parents with high scores on Restrictiveness had children who more frequently used an evasion strategy for solving interpersonal problems.

A study conducted by Duvall (1990) showed that marital discord often negatively affects parenting practices while a high level of marital satisfaction leads to effective parenting. Duvall examined marital satisfaction as it relates to effective parenting among 72 husband–wife dyads with a preschool child, using the Rickel Modified Child Rearing Practices Report. The results demonstrated that husbands' marital satisfaction was related to greater satisfaction with their wives' parenting. Marital satisfaction for wives was significantly related to greater nurturance toward their children, greater satisfaction with their own and their husbands' parenting, and greater husband involvement in child care.

Duvall (1990) also reported gender differences between mothers and fathers: mothers scored higher on the nurturance dimension than did fathers, and fathers were more restrictive in their self-reported parenting style than mothers. Marital satisfaction was not associated with parental agreement on child rearing; therefore, rather than it being an index of marital functioning, such agreement may only represent concordance with a standard of good parenting.

In a study of 216 unmarried college students, Silverman and Dubow (1991) continued work on gender differences with the Rickel Modified Child Rearing Practices Report. It was found that the unique predictors of nurturant child-rearing attitudes differed for males and females. Psychological well being was the primary predictor of nurturance for females, whereas for males, experience with children predicted nurturance.

Recently, Arnold, O'Leary, and Edwards (1997) examined the variables that moderate the effects of father involvement and parental discipline practices of 71 couples who have children with attention-deficit/hyperactivity disorder. One of the variables studied was similarity in child-rearing views as measured by correlating couples' responses on the Rickel Modified Child Rearing Practices Report. Arnold found that father involvement had a negative effect on mothers when parents had dissimilar child-rearing views. However, the effect of father involvement became more positive as couples' views became more similar.

Cross-cultural studies conducted in the Netherlands and the Caribbean tested the generalizability of earlier findings on the Rickel Modified Child Rearing Practices Report. In the Netherlands, a study conducted with 239 Dutch parents provided a replication of the two-factor solution. Restrictiveness and Nurturance, two reliable scales measuring important constructs in socialization were again identified. In addition, direct observation of parent–child interaction was conducted. The results indicated that parental self-reports corresponded to parental behavior in interactions with children (Dekovic, Janssens, & Gerris, 1991).

The Rickel Modified Child Rearing Practices Report was administered to 628 Afro-Caribbean parents in Barbados and provided additional cross-cultural data (Payne & Furnham, 1992). The researchers found that those items with the highest factor loadings in the Rickel and Biassati (1982) U.S. study also tended to load heavily on the same Nurturance and Restrictiveness factors in the Afro-Caribbean sample. Payne and Furnham also found that fathers' nurturant scores were significantly lower than mothers' scores on this dimension. However, these results were understandable given the predominance of mother-headed households in this community. It was also revealed that parents in nonmanual occupations were less likely to endorse restrictive parenting styles.

Parenting styles that correlate with alcohol abuse have also been identified. Nurturance and restrictiveness of parents toward their children have been related to whether the parent is presently abusing alcohol. The Rickel Modified Child Rearing Practices Report and a family assessment measure was administered by Packer (1992) to 26 "prerecovering" alcoholic fathers and 34 recovering alcoholic fathers. Packer found that prerecovering alcoholic fathers were significantly more restrictive than recovering alcoholic fathers, but he found no differences in nurturance levels. Self-reported nurturance was positively related to healthy family functioning, whereas restrictiveness was negatively associated with healthy family functioning.

There appears to be a significant probability that parents who abuse their children were subjected as children to parenting that was high in restriction and low in nurturance. Wiehe (1992) conducted a study in which a group of 153 abusing and 141 nonabusing parents were given the Rickel

Modified Child Rearing Practices Report. Instead of answering how they would behave in a given parenting situation, participants were told to answer how they thought their parents would have reacted in rearing them. The results of the study demonstrated that abusive parents rated their own parents as high on restrictiveness and low on nurturance, compared to nonabusers.

These findings provide evidence for a theory of the intergenerational transmission of abuse. In addition, the findings suggest a possible explanation of the ways in which abuse is transmitted and the means to prevent it. In their extensive review of the literature on intergenerational abuse, Kaufman and Zigler (1987) suggested that the rate of transmission is about 30%, plus or minus 5%. That is, one third of parents who were neglected, or physically or sexually abused as children, will perpetrate some form of maltreatment on their own children.

In recent years, documentation of the intergenerational effects of child maltreatment have suggested that the majority of parents abused as children do not abuse their own children (Kaufman & Zigler, 1987). The various findings from developmental, prevention, and child maltreatment research, as well as clinical practice with families, suggest that problematic parent–child relationships are a much more common outcome than maltreatment (Becker-Lausen & Rickel, 1995; Rickel & Becker-Lausen, 1995).

Many studies have linked child sexual abuse to interpersonal difficulties (Courtois, 1988; Elliott & Gabrielsen, 1990; Finkelhor, Hotaling, Lewis, & Smith, 1989). Broader forms of maltreatment have also been found to be related to interpersonal difficulties, with depression and dissociation shown to be mediator variables between childhood maltreatment and later negative life experiences, including interpersonal difficulties (Becker-Lausen, Sanders, & Chinsky, 1995). Results showed the broader maltreatment experiences were related to later interpersonal difficulties, with depression the primary mediator between them, although dissociation also showed small mediating effects.

The direction of the paths among childhood maltreatment,

depression, and interpersonal difficulties may be questioned on the grounds that a depressed subject may see both their childhood and their current relationships more negatively than others do. However, in addition to work (Alloy & Abramson, 1979; Layne, 1983) demonstrating that depressed individuals actually view the world more realistically than nondepressed people (the latter showing an optimistic bias), other studies, both prospective and retrospective, have been supportive of the directionality of the paths proposed by Becker-Lausen et al. (1995), for child maltreatment, depression, and interpersonal difficulties (Briere & Runtz, 1988a; Browne & Finkelhor, 1986; Dodge, Bates, & Pettit, 1990; Fichman, Koestner, & Zuroff, 1994; Webster-Stratton & Hammond, 1988; Widom, 1989a).

In previous chapters we discussed studies (Dodge et al., 1990; Vissing, Straus, Gelles, & Harrop, 1991) connecting physical abuse to externalizing and internalizing behaviors in children that report distinct cognitive pathways through which these outcomes develop. That is, harmed children who were aggressive were likely to develop "biased and deficient patterns of processing social information, including a failure to attend to relevant cues, a bias to attribute hostile intentions to others, and a lack of competent behavioral strategies to solve interpersonal problems" (Dodge et al., 1990, p. 1682).

However, as we suggested previously, when child maltreatment occurs within a family, it always happens within a particular social context, the existence of which cannot be ignored. Next, we turn to research studies that add to our understanding of the complex ways in which family dynamics, parent–child relationships, and societal factors interact to produce individual outcomes.

Parent–child relationships. Research into parent–child interactions suggests children's social development is about equally affected by mothers' and fathers' interactions. Parental influence begins early to facilitate or hamper children's peer relationships, problem-solving ability, emotional reactions, and overall adjustment (Barth & Parke, 1993; Bhavnagri & Parke, 1991; Dickstein & Parke, 1988; Rueter & Conger, 1995). Studies have documented that parent–child interaction may lead to the intergenerational transmission of such negative outcomes as parental rejection (Whitbeck et al., 1992). Harsh parenting has also been shown to be transmitted across generations, primarily through direct modeling of parenting practices, but also, for male children, related to socioeconomic factors (Simons, Whitbeck, Conger, & Wu, 1991; Whitbeck, Simons, & Conger, 1991). Furthermore, the quality of early parent–child relationships has been found to persist across time: childhood experiences such as parental rejection or harsh discipline from parents are associated with poorer parent–child relationships in later life.

A review of resiliency studies, conducted across generations with different ethnic and cultural groups (Werner & Smith, 1992), suggested a variety of factors that may mediate or moderate negative outcomes for children, including child factors such as temperament, planning ability, and scholastic aptitude, as well as family factors such as the provision of responsible chores; a self-confident, educated mother; and the presence of supportive, extended family members. Boys typically have the greatest difficulty in the first decade of life, whereas girls become more susceptible to problems in the second decade. However, in adulthood, females again appear to regain the greater resiliency evident in the early years.

For adolescents, parental attitudes and influence have been linked to a variety of outcomes, including the effects of parental hostility on teens' delinquent behavior, and the cross-gender, reciprocal effects of psychological distress (i.e., mothers with sons; fathers with daughters) (Conger & Conger 1994). For male adolescents, a relationship has been further identified between the mother's stress-related depression, subsequent poor discipline resulting from depression, and adolescent adjustment problems (Conger, Patterson, & Ge, 1995; Ge, Conger, Lorenz, Shanahan, & Elder, 1995).

Adolescents' success in school has been linked to *authoritative parenting* (firm control combined with responsiveness to and open communication with the teen), parental encouragement, and parental involvement in school activities (Dornbusch & Wood, 1989). However, studies with multiethnic participants reveal that Asian, African American, and

Hispanic adolescents are more likely to report parents who used *authoritarian* (high control, low responsiveness) child-rearing styles, and that the relationship between authoritative parenting and school success is greatest for White subjects; some researchers have suggested that the influence of peers on ethnic minority teens may reduce the effect of parental influences (Dornbusch, Ritter, Leiderman, Roberts, & Fraleigh, 1987; Steinberg, Dornbusch, & Brown, 1992).

Values socialization has also been identified as an important factor in early adolescent delinquency. Teens who endorsed altruistic values were less likely to have friends who engaged in deviant behavior, whereas values related to success and affluence did not affect the degree to which teens associated with those who were involved in deviant activities (Whitbeck, Simons, Conger, & Lorenz, 1989).

The structure of the family has also been found to influence adolescent outcomes, particularly high school completion and educational attainment. Studies of large, national samples have documented a relationship between disruption of a two-parent family during adolescence and the likelihood of high school graduation. Those at age 14 who live with one parent, with a parent and stepparent, or with neither parent were less likely to finish school, and these effects were independent of number of siblings, school dropout rate, and gender (Astone & McLanahan, 1991; Sandefur, McLanahan, & Wojtkiewicz, 1992).

Just as parents affect children, the presence or absence of children has been shown to affect adults' psychological well being. McLanahan and Adams (1989) have documented that parenthood has become an increasingly stressful experience over the past several decades. Looking at data on parenting from 1957 to 1976, they found that parenting decreased quality of life and increased psychological distress, and that much of the effect on women, specifically, could be attributed to changes in employment and marital status. These changes did not account for men's experience of diminished well being associated with parenthood, although their experience was similar to women's decline in well-being.

Societal Factors

Studies with large, national samples have repeatedly documented the effects of role accumulation and *role strain* (i.e., feeling pulled in a variety of directions by demands from overlapping or conflicting societal roles) on adults' marital quality, quality of life, and psychological distress, with parents reporting less happiness, less satisfaction, and greater levels of worry, anxiety, and depression than those adults without children (McLanahan & Adams, 1987). Furthermore, in one national study, adults 50 and older with grown children reported few positive effects of having had children, compared to those who have not (Glenn & McLanahan, 1982). Such findings emphasize the importance of building greater social support and respite opportunities for parents in today's world where, frequently, extended family no longer are available to provide such support.

Ethnicity and gender effects in stress and coping have been documented in some studies. Findings from a large sample of Black adults (Neighbors, Jackson, Bowman, & Gurin, 1983) indicated that prayer was a significant coping mechanism, particularly for the elderly, lower income groups, and women. However, informal support structures were also extensively used, and women were more likely than men to seek formal professional help. Studies of White families (Simons, Lorenz, Wu, & Conger, 1993) suggest that use of social networks has only an indirect effect on their parenting behavior, and that such social support is not an adequate buffer against the stress of economic hardship. Intergenerational trends in a large ($N = 7,969$), multiethnic sample of women aged 15–44 indicated that subjects who spent a portion of childhood in a single-parent home were more likely to marry early, have children at a young age and out of wedlock, and to experience marital disruption as adults (McLanahan & Bumpass, 1988). These findings were consistent across ethnic groups except that for Black women, early marriage was not related to family background.

Economic conditions have repeatedly been shown to have dramatic effects on family functioning. In one large national survey (N = 3,488), parental behaviors did not appear to mediate the negative effects of economic disadvantage (Thomson, Hanson, & McLanahan, 1994). Likewise, economic strain has been shown to directly affect parenting by reducing parental involvement, and to indirectly affect it by reducing spousal support, which is associated with supportive parenting (Simons, Lorenz, Conger, & Wu, 1992). Economic hardship in White, rural intact families has been shown to lead to parental dysphoria, marital conflict, and disruption in parenting skills (for both mothers and fathers), which in turn have been linked to adolescent internalizing and externalizing behaviors, problematic adjustment, and psychological distress (Conger, Ge, Elder, Lorenz, & Simons, 1994; Conger et al., 1993; Conger et al., 1992).

Changes in family structure in recent decades have increased the degree to which economic factors affect child outcomes. Women's poverty rates increased relative to men's for all age groups between 1950 and 1980, for both Black families and White families, according to one large-scale study (McLanahan, Sorensen, & Watson, 1989). Children growing up in single-parent homes are not only more prone to dropping out of high school, as noted previously, but also more likely to earn lower wages and more likely to rely on welfare as adults, perpetuating cycles of poverty (Astone & McLanahan, 1991; Garfinkel & McLanahan, 1986).

Another significant trend has been that of grandparents rearing children of substance-abusing parents. Burton's (1992) study of Black grandparents rearing children of addicted parents documented the psychological, physical, and economic costs of this stressful role in later life (participants were aged 43 to 82 years). Although most grandparents found it emotionally rewarding to parent their grandchildren, they showed a heightened risk of heart attacks, alcoholism, and depression, and were more likely to smoke. Needs documented for this population included child care, health care, and some form of counseling services; that is to say, their needs are essentially the same as those of many U.S. families today.

Findings from the 1993 Current Population Survey (CPS)

reflect the deepening poverty for families in the United States, where 26% of children under the age of 6 live in poverty (Knitzer & Aber, 1995). For the 1993 CPS, the poverty line was set at $11,000 for a family of three and $14,000 for a family of four. But these strikingly low income levels tell only half the story. While poverty rates for children under age 6 grew substantially between 1987 and 1992, producing the highest rate for these children in more than 25 years, half of these children live in families with incomes which are only 50% or less of the poverty line numbers. That is, 12% of U.S. children under 6 live in households where the annual income for a family of three is $5,500 or less, and $7,000 or less for a family of four.

As Knitzer and Aber (1995) noted, 57% of these poor children under age 6 live in families where one or both parents work. In 18% of poor families, at least one adult has a full-time job; in 39%, adults hold part-time jobs. Nearly 40% of poor families with children under 6 receive no public assistance at all and are entirely dependent on their own earnings. Likewise, just 52% of families in poverty with children under 6 receive public assistance; one third of these families earn income in addition to their assistance.

The picture of the working poor that emerges from these figures contrasts starkly with the images of the poor which have been perpetuated for political purposes. The fact is that, at the time of the 1993 CPS report, a full-time, year-round minimum-wage job would provide less than $9,000 in annual income, if the job included sick leave and paid vacation, or if the employee took no days off all year. (Of course, many minimum wage jobs provided no leave or other benefits.) The recent small increase in the minimum wage, while long overdue, does little to reduce the numbers of families who will still be unable to rise above the poverty line, no matter how hard they work.

The National Research Council (NRC) Panel on High-Risk Youth (1993) summarized these changes as follows:

> The combination of financial insecurity for an increasing proportion of families, increased work effort by parents

seeking to maintain their living standard, and the demographic changes that have so dramatically increased the number of children and adolescents living in single-parent households result in increasing numbers of adolescents who do not receive the nurturance necessary for positive development. The consequences are not inescapably negative.... However, the adverse outcomes—the failure rates—are unacceptably and unnecessarily high. (p. 56)

Despite numerous reports documenting these trends, in the 104th Congress the welfare bill passed will increase child poverty rates by an estimated 1 million children and nationwide by 12% (The Personal Responsibility and Work Opportunity Reconciliation Act of 1996, Pub. L. No. 104–193). The bill ends any federal guarantee of cash assistance to poor children and families (by block-granting funds to states); cuts off aid to children after 5 years, regardless of whether the parents have found work; drastically reduces food stamp funding; denies benefits to children and adults who are legal immigrants; and ends cash assistance to more than 300,000 children with serious disabilities.

This bill reflects a punitive approach to poor families, ignores the realities of the workplace, and provides little support for a viable transition to work. That such legislation should even be contemplated in an era in which the importance of preventive approaches is well known should cause social scientists to reflect on how we might better promote a prevention agenda.

As the NRC (1993) panel noted, even a return to strong economic growth will not alter the decline for most poor families, particularly young families. A combination of social forces, including inner-city deterioration, discrimination, crumbling public school systems, single-parent households, and low-paying jobs, makes rising out of poverty a nearly impossible feat for many young people. Thus, substantial investment would be required to improve the situation: Among the recommendations of the NRC are job-skill enhancement, entry employment opportunities, and child care.

Income-transfer programs are suggested to supplement salaries of low-income working families so that they can afford safe housing and health care.

Teen Pregnancy: An Outcome of and Factor in Downward Spirals

More than half of unmarried U.S. adolescents report having had sexual intercourse by age 18, and the age of initiation of sexual activity is dropping; one study found 21% of teens aged 11 to 14 had engaged in sexual intercourse (U.S. Public Health Service, 1993). About 20% of these sexually active teens get pregnant each year (Adler, 1994). As was highlighted previously, U.S. teen pregnancy rates are more than twice those of England, Norway, and Canada; three times those of Denmark and Sweden; and seven times those of The Netherlands, even though U.S. teens are not more sexually active than their European counterparts (Alan Guttmacher Institute, 1986). Because sexual activity among U.S. teens is no more prevalent than in other Western countries, it appears that prevention of the consequences of sexual activity among our teens is woefully inadequate.

Research on teen pregnancy has long suggested that it is both an outcome and a factor in the perpetuation of poverty cycles. Numerous studies have shown that the fatalistic beliefs and diminished expectations for the future that accompany unemployment, poverty, and lack of educational opportunity are associated with sexual promiscuity in both urban Black and blue-collar White families (Butler, Rickel, Thomas, & Hendren, 1993; Chilman, 1986; Kessler & Cleary, 1980; Rubin, 1976). Early research (Jessor & Jessor, 1975) suggested that sexually active teens had lower grade point averages, lower achievement expectations, and less acceptance of parental controls. Sexually active girls were more likely to view their parents as unsupportive, socially critical, and hostile.

Recent findings indicated that, among sexually active girls, the independently predictive variables for pregnancy intention have been shown to be low self-esteem and lowered educational aspirations (Adler, 1994). An earlier study by Barth, Schinke, and Maxwell (1983) found lower self-esteem in pregnant and parenting teens, compared to nonpregnant, nonparenting peers. They also found slightly higher rates of depression in the pregnant adolescents. Zonger (1977) reported that pregnant adolescents experienced greater feelings of inadequacy and unworthiness. Further research into the psychological factors that distinguish pregnant or parenting teens from their nonpregnant or nonparenting peers is warranted to improve the understanding of the complexity of this outcome for the individual child-bearing adolescent.

Teen Pregnancy and Maladjustment

Thomas and Rickel's study (1995) of 420 adolescents in a high school population, described in chapter 4, found that those who were pregnant or parenting were significantly more maladjusted than matched controls who were neither pregnant nor parenting. Seventy-nine percent of the 179 pregnant or parenting teens in the study scored in the clinical range on the MMPI, using adolescent norms (the MMPI-A was not used because the adolescent form was not yet available at the time of the study). Just 21% of the sample scored in the normal range.

Furthermore, using a discriminate function analysis based on MMPI scores, Thomas and Rickel (1995) were able to correctly classify 80% of the entire sample ($p < .001$). High scores on the MMPI scales for Paranoia, Masculinity–Femininity, Schizophrenia, and Psychopathic Deviance, as well as the validity scales L and F, correctly identified pregnant and parenting adolescents, whereas low scores on those scales were predictive of the matched control nonpregnant and nonparenting adolescents.

Childhood Trauma and Sexual Behavior

Research into teen pregnancy long ago established that there is a greater incidence of sexual intercourse among teens who are unhappy at home, who feel they have poor communication with their parents, and who come from single-parent homes (Fox, 1979; Jessor & Jessor, 1975; Thomas, Rickel, Butler, & Montgomery, 1990; Zelnik, Kantner, & Ford, 1982).

According to Briere (1992), the correlary is also true: many adults mistreated as children report engaging in frequent, short-term sexual relationships with multiple partners, which appears to stem from a need to reduce tension, avoid feelings of emptiness, and distract from the recall of painful abuse experiences. Maltreatment victims report that this sexual activity is often precipitated by periods of depression, loneliness, or perceived abandonment or rejection by others, as well as by memories of abuse.

In the previously described study by Becker-Lausen, Sanders, and Chinsky (1995), a relationship between a history of maltreatment and subsequent negative life outcomes, such as revictimization, interpersonal difficulties, and other stressful life experiences of college students, was found to be differentially mediated by dissociation and depression. Further analysis of the college sample (Becker-Lausen & Rickel, 1995) indicated that dissociation, but not depression, was significantly related to reports of becoming pregnant in high school. Child maltreatment history alone did not correlate with these reports; however, for male teens, child abuse history did correlate with reports of a girlfriend's becoming pregnant. Neither dissociation nor depression scores were related to these reports by teen males. Although high-risk sexual behavior has been found to be prevalent in the college population (Fisher & Fisher, 1992; Fisher & Misovich, 1992), the 1995 Becker-Lausen and Rickel data base had no other information on the variable, and the number of teen pregnancies was very small.

Child Maltreatment and Psychopathology

Several studies have shown increased psychopathology associated with higher levels of maltreatment in childhood (Kolko, 1992; Marshall, 1989). With the exception of psychotic disorders such as schizophrenia, perhaps the most serious mental disturbance is *dissociative identity disorder,** formerly termed *multiple personality disorder.* The disorder has been linked to severe child abuse in numerous studies (Coons & Milstein, 1986; Kluft, 1985; Putnam, Guroff, Silberman, Barban, & Post, 1986). Elevated levels of dissociation and of depression have been identified in abuse victims in studies of both clinical (Chu & Dill, 1990; Sanders & Giolas, 1991; Webster-Stratton & Hammond, 1988) and nonclinical populations (Becker-Lausen, Sanders, & Chinksy, 1995; Briere & Runtz, 1988b; Sanders & Becker-Lausen, 1995).

Further evidence of adult psychosocial maladjustment in both male and female victims of childhood abuse is provided by Hunter (1991), who found adult victims of child sexual abuse manifested low self-esteem, sexual maladjustment, problems in interpersonal relationships, and general emotional maladjustment, based on their scores on measures of psychosocial adjustment, including the MMPI.

Implications of Research Findings

Few studies have closely examined the relationship between childhood maltreatment and later sexual behavior that puts an individual at risk for HIV infection, other sexually transmitted diseases, and unplanned pregnancy. In one such study, adolescents with elevated scores on a measure of high-risk sexual behaviors reported parents who were more coercive, less available, and less supportive than the parents of youth who reported lower levels of these behaviors (Biglan et al., 1990). The relationship between childhood sexual abuse and current HIV status has been assessed in some studies. For example, adult men sexually abused as children had double the rates of HIV infection of nonabused men, according to one study (Zierler et al., 1991). Another study found 65% of HIV-infected subjects had been sexually abused

---

*The validity of the dissociative identity disorder diagnosis has been the subject of an ongoing debate in psychology (Gleaves, 1996).

(Allers & Benjack, 1991). Furthermore, according to Briere (1992), "For such individuals, 'inappropriate' or 'excessive' sexual activity is . . . a consciously or unconsciously chosen coping mechanism invoked to modulate painful internal experience" (p. 67–68).

In a longitudinal study of youth, Cunningham, Stiffman, Dore, and Earls (1994) evaluated sexual risk behaviors and their change over time in participants with histories of sexual abuse and with participants who had been physically abused. They found that both participants who experienced physical abuse and those who experienced sexual abuse were more likely to engage in several forms of risky sexual behavior. Participants with histories of any of these forms of maltreatment were also more likely to maintain or increase their risky behavior over the 3-year period of the study, from late adolescence into early adulthood.

Although these prior studies have illuminated the complexity of the issues, none has investigated the mediator variables between childhood maltreatment and sexual behavior in adolescence and young adulthood. Determining the interactions among these variables may help in the design of intervention efforts for prevention of HIV and other sexually transmitted diseases and pregnancy prevention.

Data from the Hunter (1991) study in the previous section was compared to the Thomas and Rickel (1995) data. Sexually abused adult females in the Hunter study and pregnant or parenting teens in the Thomas and Rickel study were found to have in common higher scores (compared to control groups) on the MMPI scales of Paranoia, F, Schizophrenia, and Psychopathic Deviate. Hunter's adult child abuse victims also had elevated scores, compared to controls, on K, Hypochondriasis, Depression, Hysteria, Psychasthenia, Mania, and Social Introversion. These victims' T scores were elevated more than two standard deviations (SDs) above the mean on two scales: Psychopathic Deviate and Schizophrenia. Nonvictims had no T scores on any scales that were greater than two SDs above the mean on any scale. Two scales were not significant for victims in the Hunter study but were significant for the pregnant and parenting teens in the Thomas and Rickel study (compared to the matched controls): L and Masculinity–Femininity. Adult male and female victims of childhood sexual abuse in the Hunter study had similar MMPI profiles. However, male participants had two additional T scores that were greater than two standard deviations above the mean: Masculinity–Femininity and Psychasthenia. The control group showed no T scores on any scale that were greater than two SDs above the mean.

Thus, these sexual abuse victims (Hunter, 1991) display similar levels of maladjustment to those of the pregnant and parenting teens in the Thomas and Rickel (1995) study. However, the sexual abuse victims' symptomatology appears to be more severe. If sexual abuse is understood to be at the severe end of an abuse–neglect continuum, then one would expect to find more severe pathology in its victims. Similarly, if child maltreatment were measured as a continuous variable, psychopathology should be reduced in a sample of victims of general childhood maltreatment, compared to a sample of a specific type of severe maltreatment, such as sexual abuse. Psychopathology would be reduced in the former sample by the presence of victims of less severe forms of abuse, such as overly restrictive or punitive parenting, or parental substance abuse.

Such an approach would take into account the coexistence of various forms of abuse and neglect. For example, in a review of 42 studies of short- and long-term effects of child sexual abuse, Beitchman, Zucker, Hood, DaCosta, and Akman (1991) found that promiscuity was among the most common sequelae for adolescents, although survivors of sexual abuse also exhibited other symptoms of psychopathology typically found in clinical samples. The prevalence of severe family pathology co-occurring with sexual abuse led the authors to conclude that the specific impact of sexual abuse over and above a dysfunctional home environment was difficult to determine.

In fact, when child maltreatment is measured as a continuous variable, the level of reported abuse and neglect increases with the degree of psychopathology of the sample. Using the Child Abuse and Trauma Scale, a continuous measure of child maltreatment (Sanders & Becker-Lausen, 1995), an inpatient psychiatric sample of adolescents reported twice the level of abuse as that reported by a sample of college students; a sample of patients diagnosed as having multiple personality disorder reported twice the level of abuse of the hospitalized adolescents, or three times that of the college students (Becker-Lausen, Sanders, & Chinsky, 1995; Sanders & Giolas, 1991).

Sexual Behavior Model

Few studies have attempted to examine the childhood experience of abuse and neglect as an antecedent of high-risk sexual behavior and teen pregnancy. Sexual abuse has often been examined separately; however, many in the field are now recommending that maltreatment should be considered on a continuum (Elliott, Briere, McNeil, Cox, & Bauman, 1995; Finkelhor & Dzuiba-Leatherman, 1994; Sanders & Becker-Lausen, 1995). The substantial overlap between the MMPI data on pregnant and parenting teens and sexual abuse victims, described previously, bears further investigation. Furthermore, neither Thomas and Rickel (1995) nor Becker-Lausen, Sanders, and Chinsky (1995) found a relationship between depression and teen pregnancy, although earlier work suggested there might be an association (Barth, Schinke, & Maxwell, 1983).

Based on data from Hunter (1991), Thomas and Rickel (1995), and Becker-Lausen, Sanders, and Chinsky (1995), we initially (Becker-Lausen & Rickel, 1995) proposed a model similar to the one shown in Figure 1.

In our work we have frequently expanded the outcome variable to include other forms of high-risk sexual behavior, so that the model predicts that (a) child maltreatment leads to dissociation in some individuals, reflected in elevated Schizophrenia scores, mediating the outcome of high-risk sexual behavior; (b) child maltreatment leads to a rejection of conventional norms by some adolescents, reflected in an elevated Psychopathic scale, which then also mediates their risk of early sexual activity; (c) child maltreatment results in

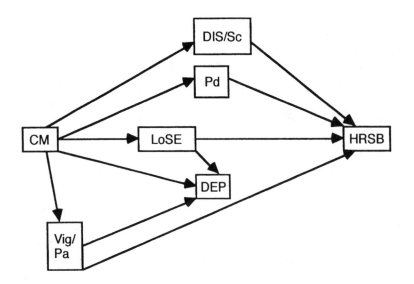

Figure 1.   Model of child maltreatment and high-risk sexual behavior. CM = child maltreatment. HRSB = high-risk sexual behavior. Vig/Pa = Vigilance/Paranoia scale. DIS/Sc = Dissociation/Schizophrenia scale. Pd = Psychopathic scale. LoSE = low self-esteem. DEP = depression. From Becker-Lausen & Rickel (1995). Reprinted with permission of the publisher.

lowered self-esteem, which independently mediates depression and high-risk sexual behavior; and (d) child maltreatment increases vigilance, which manifests as elevated Paranoia scores, for some related to sexual activity, but for others, related to depressive symptomatology.

Tests of the model. Our ongoing research efforts have included attempts to test various aspects of the model proposed above. To begin to examine the relationship between child maltreatment history and high-risk sexual behavior, Gleeson (1996) studied college students' reports of maltreatment in childhood, dissociative experiences, and high-risk sexual behavior. Using measures designed for the University of Connecticut AIDS Risk Reduction Project (Fisher & Fisher, 1992; Fisher & Misovich, 1992) together with a broad measure of child maltreatment history (the Child Abuse and Trauma scale, Sanders & Becker-Lausen, 1995), Gleeson found that child maltreatment history was related to motivational measures, but not to specific behavioral indicators relevant to high-risk sexual behavior. That is, child maltreatment history was related to distorted beliefs and attitudes about AIDS, AIDS transmission, and prevention (such as believing prevention poses a threat to a relationship or holding faulty beliefs that one can determine AIDS status from an individual's appearance). Maltreatment history was not related to condom use or other behavioral factors. These findings suggest further research to explore cognitive processes by which negative childhood experiences are translated into distorted perspectives that ultimately increase one's risk of negative outcomes, in line with studies such as Dodge, Bates, and Pettit (1990) where physically harmed children were more likely to develop "biased and deficient patterns of processing social information . . ." (p. 1682).

To continue this line of research, Becker-Lausen and Gleeson (1996) compared Gleeson's (1996) data on college students ($N = 336$) to data collected on 518 low-income mothers aged 18–50 archived with the National Data Archive on Child Abuse and Neglect (Zuravin, 1989; Zuravin & DiBlasio, 1992). Becker-Lausen and Gleeson proposed that a relationship between child maltreatment and risky sexual behavior would not be bound by race nor class. Based on research on pregnancy intention (Adler, 1994), a difference was predicted in incidence of adolescent pregnancy, resulting from the lack of incentive to delay pregnancy where poverty interferes with a young woman's chances of pursuing educational or career goals.

The two samples proved to be dramatically different on demographic variables, as the authors (Becker-Lausen & Gleeson, 1996) expected: 71% of the college students were White; 80% of the low-income mothers were Black; students were middle- and upper-middle class compared to lower-class mothers; 55% of the students were Catholic and 80% of the mothers were Protestant; students were primarily from New England and the mothers were in Baltimore; and 100% of the college students, by definition, had completed high school, compared to 41% of the mothers who had completed high school or been educated beyond it.

These extremely diverse groups both showed evidence of a relationship between the experience of maltreatment in childhood and high-risk sexual behavior. The relationship for the college students in Gleeson's (1996) study was described previously. For the low-income mothers in Zuravin's database (1989) reports of maltreatment in childhood, such as having been beaten, having been sexually molested, having gone hungry or without adequate clothing, and having witnessed domestic violence, were significantly related to lack of birth control use and to a greater number of sexual partners.

Pregnancy and child birth before the age of 18 was about 20 times more common for the low-income mothers than for the college students, whereas the rate of abortions prior to age 18 was only two times greater for the low-income women than for the college students. These findings, particularly the relatively small difference in abortions compared to the very large difference in pregnancy rates, support the contention that educational and career incentives encourage the delay of both pregnancy and child birth.

Also significant in this study was the fact that sexual abuse history was highly intercorrelated with other forms of maltreatment in both of these diverse samples. Thus, we advocate, as have others, that child maltreatment history is best studied as an aggregate of maltreatment experiences, rather than a focus on any specific form of abuse (Becker-Lausen, Sanders, & Chinsky, 1995; Elliott, Briere, McNeil, Cox, & Bauman, 1995; Finkelhor & Dzuiba-Leatherman, 1994; Sanders & Becker-Lausen, 1995).

We continue to explore these pathways through our ongoing research program. Research currently underway includes studies of the Rickel Modified Child Rearing Practices Report (CRPR) and its relationship to the Child Abuse and Trauma (CAT) scale (Sanders & Becker-Lausen, 1995) with both clinical and nonclinical populations. We are examining how these two measures relate to individual outcomes that may be relevant to intimate relationships, such as loneliness, interpersonal difficulties, trust, and traumatic symptomatology. We are also exploring further the relationship between these measures and the scales of the Minnesota Multiphasic Personality Inventory, using the revised, updated version (MMPI-2).

Preliminary findings from these ongoing studies have added data supporting the validity of both the Rickel Modified CRPR and the CAT scale. For example, in a study by Mallon-Kraft (1996), college students' reports on the CRPR of their parents' child-rearing practices were significantly correlated with parents' self-reports of their child-rearing practices, a finding that held for both the Nurturance and the Restrictiveness factors of the CRPR. In this same study, scores on the CAT scale completed by the college student were significantly correlated with the father's report of his restrictiveness, but were not correlated with father's report of nurturance. The reverse was true for mothers: college students' CAT scores were inversely correlated with mothers' own reports of nurturance, but were not correlated with mothers' reports of their restrictiveness.

Implications for Policy and Practice

All too frequently, teen pregnancy is the beginning of a downward spiral leading to poverty and family dysfunction, or a perpetuation of poverty and dysfunction from one generation to another. The potential for sexually transmitted diseases through risky sexual practices, particularly the risk of HIV-infection, lends yet another tragic outcome to potentially devastating consequences of adolescent sexual practices (Ruder, Flam, Flatto & Furran, 1990).

To the extent that teen sexual activity cannot be controlled, we must do all we can to encourage safe sexual practices. When we are unable to prevent teen pregnancy, it is critical that we intervene with young, inexperienced parents to help them better nurture their children, delay additional pregnancies, and improve the quality of their own lives.

We know from many sources, such as the Detroit Parent Project and Head Start-type programs, that parents can be helped to improve their child-rearing skills while enhancing their own lives. Efforts to support families have the potential to prevent numerous problems, including child maltreatment, family violence, substance abuse, maternal and child health problems, and welfare dependency (Browne, 1987; Holden & Zambarno, 1992; Lewinsohn, Rohde, & Seeley, 1996). Communities must come together to build coalitions that support prevention of major social problems. Providing affordable housing, access to health care services, and education and job opportunities all are critical to the health care survival of our communities today (Institute of Medicine, 1994).

Theoretical Models of Intergenerational Outcomes

We have attempted in this chapter to review various factors related to intergenerational transmission of outcomes that affect the child's development, including aspects of the parents and the environment. From what has been described, we have proposed a theoretical model of these interactions, shown in Figures 2 and 3. The model has been divided into two figures for easier comprehension. Central to the model are the two constructs of parental nurturance and parental restrictivenesss, and the concept that high-risk sexual behavior in adolescence is a key outcome variable predisposing the next generation (looping back to Figure 2) to the many negative outcomes described in the model.

Figure 2 provides the foundation at the beginning of the child's life: The prenatal environment is affected directly by environmental hazards and indirectly through their potential effect on genetic material; genetic factors interact with the prenatal environment, and directly and indirectly affect birth outcome. Parental stress level also affects prenatal environment, and parental stress is influenced by socioeconomic status (SES), either positively through economic and other resources, or negatively through economic stress and poverty. In the same manner, SES affects the prenatal environment

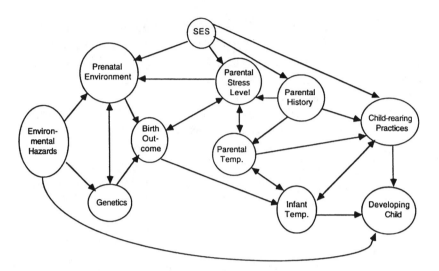

Figure 2.   Biopsychosocial antecedents of child-rearing practices. From B. Ryan, *The Family–School Connection.* Copyright 1995 by Sage Publications. Reprinted with permission of the publisher.

more directly, through access to economic resources such as adequate prenatal care and nutrition.

Birth outcome (e.g., neonatal health), then, interacts with parental stress levels, which in turn interact with temperament. Birth outcome also affects infant temperament (e.g., prenatal cocaine exposure makes neonate difficult to soothe), which interacts with parental temperament, and in turn, parental temperament affects the parent's child-rearing practices, and the infant's temperament then interacts with the parent's child-rearing practices (e.g., impatient parent under stress has difficulty responding with nurturance to infant's fussiness).

SES continues to be an important factor, influencing the parent's own childhood history, including the child-rearing practices they learned from their own parents. The parent's history, particularly one of maltreatment in childhood, affects the level of stress as a parent. The experience of parenting may revive past traumatic experiences, or it may evoke positive and happy feelings.

The developing child, then, is directly or indirectly affected by all of these factors, as well as by their own temperament,

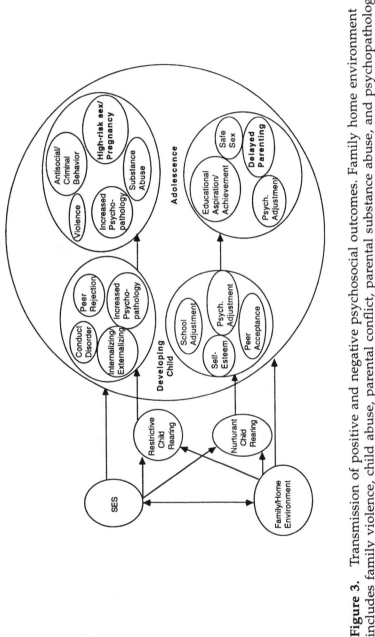

Figure 3. Transmission of positive and negative psychosocial outcomes. Family home environment includes family violence, child abuse, parental conflict, parental substance abuse, and psychopathology. SES = socioeconomic status, and includes factors such as poverty, and economic stress vs. economic resources.

by the parents' child-rearing practices, and the continuing possibility of environmental hazards (e.g., lead paint, dangerous neighborhoods, school violence, heavily trafficked streets).

Moving to Figure 3, we have divided child-rearing practices into the constructs of restrictive and nurturant parenting, as we described previously in this chapter. Described in Figure 2, child-rearing practices are moderated by factors such as the parent's socioeconomic status (i.e., positive outcomes of nurturing parenting may be offset by the child's exposure to conditions of poverty or, conversely, may be enhanced by the advantages of higher status). Furthermore, the family or home environment will moderate the effects of nurturing or restrictive parenting. For example, a boy who sees his nurturant mother being beaten by his father may be vulnerable to externalizing behavior, conduct disorder, or other negative outcomes, despite his mother's parenting skills. On the other hand, a girl with restrictive parents whose home is otherwise relatively free of stressors may do well in school, build a positive self-concept, and be able to make the most of learning experiences outside the home.

Figure 3 was designed with the various negative or positive outcomes shown in clusters to simplify the concepts presented. Numerous paths could be drawn among SES, home environment, and child-rearing practices, and all the various outcomes, but the diagram would then be impossible to decipher. Instead, Figure 3 depicts SES and home environment interacting with one another as moderator variables affecting child rearing, potentially leading to any of the various positive and negative outcomes listed in the clusters, with onset during childhood or adolescence.

Restrictive and nurturant child rearing are shown leading to negative or positive outcomes respectively. Thus, we believe that these child-rearing styles are capable of mediating the effects of home environment and SES. Research so far suggests that, were restrictive or nurturant parenting to exist in a vacuum, they would lead in this straightforward manner to negative or positive child outcomes. Because they exist as one of multiple influences on the child, we propose that the outcome for the child will result from the interaction between these child-rearing styles and the environment.

As Thornberry remarked following his 5-year study of 4,000 youth in three U.S. cities: "Violence does not drop out of the sky at age 15 . . . . It is a part of a long developmental process that begins in early childhood" (Kantrowitz, 1993, p. 46). Thornberry found that just 15% of the teens studied committed 75% of the violent offenses. He discovered that the most violence and abuse occurred where parents were unemployed, had dropped out of high school, and began having children in their teens.

We suggest, as did Forehand, Armistead, and Klein (1995), cited previously in this chapter, that the process begins well before early childhood. The major policy implication is the need for multidisciplinary approaches to prevention, approaches that would involve major social systems—education, health care, mental health, child protection, and juvenile justice. Not one of the variables discussed is beyond society's control, but if we ignore any one of them—for example, prenatal care for young mothers—our efforts to intervene later with preschoolers are likely to be inadequate.

Research efforts to demonstrate these pathways may have the potential to serve as a foundation for the development of prevention programs in managed care settings, particularly health maintenance organizations (HMOs). We believe that with the privatization of public sector medicine (i.e., Medicaid), already underway, such a prevention initiative is timely. In fact, the National Committee for Quality Assurance, a Washington-based nonprofit organization that accredits HMOs, has developed standards for behavioral health treatment in managed care settings. Primary, secondary, and tertiary prevention are components of these standards.

Summary and Conclusions

As researchers and practitioners, we must stress the importance of adequate assessment of the needs of patients (e.g., trauma history, level of maladjustment, symptomatology) at the outset of prevention efforts, as well as the importance of ongoing evaluation of a program's success. This approach has been shown to be effective in other interventions as divergent as substance abuse treatment (Babor et al., 1991) and preschool intervention programs (Rickel & Allen, 1987; Rickel & Becker-Lausen, 1995; Rickel, Dudley, & Berman, 1980). Our ongoing research may provide the basis for a similar approach to the prevention of high-risk sexual behavior and its negative outcomes, which carry a heavy price tag for the individual and society, from a moral and psychological, as well as from an economic standpoint.

In this chapter we have outlined the relationships among problems of parenting, environmental factors in the home and in the broader community, and intergenerational transmission of positive and negative outcomes. We have seen how forces shape the family's experiences internally, through interpersonal interactions, and externally, through interaction with the society at large. Factors such as economic pressures on adults (e.g., "downsizing" and attendant layoffs) can affect outcomes for the children and youth in the home. Adolescent pregnancy has been presented as a pivotal issue that results from negative environmental forces and, in turn, perpetuates them. A model of these relationships was proposed, and it indicated that negative outcomes for the child, and ultimately for the adolescent and adult, are the end points of a dual pathway that begins before birth.

6

Implications for Public Policy

> Never doubt that a small group of thoughtful,
> committed citizens can change the world; indeed,
> it is the only thing that ever has.
> —Margaret Mead

After an initial discussion of the devastating effects on children of the recent welfare reform legislation, we review in this chapter the history of the prevention movement in the United States, including interventions for developmental delay; treatment of mental disorders in children; legislative and judicial responses to child development, maternal and child health, and additional family issues; the White House conferences on children and other executive branch actions related to child and family policy. The community mental health movement is outlined, and the current political climate for children and families is presented.

Although interest in prevention has continued to increase among researchers and clinicians for the past 2 decades, the public's understanding, acceptance and commitment to prevention programs appears to be declining. Ironically, just as the study of childhood trauma has burgeoned (Briere, 1992; *Children of War*, 1992; Herman, 1992), the national commitment to prevention of child maltreatment came into jeopardy. The Child Abuse Prevention and Treatment Act, first passed in

1974, was eliminated in the House welfare bill in the 104th Congress but passed separately later. The compromise welfare-reform bill, the Personal Responsibility and Work Opportunities Reconciliation Act of 1996, also abolished federal entitlements that, for decades, have guaranteed assistance to individuals and families in times of need. Following are details of this Act's wide-ranging consequences for children and families.

At the most basic level, the entire concept of prevention was threatened by the 104th Congress' cuts to basic assistance, including food, shelter, and medical care for poor families. Social scientists, public health researchers, and pediatricians were left shaking their heads at the apparent lack of understanding on the part of legislators of the relationship between basic preventive measures and societal outcomes such as teen pregnancy, delinquency, and substance abuse. These relationships have been recognized for the better part of this century, so it is timely to consider the Act in context with the history of prevention in this country.

Turning Back the Clock: The Personal Responsibility and Work Opportunity Reconciliation Act

The Personal Responsibility and Work Opportunities Reconciliation Act of 1996 eliminated Aid to Families with Dependent Children (AFDC), Emergency Assistance to Families With Children (one month per year of temporary aid), and JOBS (a work and training program). Block grants given to states with few strings attached replaced these federally mandated programs. States must operate an assistance program for families, but it need not be cash aid, and it may be disbursed by private charities, religious organizations, or other private groups.

In the past, states had considerable flexibility in setting eligibility guidelines and levels of assistance, but federal law required that they provide cash aid to all children and families who met basic criteria. Under the new law, states are no longer required to provide cash aid, although they may choose to do so. States also no longer must provide matching funds in order to receive federal dollars, as was the case with AFDC, JOBS, emergency assistance, and past child care programs related to welfare. Federal funds under this law cannot be used by any family for more than a total of 5 years. Once this time limit is met, states will not be required to provide anything to children in such families. Parents who are minors may only receive support if they live at home or in an adult-supervised setting, and they must be in high school or an alternative program if their child is 12 weeks or more in age.

Financial Impact

Total cuts from the Act were projected in 1996 to total $54 billion through the year 2002, with $23 billion coming out of the Food Stamp Program, and nearly $3 billion cut from child nutrition programs. In addition, a new definition of childhood disability restricts eligibility for Supplemental Security Income (SSI), which could result, by the year 2002, in more than 300,000 children being denied SSI funding because of this change. Medicaid will also be denied these children, unless they qualify under other criteria. The Congressional Budget Office estimated that as many as 50,000 children may lose their Medicaid benefits because of this shift.

In addition to these cuts, legal immigrants, including children, will be denied billions of dollars in assistance under this law. Legal aliens are no longer eligible for SSI or Food Stamps. As of January 1, 1997, states were also allowed to deny welfare, social services, and nonemergency Medicaid to legal immigrants.

Work Demands That Leave Children in the Lurch

Work requirements were significantly increased in the new law, with little support for programs that might make them feasible. The Congressional Budget Office estimated the work portions of the bill were short by about $13 billion. Within 2 years of receiving aid, adults are required to participate in work activities, and by 2002, 50 percent of a state's caseload is expected to be working at least 30 hours per week. However, the degree to which educational pursuits may be considered work was sharply limited. All families are expected to participate in work, although states may exempt parents with a child under 1 year of age, and parents of children under 6 cannot be penalized for failure to meet work requirements because they have been unable to find or afford child care for those children.

The key issue of child care is inadequately addressed in the law. The Act abolished the previous guarantee of child care assistance to families on welfare who begin work or pursue training, eliminated the prior one-year transitional child care for families who leave welfare to work, and ended the "at-risk" child care that formerly could be provided to families who would need welfare if they could not get help with child care. Funds for child care were to be provided under the new law to states as *capped entitlements* (i.e., guaranteed amounts that cannot be increased above a certain "cap") and in block grants, but the Office of Management and Budget (OMB) estimated that child care funding was $2.4 billion short of what would be required if welfare work provisions were met. Some of the funds are discretionary, meaning that Congress may decide to appropriate still less, so that the shortfall could be even greater than OMB estimated.

Policy Makers Concerned for Children Resign Posts

As the effects of these changes on children become clear, some Clinton administration officials found they could not support the Act's implementation. Wendell E. Primus, deputy assistant secretary of Health and Human Services (HHS), resigned in 1996 after analyzing the effects of the legislation on children. He was followed by Peter B. Edelman, acting assistant secretary of HHS (and husband of Marian Wright Edelman, head of the Children's Defense Fund). Mary Jo Bane, an assistant secretary at HHS whose welfare research had been cited by legislators on both sides of the aisle, resigned with Edelman, both declaring the law's effect on children as the reason for their exit. HHS Secretary Donna Shalala, opposed to the bill initially, supported the Act once President Clinton signed it, but openly suggested in 1996 that if Clinton were reelected, the immediate goal would be to change the law ("Acts," 1996).

Historical Overview

In light of these sweeping changes in public laws affecting children and families, an historical perspective may help our understanding of where the United States was at the turn of the last century, and where we may be heading as we begin the next one.

Developmental Delay

In the last century, Victor, the "Wild Boy of Aveyron" spurred interest in developmental delay, the first recognized disorder of childhood. Found running naked in the woods of southern France in the 19th century, the "Wild Boy" was initially captured and confined by a fearful community. Jean Itard, a French physician, worked hard at rehabilitating Victor, insisting that it was the environmental effect of his time spent in the woods, and the lack of adequate stimulation, that had caused Victor's developmental delay. Although Itard grew frustrated and eventually gave up on Victor, his work led others to the realization that developmentally delayed children could be trained (Rosen, Clark, & Kivitz, 1976).

Although interest in educating the developmentally disabled blossomed in the United States, largely through the efforts of advocate Edward Sequin, the ambivalence of society toward delayed children remained strong. Thus, while facilities dedicated to training and educating these children were built, the facilities' locations were commonly isolated and remote, distinctly outside the mainstream of society.

The 20th century brought further changes, among them the use of intelligence testing, the growth of developmental theory, and the effort to bring developmentally delayed children into the larger society. Parent advocacy has played a key role in the progress that has been and continues to be made in our understanding and treatment of developmental delay.

As the century closes, controversy swirls around one of the mainstays of the field, intelligence testing. In the latter part of this century, it has become increasingly clear that standardized IQ tests discriminate against African American children, leading to the inappropriate diagnosis of developmental delay for too many Black children. In California, the case of *Larry P. v. Wilson Riles* (1972) established that African American children could not be classified as mentally retarded on the basis of the IQ test alone.

At the same time, at the end of this century, the first large wave of children prenatally exposed to crack cocaine (frequently mixed with alcohol, tobacco, amphetamines, and/or marijuana) are reaching the public school system. Among White and ethnic minority children, the effects of drug exposure on early development are just beginning to be understood (Scherling, 1994). However, it is clear that the subsequent environmental hazards of continued drug and alcohol use, multiple placements for the child, and poverty play havoc with the development of an infant who is already rendered more vulnerable by prenatal factors (which often include lack of prenatal care and inadequate nutrition).

In Los Angeles County, by the 1990s the problem of prenatal exposure to crack cocaine was already becoming apparent, as the following story illustrates: One African American mother came to the county hospital requesting that her daughter be given intelligence testing because she was convinced her 7-year-old girl was severely delayed. The public school had refused to test the girl, citing the *Larry P. v. Riles* (1972) ruling. The youngster was having severe conduct problems, and was beginning to be seen as conduct disordered by the school. At the time of the appointment at the county hospital, the mother was reporting that the child was experiencing seizures, mostly at night. The mother told clinicians she had used large amounts of crack, alcohol, and other drugs daily throughout the pregnancy; and had also been severely beaten by the girl's father during the pregnancy. She had left the relationship and had since been through several treatment programs, reporting that she had been sober for more than a year.

The child had been in the care of family members throughout her life. No one had ever explored the child's neurological or intellectual status until this point, when she was 7. Her tested IQ was below 70, her vocabulary was minimal, her mother's ratings of her ability to perform developmentally appropriate tasks supported the IQ test results, and she had severe problems with impulse control. Efforts to obtain neurological examinations for the seizures were frustrated by the fact that none of the pediatric neurologists in the city in which the child lived accepted Medicaid patients; and the waiting list for the county neurology clinic was several months.

Thanks to her mother's advocacy, this child became eligible for the special services she so badly needed. Unfortunately, however, the neglect of this child's problems is not uncommon; in the 1990s, the public schools in large cities are simply overwhelmed by the sheer numbers of children needing special attention. Furthermore, many fear that cuts to Medicaid coming out of the 104th Congress will halt services that have in the past helped keep children with severe delays at home with their families.

Mental Disorders

The first psychological clinic for school-aged children was established by Lightner Witmer in 1896 and primarily served children and adolescents with developmental or physical disabilities. This landmark work by Witmer became the foundation for the field of clinical psychology. In the first year of operation, an estimated 24 cases were seen in the clinic; ages ranged from 3 to 16, and presenting problems included learning and speech difficulties, hyperactivity, and physical abnormalities such as hydrocephalus (McReynolds, 1996). The clinic began to grow rapidly around 1907, becoming a prototype for clinics being established both in universities and in public school systems. In fact, the latter were the primary source of referrals for Witmer's clinic, establishing early the importance of the connection between school systems and children's clinical services.

Witmer's primary interest, however, remained with developmentally delayed children. Nevertheless, significant aspects of his approach included an emphasis on parental involvement and even occasional treatment of a parent's psychological problems and, consequently, a focus on structuring the home environment to support behavioral change in the child (McReynolds, 1996).

In 1907, the first child guidance clinic was established by the physician William Healy in Chicago (Routh, 1996). The Juvenile Psychopathic Institute began with the premise that juvenile delinquents were youth with treatable mental problems. At the beginning of the century, this was a novel idea, but one which for much of the 20th century has been an accepted axiom. Only at the end of this century are we now witnessing the rejection of this idea by the public, as legislators call for more jails and for adjudicating youthful offenders as adults.

Between 1980 and 1994, the number of inmates in state and federal prisons increased three-fold, from 329,821 to more than 1 million (Kupers, 1996). American society has come full circle; rehabilitation is no longer even a goal in the federal penal system. Those brave enough to work as clinicians with youthful offenders in this punitive climate often are lurching forward day by day, pasting Band-Aids on the gaping wounds left by massive social policy failures. More juveniles today are being transferred to the adult criminal justice system, where they face harsher consequences and exposure to more experienced offenders and to victimization.

At the same time, researchers are learning more about the effects of the massive doses of violence on our youth, whether it is at home, in the media, or in the streets. At the research and clinical level, the environmental effects of poverty and violence on children have probably never been clearer or better understood, although there is still much to learn. Problems with emotional regulation, an increase in aggressive behaviors, negative self-image, symptoms of post-

traumatic stress disorder, and difficulties in interpersonal relationships all have been documented in research with
children and youth exposed to violence. In addition, there is
some evidence that the parenting capacity of caretakers is
also negatively impacted by violence (Osofsky, 1995). It is
truly ironic, then, that at this time the public and its representatives seem largely oblivious to this knowledge.

A poll conducted by the *Washington Post* (Morin, 1995)
found that White Americans believed African Americans
were as well off as Whites and that there was little discrimination. This staggering finding, completely at odds with reality, provides some clue as to what is going on in the American conscience. In May, 1996, a week-long series on race
relations on ABC's *Nightline* further explored this issue. On
national television, White Americans repeatedly voiced some
variation of this belief—that racism is no longer a problem
in the United States—while African Americans spoke of their
continued personal experiences of discrimination at all levels
of society.

Thus, ignorance may be one source of the harsh policy decisions observed in the 1990s. However, there are probably
multiple explanations. Observing shifts in Canadian social
policy similar to those in the United States, a group of Canadian researchers examined causal attributions related to
welfare recipients (Hilbers, Graham, Wilson, O'Connor, &
Duck, 1996). As predicted, when welfare status was attributed to controllable, individual internal causes, participants
viewed welfare recipients as more responsible for their situation, felt more anger toward them, and were less likely to
want to help them. Furthermore, political orientation affected
response: self-identified conservatives were more likely to attribute welfare status to individual, controllable causes, more
likely to report anger toward the welfare recipient, less likely
to feel sympathy, and less likely to want to help the recipient.
These findings were supportive of earlier work by Zucker
and Weiner (1993).

On the other hand, Hilbers et al. (1996), also found that
individuals who fear they may need assistance in the future
were more likely to feel sympathy and less likely to feel an-

ger toward recipients. These latter findings have implications for future U.S. elections, as more families are touched by layoffs associated with downsizing, defense cutbacks, and other spending cuts.

Several authors have suggested that, since the late 1970s, conservative politicians have systematically encouraged the White middle and working classes to blame the poor and ethnic minorities for economic difficulties (Edsall & Edsall, 1991; Freedman, 1993). The attributions include Whites blaming job losses on affirmative action effects, and believing that the deterioration of society is the fault of immigrants and people of color. Using rhetoric that encourages these beliefs, conservatives have both diverted attention from the increasing inequality reflected in the widening gap between the upper socioeconomic groups and the rest of the populace, while simultaneously dividing traditional coalitions of labor, ethnic minorities, and women.

Returning to the earlier part of this century, the first child guidance clinic with a full range of services for children, families, teachers, and others involved with the child, opened in Boston in 1921. During the 1920s, child guidance clinics organized by the Commonwealth Fund were developed across the country. They used Healy's staffing model, which consisted of a psychiatrist, a psychologist, and a social worker (Routh, 1996).

Only in the 1930s did children become the subject of serious study in the field of mental health research. In 1934, the Society for Research in Child Development was formed by researchers studying child development without a clinical focus, and Leo Kanner authored the first textbook on child psychiatry, published in 1935. Nearing the middle of the century, child psychopathology began to be defined and described. In the 1940s, while Beata Rank was chronicling the "atypical" child in Boston, Leo Kanner was defining what he termed *early infantile autism* in Baltimore.

World War II and its aftermath, particularly the establishment of the Veterans Administration and its training programs, marked a period of renewed emphasis in clinical psychology on evaluation and treatment of adults. After the

1949 Boulder Conference set standards for the scientist–practitioner training model in clinical psychology, the dominant theme in the field was, for a time, adult psychopathology. However, the publication in 1959 by Alan Ross of *The Practice of Clinical Child Psychology*, and the founding in 1962 of Section 1, the Clinical Child Section of the American Psychological Association's Clinical Division (Division 12) both served to re-emphasize the continued importance of child psychology to the field (Routh, 1996).

Legislative and Judicial Efforts

Child development researchers, meanwhile, were providing a base of knowledge, delineating the "healthy" or "normal" course of development. These efforts were instrumental in stimulating federal initiatives such as the Mental Health Act of 1946, which clearly established mental health as a federal responsibility.

Some 50 years later, one of the few encouraging outcomes of the 104th Congress was the unanimous passage by the Senate of S.1028, a bill that included a provision to make mental health insurance equivalent to medical insurance benefits. S.1028, which ensured that health insurance would not end when workers changed jobs, was amended in the Senate by the Domenici-Wellstone measure for mental health parity. The amendment prohibited health plans from requiring co-pays, deductibles, or lifetime limits for mental health benefits unless the same restrictions were applied to medical benefits. Although the amendment was significantly modified by the Senate-House Conference Committee, its passage in September, 1996 was a milestone in the history of mental health services delivery, marking the growing acceptance of the significance of mental health care provision.

From mid-century until the 1980s, national efforts for child health and welfare continued to grow. In 1963, the National Institute of Child Health and Human Development was established to conduct research and training in maternal and child health, in special maternal health requirements, and in human development. Other landmark federal initiatives have included the establishment of Project Head Start in 1965 and the Office of Child Development in 1969, the Report of the Joint Commission on the Mental Health of Children in 1970, and the Child Abuse Prevention and Treatment Act, signed into law in 1974.

Along the way, however, defeat of key legislative proposals has also served to shape U.S. policy on child and family issues; for example, the defeat of the Comprehensive Child Development Act of 1971, which would have created a nationwide network of child care centers with a federal commitment to quality, funding, and training. Reflecting on his experience with this legislation, Zigler (Zigler & Muenchow, 1992) outlines the effect the defeat of this bill had on policy:

> But I remain troubled by the opportunity we lost. Child care remains a massive problem in this nation. More than two decades later, we still have three separate systems for child care—Head Start for children from poverty-level families; federally funded care with no federal standards for children from other very low-income working families; and a hodgepodge of frequently unreliable arrangements of mixed quality for everyone else. Had the defenders of children—advocates, congressional supporters, and, most especially, the President of the United States—been a little more willing to compromise in 1971, millions of Americans would be better off today. We had the opportunity to develop a quality child care system, but we let it slip by. (pp. 148–149)

Similarly, repeated failures to pass federal initiatives for key issues such as child support enforcement and the consolidation of services for families and children have continued to put the United States behind most other industrialized countries in the arena of child and family policy (Tomes & Rickel, 1996).

For example, the Family and Medical Leave Act of 1993 was finally signed into law by President Clinton as the first act of his presidency on February 4, 1993. The bill had been introduced as legislation seven times, had been the subject of 17 Senate committee hearings, was passed by Congress three times (1990, 1992, and 1993), and was vetoed twice by President Bush. The bill was first introduced in 1985, and by 1993 had the backing of 240 organizations and associations. However, the legislation had been seriously limited by that time through the compromises encountered in this legislative labyrinth. That is, 95% of employers were not affected by the bill, which was limited to companies with greater than 50 employees. Nevertheless, the passage set a significant precedent for the importance of family commitments within the work environment, particularly the guarantee of job security when family or medical leave is necessary.

Many of the witnesses at congressional hearings told horror stories of job loss resulting from leave taken for family emergencies, which created situations in which income and health insurance were lost at the same time the family was hit by medical and financial crises. Although several industrialized European countries have much more liberal policies (e.g., paid rather than unpaid leave), the job security provided by the bill was considered key to establishing a family-friendly workplace.

Judicial response from mid-century until the 1980s also tended to provide strong support for the needs and rights of children. In 1954, the U.S. Supreme Court, in *Brown v. Board of Education*, struck down the "separate but equal" justification for segregated public schools. In 1969, students were declared persons under the law, with rights of free expression that must be respected by states, by the Supreme Court in *Tinker v. Des Moines Independent School District*.

Equal educational opportunities for children have also been judicially mandated at the state level. In 1972, *Mills v. Board of Education* (D.D.C. 1972) led the state to conclude that mentally and emotionally disabled children could not be excluded from attendance at a regular public school unless adequate alternative services were provided. That same year, in the case of the *Pennsylvania Association for Retarded Children v. Commonwealth* (E.D. Penn. 1972), the court specified that a free, public program of education and training, tailored to the needs of the child, must be provided to children in need.

A district's claim of insufficient funds was not accepted as a legitimate reason for failure to provide services.

On the other hand, the courts and the American public have consistently approved the use of corporal punishment with children. In 1977, the Supreme Court upheld the use of corporal punishment in the schools, ruling that the eighth amendment ban on "cruel and unusual punishment" does not apply to school children (*Ingraham v. Wright*, 1976). Despite this ruling, by 1994, 26 states had legislation prohibiting corporal punishment in schools, and 11 states had local rulings banning it for more than one half of the children in their public schools. Furthermore, most Catholic schools have now prohibited the infliction of pain as a disciplinary strategy (Hyman, 1994).

A ban on the use of corporal punishment in the home has been much slower to find acceptance in the United States, and the issue is fraught with controversy (Hyman, 1994). Meanwhile, in Europe, Sweden first banned corporal punishment by schools in 1958, which was followed 2 decades later by a ban on the use of physical punishment by parents in 1979. Particularly noteworthy in the Swedish approach is that the law is not punitive: if a parent breaks the law, the authorities do not swoop in and remove their children, nor do they fine them or threaten them with jail time. The response instead is one of assistance to the family, reflecting strong beliefs that parents who hit are likely to be stressed, misguided, or lacking in the necessary skills to parent effectively (Hyman, 1994). At least five other European nations have enacted similar laws to those of Sweden (Denmark, Norway, Finland, Poland, and Austria).

In the United States, the trend continues to move in the opposite direction, most recently with the introduction of a Parental Rights and Responsibilities Act (PRPA) in several state legislatures and in both houses of the 104th Congress. Purported to ensure parental protection from government interference with personal child-rearing philosophy, the bill in reality raised major issues about society's ability to protect children from maltreatment.

The PRPA specified the parental right to direct health care, education, discipline, and religious teaching. Parents' rights to use "reasonable corporal punishment" are defended by the bill. Most child advocacy groups opposed this legislation on the grounds that it is unnecessary, because the U.S. Supreme Court has already set the precedent intended by the bill. Furthermore, the bill is potentially harmful to abused and neglected children, limiting the ability of society to intervene in suspected cases of abuse. Conflicts between this bill and existing laws raised numerous issues of unforeseen consequences of this bill for the future protection of children.

Executive Branch Response

Eight White House conferences on children held during this century have reflected the changing views of child advocates regarding the most salient problems of children. In 1909, the first conference focused on the care of dependent children. The conference resulted in the establishment of the federal Children's Bureau, charged with information gathering and the support of research on child development.

The second conference, 10 years later, emphasized careful reporting and statistical analysis of child and maternal health problems, rather than the creation of new programs. In 1930, a White House Conference on Child Health and Protection was marked by controversy over who was best able to determine how a child should be raised—the parents or the "experts." The conference concluded that parent education was the best avenue for change within families.

By 1950, the fourth White House conference reflected 2 decades of changing attitudes by emphasizing that professional expertise was particularly important in shaping the development of healthy children. The 1960 conference focused on the increasing violence in the United States, specifically for adolescent individuals and youth gangs. Moving back to the attitude that the parents are the preeminent influence on children and youth, the conference stressed the need for research into the underlying causes of broken families and, once again, for parent education. The 1960 conference emphasized early intervention to teach parenting skills, recommending education for preparenting high school students.

In 1970 and 1971, the problems of adolescents had gained sufficient attention to warrant the holding of a conference for youth separate from the one for children's issues. Once more the emphasis appeared to be shifting back to the experts, with increasing numbers of children in day care settings, under the influence of teachers trained in early childhood education. However, this time the conferences urged cooperation between families and extrafamilial experts, to maximize the child's development.

These conferences, which emphasized economic, social, and educational reforms for children, recommended preventive measures which, for the most part, have never been implemented. Together with other executive branch efforts, such as the Office of Child Development, these conferences failed to advance prevention efforts sufficient to make a dent in the emotional problems of children and youth in the United States. These problems have continued to mount, leading a National Research Council panel of experts to conclude in 1993 that social systems in America had completely failed our youth.

Dispersion of responsibility across federal agencies, with poor coordination of program and research efforts, is a significant part of the problem. Head Start, the only child-focused program to attract and retain key staff and innovative programs, is also the only major federal effort that has been housed in the Administration for Children, Youth and Families or its forerunner, the Office of Child Development.

Other programs, such as Aid to Families with Dependent Children (AFDC), Women, Infants and Children (WIC), and Title I of the Elementary and Secondary Education Act, have been spread throughout federal agencies. In the past, advances for children have been segmented and discontinuous, rather than comprehensive approaches such as those for veterans, the elderly, and the unemployed.

Most recently, this fragmenting of child programs has made it easier for Congress to make significant changes in these services without the public recognizing the full impact on the nation's children. In the 104th Congress, while the public worried about Medicare, taxes, and putting welfare recipients to work, the drastic cuts to services for children were so numerous it was nearly impossible to track them all.

For example, in July, 1995, after an initial veto, President Clinton signed a bill rescinding $16.4 billion in already appropriated funds for the 1995 Fiscal Year. This left programs 10 months into their fiscal year experiencing drastic cuts in the committed budgets, including $20 million from the WIC Program, $5 million from Healthy Start, $2 million from the child care/development block grant; $16 million from Safe and Drug-Free Schools, and $872 million from summer youth employment. In addition, $131.8 million was cut from the 1995 budget of the National Science Foundation for academic research.

A number of studies have highlighted the importance of interagency collaboration and integration of services for children and families (Duchnowski & Friedman, 1990; Mordock, 1990; Zahner, Pawelkiewicz, DeFrancesco, & Adnopoz, 1992). Such integration has been found to be a significant factor in the success of programs for a wide range of problems. For example, a study of 100 children and adolescents, aged 9 to 19, with emotional or behavioral disorders, examined the effectiveness of six model, community-based programs designed to prevent the need for residential placement (Epstein, Cullinan, Quinn, & Cumblad, 1994). Most of the children and youth lived with one parent (59%), and 22% lived with both parents. Academic difficulties were common: 77% had a special class placement; 55% were considered underachievers. The prevalence of factors such as divorce, poverty, alcoholism, violence, mental illness, and crime in the lives of these children and youth led the authors to conclude that interagency collaboration was essential for work with this population.

Similarly, work with conduct-disordered youth has led to the finding that successful intervention depends on the ability to address multiple factors and the interactions among them. A comprehensive strategy that includes interagency collaboration and work with families has been found to be the most effective (Becker-Lausen & Rickel, 1997; Illback et al., in press; Short & Shapiro, 1993). In fact, a nationwide survey of 15 providers of individualized assistance programs for seriously emotionally disturbed youth, as well as 10 consultants and state administrators, found interagency collaboration was the factor most frequently cited by this group as accounting for the success of these programs (MacFarquhar, Dowrick, & Risley, 1993).

Zahner et al. (1992) conducted a cross-sectional survey of parents and teachers of 822 children, aged 6 to 11 years. In combined reports of parents and children, 38.5% of the children were determined to be at risk of psychiatric disturbance, yet only 11% of these children received treatment in mental health settings. The researchers cited the need for interagency collaboration, as well as the need to assess children from both parental and teachers' perspectives.

A nationwide study of state mental health services revealed that 36 states reported no primary prevention activities, 7 reported some involvement, and 7 reported substantial involvement in prevention (Goldston, 1991). Interagency collaboration was found to be a factor in the commitment of those states that conducted or supported prevention activities to any degree.

Numerous model programs for interagency collaboration have been described in the literature. For example, a consortium of regulatory and treatment agencies to provide a consistent response to child sexual abuse was found to be effective in insuring a coordinated delivery of services (Peck, Sheinberg, & Akamatsu, 1995). Likewise, the Fostering Individualized Assistance Program, which provides individualized, integrated services to foster children aged 7 to 15 (at entry) to help stabilize the child placement, relies on a family specialist to establish and facilitate interagency collaboration and interactions among the child, family, and foster family (McDonald, Boyd, Clark, & Stewart, 1995). These relationships are considered crucial to the success of the program.

In San Mateo County, California, a managed care system has been designed to integrate the provision of mental health, probation, social, and education services for children (Abbott,

Jordan, & Murtaza, 1995). Funding streams are merged to create a seamless garment of services. The county, the State Department of Mental Health, and the University of California at San Francisco have all been involved in the design of evaluation criteria. After 3 years, the project showed substantial gains over more traditional approaches. Five committees enhance communication among the many agencies involved; these committees are considered the most important element of the program's effectiveness. In addition to the interagency collaboration and the committees which facilitate this process, other factors to which success is attributed include cultural sensitivity, prevention efforts, and out-of-placement alternatives.

Another model project for enhancing interagency collaboration has been designed around school transition for young children with disabilities (Rous, Hemmeter, & Schuster, 1994). Project Sequenced Transition to Education in the Public Schools, a national outreach project (which began as a demonstration project), is part of the Early Education Program for Children with Disabilities. Model programs have also been described that are state-wide, such as Vermont's interagency teams for emotionally disturbed children and youth (Pandiant & Maynard, 1993), and that are local, providing services geared to a specific population, such as Cambridge Hospital's Latino Health Clinic (Carrillo & de la Cancela, 1992).

Interagency collaboration has also been identified as a significant factor in the effectiveness of programs for a wide range of problems of children and families, including children living in families with HIV infection or AIDS (Roth, Siegel, & Black, 1994), children of parents with mental retardation (Espe-Sherwindt, 1991), and drug education programs (Pellow & Jengeleski, 1991).

Prevention

Nearly 40 years ago, Albee (1959) pointed out that the number of individuals needing psychological services is far greater than could ever be accommodated by the clinicians practicing at any given time. This is equally true today, despite the proliferation of programs in clinical psychology, social work, marriage and family therapy, and numerous other forms of clinical training.

In the 1960s and 1970s, the community mental health movement developed as a response to this concern. Comprehensive care facilities for mental patients were proposed as a means of reaching large numbers of patients in need of services. At the same time, the needs of children and youth were beginning to be recognized as a social issue. Many believed that the convergence of community mental health with the recognition of children's needs would lead to a groundswell of prevention programs for the young (Rickel, 1986).

When President Kennedy recommended in 1963 that mental health should emphasize community-based prevention and treatment, Congress responded by passing the Mental Retardation Facilities and Community Mental Health Centers Construction Act that same year. The Act quickly established comprehensive community mental health centers nationwide, which led to an examination of appropriate roles for professionals, as well as nonprofessionals, in designing mental health care. The well being of the entire community became the focus of attention in this rapidly changing environment.

Spurred by these changes, a group of clinical psychologists met in 1965 to discuss training approaches that would prepare psychologists for the new roles created by the comprehensive centers. Many psychologists at the meeting were actively involved in community mental health; the Boston meeting marked the emergence of community psychology as a specialty area of psychology.

The mandate that attendees carried away from that meeting was two-fold. Community psychology was to address (a) prevention of mental disorders, and (b) the ecological context in which mental health or illness occur. The study of prevention was to be modeled after the concepts of public health; exploration of ecological context would include research into the impact of social institutions and other environmental factors on an individual's mental well being (Iscoe & Spielberger, 1970).

Buoyed forth by new ideas, supported by federal policy and professional commitment, the new community psychologists in the early 1970s were filled with optimism. A full investment in prevention could potentially eliminate most of the major social problems: crime, poverty, hunger, racism, alcohol and other drug misuse, school drop-outs, teen pregnancy. However, 25 years later, Americans find all these problems are not only still with us, but many have worsened. Some congressional leaders have claimed that it was the very creation of social programs to address these problems that somehow caused them to worsen. At best, they claim that "throwing money at the problem" has not worked. At worst, they suggest that providing a small subsistance of food and housing to children and (primarily) to their mothers has caused an increase in violence, drug use, teen pregnancy, and unemployment.

Besides the latter argument being a rather outrageous example of *post hoc, ergo propter hoc* reasoning, there are also many faulty assumptions underlying this charge. In reality, despite federal policy and commitment from the mental health community, the Community Mental Health Centers Act of 1963 led to relatively little preventive activity in mental health. By the late 1970s, a survey on primary prevention programming conducted with community mental health centers in a three-state area found the median amount of staff time spent on primary prevention programs was just 5% (Klein & Goldston, 1977). For secondary prevention activity, median reported staff time was 10%. The study uncovered numerous barriers to prevention programming, including problems with funding, gaining community acceptance, lack of knowledge and skills, evaluation difficulties, competition with direct services, staffing limitations, lack of administrative or staff interest and support, and difficulties with the setting of goals and priorities related to prevention.

Throughout the 1980s, community mental health centers (CMHCs) turned more and more toward tertiary treatment, reimbursable through client fees and insurance payments, and away from prevention efforts, as federal cutbacks for social programs steadily eroded funding. Into the 1990s, CMHCs have found themselves increasing fees, cutting back services, and in some cases closing their doors, as they move ever further from the original idea of making services accessible to communities and their members.

Current threatened cuts to federal programs such as child abuse prevention (including family support approaches), as well as to the more basic primary prevention public health services such as welfare subsistence, nutrition, housing, and medical care programs, will likely leave CMHCs struggling to stay afloat by wading further into the managed behavioral health care environment. Funding problems, staffing limitations, and competition with direct services may all but eliminate prevention programming as we move into the 21st century. Some of the most innovative agencies are already exploring alternative funding sources.

Obtaining funding from charitable organizations or private industry, however, frequently requires a rigorous cost–benefit analysis to demonstrate program effectiveness (Price & Smith, 1985). Evidence is gradually accumulating for the cost effectiveness of some types of programs, such as pre-school interventions with high-risk kids (Barnett, 1993). The latter study followed Head Start preschoolers for 25 years and found that an initial investment of $12,000 per child saved society approximately $70,000 per individual, because the participants as adults were better off in every category than their matched control counterparts. That is, recipients of the preschool intervention were less likely to drop out of school, less likely to be arrested, less likely to be on welfare, more likely to be employed, and so forth.

More evaluative studies must be undertaken to amass documentation for the usefulness of prevention. Longitudinal research must begin sooner if social science is to convincingly demonstrate the efficacy of prevention approaches. The difficulties of evaluation, cited as a barrier to prevention programs, may be countered with incentives and technical assistance from researchers and theorists who can translate sound evaluation research theory into prevention practice (Lorian, Iscoe, DeLeon, & VandenBos, 1996).

Of the other barriers to prevention discussed previously, three have relevance to the training of professionals who will work in prevention settings. Lack of knowledge and skills, lack of interest and support among administrators and staff, and difficulties setting prevention goals and priorities, can be modified or reversed with careful attention to the training of professionals who will enter community settings in the future. Despite increases in applied psychology programs, training tends to emphasize skill development rather than education in theories of prevention programming and research. Although such approaches serve to increase interest and support for prevention, they do not adequately prepare practitioners to set goals and priorities for prevention because a sound theoretical grasp of a social problem is essential for appropriate goal setting. For example, although theories of intergenerational transmission of negative outcomes are being developed in trauma research, in developmental psychology, and in treatment literature, the teaching of these theoretical approaches frequently is overlooked in community psychology. In fact, even across all four of these fields of inquiry (trauma, development, treatment, and community), there is little integration of findings (Becker-Lausen & Rickel, 1995; Rickel & Becker-Lausen, 1995).

In child psychology, the emphasis continues to be on individual, child-oriented approaches to intervention, with too little attention paid to training in systemic intervention. However, programs directed at parent–child interventions, such as Head Start and the Detroit Preschool Project, have been among the most successful (Rickel & Lampi, 1981; Zigler, 1994), particularly when they include extended intervention with larger systems (e.g., advocacy for mothers seeking job training or social services; child care and social support for working mothers). Systemic approaches can best be taught through interdisciplinary efforts, collaboration between academic and applied settings, and other such endeavors.

Throughout the 1980s, it appeared that the public was coming to accept that prevention could reduce health care and other costs incurred from indulging unhealthy lifestyles. Even into the 1990s, alcohol consumption appeared to be declining, particularly among adults driving cars (Evans, 1990). In the 1990s, a major public health campaign is also underway to reduce smoking, which also has steadily declined. Low-fat diets, exercise regimes, and stress-reduction classes all attest to the acceptance of prevention by large numbers of Americans.

Ironically, when interest in prevention is increasing on some fronts, attention toward children is waning. Support for preventive approaches to mental health needs, particularly child and family interventions, has not been strong. Two factors influence this trend. The first is a rather obvious social class and ethnic bias: alcohol, cigarettes, cardiac disease, and cancer are problems that plague middle- and upper-middle class, predominantly White populations. In fact, cigarette smoking has declined among African American youth (Morgan, 1995).

Put more succinctly, death from alcohol, cigarettes, heart disease or cancer may be the least of the worries of inner-city minority families, for whom life holds far more immediate dangers on a daily basis. This statement in no way implies they are immune to the dangers of these public health hazards, it merely points out that when survival is routinely threatened in so many obvious ways, concern for long-term health risks are unlikely to be salient worries. Homicide is, after all, the leading cause of death for young African American men and women (Centers for Disease Control, 1992).

The second factor influencing the lack of support for child and family prevention is the low status of children in our society. In many instances, children are denied basic rights adults are granted, have no standing in court, no right to counsel, and no due process (American Bar Association, 1993). Although community psychiatry began with child guidance clinics, when community mental health centers came along in the 1960s, many of them absorbed child guidance clinics in surrounding areas. The result was reduced services for children; by 1970, only 30% of CMHCs offered services to children (Westman, 1979).

Despite White House conferences, federal initiatives, and active researchers, children still are badly treated in our society. Evidence of maltreatment comes from every arena in which children are found. Children are the subject of child custody disputes, and are sometimes torn apart by parental conflict. Judges often order children to visit parents against their will; too often, children are not even consulted in making such decisions, regardless of their age or willingness to speak. As a consequence of these and other activities regarding children's rights, a proliferation of children's law centers, which provide pro bono attorneys to advocate for children's needs, is occurring around the country (American Bar Association, 1993). Supervised visitation centers also have sprung up in recent years, particularly in urban areas.

Clinicians have a great deal to offer to these settings, which are often run by attorneys. A few children's law centers, such as the Children's Law Center in Connecticut, are organized with a clinician–attorney model, where cases are approached jointly by an assigned attorney and an assigned clinician, with both learning from one another as they proceed. Training conducted by these centers also is a fertile field for clinicians to lend their expertise because judges and attorneys may lack understanding of child development and of family dynamics.

Children are the poorest members of our society. We have already noted that 1 in 4 now lives in poverty (Children's Defense Fund, 1996). Traditionally, children have received only 10% of the money allocated for community mental health centers (Rickel, 1986), although they are one third of the U.S. population.

In the 104th Congress, the U.S. House of Representatives attempted to eliminate a federal commitment to child abuse prevention, despite the fact that child abuse and neglect reporting increased 50% between 1986 and 1992 (McCurdy & Daro, 1993). As mentioned previously in this volume, child fatalities from abuse and neglect also increased 49% during that same time frame, suggesting that it is not just an increase in reporting, but rather increased numbers of cases, as well as escalating severity of abuse, that we are witnessing.

In general, American children may be better off today than they were 200 years ago, when infanticide was not only permitted, but accepted as the right of a father to manage his property (Zigler & Gordon, 1982). As early as 1789, the newly developing textile industry in the northern states began employing children. By the turn of the last century, large numbers of children and youth worked in factories or became apprentices to tradesmen. Among the worst settings for abuse of child labor were 12-hour shifts for boys working with hot furnaces in the glass industry; garment industry tenement "sweatshops," employing whole families; jobs in the coal fields where boys breathed coal dust in 10-hour shifts; and the tobacco industry, which employed children under 10 to make cigarettes and cigars. Numerous other industries, however, were equally heartless in their treatment of children as workers (Ashby, 1984). Child labor was finally outlawed nationally in 1938.

But Americans can hardly be proud of our record with children today. Though we Americans are fond of saying children are our future, we do not often support policies that ensure the security of that future. Consequently, the United States has the distinction among industrialized countries of ranking number one for our homicide rate, near the bottom for science achievement (12th out of 14 countries), near the bottom for mathematics (13th of 14), 20th for our infant and child mortality rate (children under age 5), and 31st for our rates of low birthweight infants (Children's Defense Fund, 1996).

The Child Abuse Prevention and Treatment Act (CAPTA) of 1974, which the House bill of 1995 sought to eliminate, grew out of national rhetoric that too often only gives lip service to the protection of children. Nevertheless, the importance of this national commitment to child abuse prevention can hardly be overemphasized. Block grant approaches proposed by the House to replace CAPTA would have resulted in less funds for states and, thus, would mean the limited resources would go to overburdened and ineffective child removal and foster care systems, leaving nothing for prevention and the intensive intervention programs needed for high-risk families. Fortunately, the Senate bill (S–919), reauthorizing CAPTA, was passed unanimously as one of the final acts of the 104th Congress, thanks to a groundswell of support from child advocates and mental health professionals. President Clinton signed CAPTA on October 3, 1996.

While the poverty rate for children has steadily risen, that of the elderly has steadily fallen, from 19% in 1972 to 15% in 1982, to 12% in 1992, demonstrating that investments in programs for elder citizens have been effective in improving their style of life (Mayer & Jencks, 1995). However, it also indicates the power of effective constituent organization and lobbying, as the American Association for Retired Persons, and several other groups representing the aging population, have so powerfully demonstrated in recent years. Despite strong advocacy organizations for children, the fact that the children themselves do not vote is a major detriment to the power of their voices on Capitol Hill.

We also know from social psychology that those working with or representing groups low in status, power and influence are themselves stigmatized as low in prestige (Jones et al., 1984; Sidel, 1994). Consequently, as it is for citizens with mental illness or developmental disabilities, so also is it for children and those who represent them. In Congressional offices, for example, we often heard staffers working on the "important" issues of foreign affairs or banking make snide comments about "insignificant little subcommittees" such as the Children's Subcommittee or the Juvenile Justice Subcommittee. They insinuated that time spent on children's issues was wasted, taking away from the "real" affairs of state.

In a country where worth is determined by income, people should not be surprised by these attitudes. The judicial system also too often fails to protect the rights of children. Since the Supreme Court's decision to uphold corporal punishment, more recent decisions have continued to disregard a child's psychological "best interest." For example, decisions have been made in favor of the rights of biological parents, with courts declaring, in essence, that a child is the adult's genetic property (e.g., well-publicized cases such as the DeBoer case and that of "Baby M").

There is a consistent thread here, with U.S. judicial and legislative policy supporting the rights of adults to control children using physical force, as well as the right of adults to have possession of children based on the concept of the child as property. This policy plays out in custody disputes where children frequently are not even asked their preference, or if they are asked, too often that preference is discounted. This occurs at all age levels, not only with the very young (American Bar Association, 1993). Frequently, it is the adult with the most financial resources, toughest attorneys and, too often, the least regard for what the process is doing to the child, who winds up winning custody battles. King Solomon does not rule the courts at the end of the 20th century in America.

Disregard for the rights of children, as well as abuse, neglect, and the limited funding for child and youth mental health programs all provide direct evidence of society's failure to address children's psychological needs. Problems with the foster care, health care, and educational systems also impact children's mental health, both directly and indirectly.

Children are denied access to appropriate health care from the earliest phases of conception. More than 20% of all pregnant women in the United States receive no prenatal care during the first trimester of pregnancy (U.S. Bureau of the Census, 1995), with large discrepancies among ethnic groups. About 19% of White pregnant women fail to receive prenatal care in the first trimester, and rates for Black women, Native Americans, and most Hispanic women approach 40%. On the other hand, less than 12% of Japanese American women fail to receive prenatal care in the first trimester. Socioeconomic status is clearly a factor in these discrepancies. The prenatal care to which many women lack access is essential to the prevention of such complications as premature birth, low birth weight, and cognitive deficits. Medical attention for the mother during pregnancy also provides the opportunity for intervention when there are family violence or substance abuse problems.

Cut-backs proposed for Medicaid will likely increase the already epidemic problem of lack of care, particularly if it results in closing public and teaching hospitals, as predicted. Managed care is also adversely affecting perinatal care, with scandals erupting around mothers and babies sent home too early, with tragic results.

As children grow, their health care does not improve. About 14% of America's children under age 18 (9.6 million) have no private or public health care coverage. About 21% of U.S. children fail to receive polio immunizations by age 3, and about 15% do not obtain a measles vaccination (U.S. Bureau of the Census, 1995).

More than 65 years ago now, the 1930 White House conference asserted that a child had a right to a "secure and loving home." But multiple foster placements, abusive foster homes, drawn out termination-of-parental-rights proceedings, and lack of adequate substance abuse treatment programs designed to keep mothers and infants together during recovery all contribute to the failure to fulfill on this historic promise to our children (McKenzie, 1993; Schwartz, 1993).

Nearly half a million children are maintained in the foster care system, often until they "age out" at 18, with no workable plan for reunification, no adoption planning, and ultimately, no permanent home for the child (McKenzie, 1993). Large numbers of these long-term foster care children, particularly those from multiple placements, are in psychiatric hospital populations, in homeless populations, and in criminal populations (Mundy, Robertson, Greenblatt, & Robertson, 1989; Mundy, Robertson, Robertson, & Greenblatt, 1990; Widom, 1989a).

Foster care is poorly regulated, so that there is little assurance of quality care for children in placement. Specialized placements, where foster parents have the skills considered necessary for the large percentage of children damaged by abuse and neglect, are especially difficult to find and frequently overloaded with too many children.

Moving from foster care to an adoptive home is complicated by the agonizingly slow process of termination of parental rights, and by the lack of appropriate adoptive homes for older children, children with disabilities, and ethnic minority children. Inattention to recruitment of minority families for adoption has been an issue for the latter group of foster care children. Federal programs for adoption services, including recruitment, and pre- and postadoption support services, have been few and are dwindling, threatened by congressional cut-backs in prevention services.

Summary and Conclusions

Currently, the emotional problems of children and youth are inadequately treated at all levels. Those at risk of mental disorders receive even less attention. Looking back over the debate central to the White House conferences, that is, whether families or experts hold the key solutions, reveals a major flaw in the reasoning driving this debate. Neither the right research findings nor the right child-rearing techniques alone will remedy the problems our children and youth face today. Our historical overview suggests the solutions lie in the convergence of the multiple systems serving children and families, including the legislative, judicial, executive, direct services and research endeavors. All of these primary systems must work together to provide optimal ways to promote competence and health in our children.

At the beginning of our Congressional Fellowships, we were sent a copy of the Declaration of Independence and the Constitution to read once more before coming to Washington. We were reminded of the foundation ideas from which we were operating, for example, that the "blessings of liberty" were attempting to be secured not only for those alive at any given time, but also for "our posterity." The latter reference reminded us that from the beginning, the founders of our country recognized the critical significance of providing and caring for our children and subsequent generations. In their vision of a nation built upon ideals of equality and liberty, they understood that a democracy could not survive for long unless its youngest citizens were part of the design.

John F. Kennedy's famous quotation, "ask not what your

country can do for you; ask what you can do for your country" is said to have its roots in a notebook JFK kept in 1945, in which he wrote the following quote from Rousseau, whose ideas strongly influenced the founders of our country: "As soon as any man says of the affairs of state, what does it matter to me? the state may be given up as lost." Kennedy understood clearly the importance of an active, involved citizenry to the survival of a free, democratic state. From this understanding, he proceeded to mobilize young Americans with programs such as Volunteers in Service to America (VISTA) and the Peace Corps. In 1997, President Clinton brought together key leaders for a summit to again attempt to mobilize American citizens in the service of their country. Together with leaders such as former Presidents Carter, Bush, and Ford, President Clinton is rallying Americans to come together to repair broken neighborhoods and build stronger communities.

We began this chapter with a quote from Margaret Mead that suggests that each of us has the capacity to change the world with our actions. We spoke of our own experiences working in Congress as American Psychological Association Congressional Fellows. We have highlighted research findings that support the assertion that preventive interventions at the primary, secondary, and tertiary level have the potential to create a more healthy, productive, resilient society.

Unfortunately, funding from the federal government for preventive efforts has steadily diminished and is likely to continue to decline in the near future. Those concerned must continue to educate and lobby congressional leaders to support these preventive efforts. Social scientists must build coalitions through our professional associations, with our own colleagues and with colleagues in other professions. As private citizens, we must join with our neighbors to work for change.

Many Americans often sit with friends, discussing sociopolitical issues, and they joke about "solving the world's problems," as if such discussions are frivolous. Our own experiences in Washington, however, led us to believe that such citizen-based conversations are no joke. Quite the contrary, solutions have and will come from just such individuals who have given thought to the issues and devised creative responses.

One such person is Joe Marshall, who founded the Omega Boys Club in San Francisco and Oakland, California: By day a high school teacher, Marshall simply got tired of seeing young people lost to violence, and so he started a program, run by volunteers, to intervene with street kids to get them out of gangs, away from drug dealing, off the streets, staying in school, and even going to college. Between 1987 and 1993, the program had grown from 15 to 300 kids, 108 of whom have been placed in college.

People like Dennis James and Kevin Miller, commercial airline pilots who, discussing the plight of the homeless, had an idea for a program for high-risk youth. Using their own funds to purchase a high-performance airplane, in 1995 they started the Young Aces program, which gives young people a chance to fly aerobatic manuevers under the supervision of mentor pilots, while teaching them basic science and math concepts and supplying strong words of praise for the best elements of the youth's performance. More than 100 teens from group homes for teen mothers, from protective services sources, and from juvenile diversion programs in Southern California have flown with Young Aces. The program has become a formal segment of the Culver City Police's Juvenile Diversion Program.

Community leaders in cities around the country are working to improve the lives of children in their communities. In San Antonio, Texas, local community leaders started San Antonio Fights Back to stop violence and crime from spreading. In Vancouver, Washington, one of the fastest growing communities in the Northwest, leaders formed Community Choices 2010, a coalition of business, education, law enforcement, government, and medical and mental health groups all working together on preventive endeavors. The Northwest program, with two paid staff members and more than 2,000 volunteers, is a model of an organized community. The strategic plan includes efforts at providing support for families, improving public education, early intervention in the schools, encouraging economic growth and job development, providing initiatives to prevent school drop-out, improving cultural awareness, educating the public about health issues, and enhancing a sense of community among residents.

Those of us with professional experience with these issues, whether we are practitioners or researchers, need to support and augment such community efforts, lending our expertise where appropriate. We social scientists can provide guidance in design, implementation and evaluation aspects, and we can work to promote prevention in the community. Large-scale media campaigns to promote prevention should be undertaken as well, with anecdotal stories used to illustrate points where intervention could have or did make a difference in an individual life.

If we, as social scientists, do not make the promotion of prevention a priority, if we fail to speak out to support strong child and family policy, we leave the field open to those in politics who consider these issues just one more "insignificant little subcommittee" within the real work of the government. Each of us must choose the area in which we want to express our recognition of the need for empowerment, advocacy and representation. What is important is that we make a choice and become involved. A line from the award winning play *Man of LaMancha* may most clearly express the mandate before us: "Perhaps the greatest madness in the world is to live in it as it is and not as it should be." By taking an active role in empowerment, we confront the "greatest madness." We encourage all of you to become involved—to do whatever you can to empower and represent yourself as part of a special interest group and to advocate for citizens. Join us in doing our part in addressing the changes so critical to the practice and delivery of preventive services.

At times we may feel we are "tilting at windmills," but as Hedrick Smith concluded at the end of his book, *The Power Game*, "The power game will never be tidy. The competition will never quit. The ruckus will never quiet. But things will work better when people are encouraged to coalesce" (1988, p. 714).

Appendix

Children and the Lawmaking Process: Reflections on the Congressional Fellowship Program

This book was the result of a collaboration that began when the coauthors were Congressional Fellows together in 1992–93. The end of our fellowship class year marked the 20th anniversary of the Congressional Science and Engineering Fellowship Program, a consortium of professional science and engineering associations, of which the American Psychological Association (APA) is part. The American Association for the Advancement of Science (AAAS) has managed the program from its outset; however, APA was one of the earliest, and has remained one of the most consistent, participants.

The Congressional Fellowship Program

The Congressional Science and Engineering Fellowship Program, created in the early 1970s to provide a steady stream of science and technical expertise to the staff of congressional offices, was designed to address increasingly complex matters of public policy that contained major elements of science and technology. Typical congressional staff were not scientifically trained, and concerns were growing that staffers were increasingly reliant on lobbyists and the executive branch for information (Stine, 1994). At the same time, professional organizations were becoming more interested and eager to be involved in the political process. In our fellowship year, there were about 20 organizations sponsoring fellows. Each individual organization, such as APA, selects scientists or engineers as Fellows to be funded by the sponsoring organization for a year in Washington, and AAAS also funds one or two slots directly.

In the 1992–93 program we were two of five psychologists selected by APA to serve as Congressional Fellows; we joined 30 other Congressional Fellows who were sponsored by organizations as diverse as the American Institute of Physics, the American Veterinary Medical Association, and the Institute of Electrical and Electronics Engineers. Although we psychologists were five strong, social scientists were a definite minority in this group: two other AAAS Congressional Fellows, both with multidisciplinary doctorates, were the only other social science Congressional Fellows in our class.

When we arrived in Washington to meet our "fellow Fellows," we quickly learned we were as diverse in age, career paths, and policy interests as our organizations were different. Whether we were full professors, "fresh-out" PhD's, or engineers from industrial settings, what we had in common quickly became clear, as we stood before the group on the first day of our fellowship year giving 5-minute summaries of who we were, where we'd been, and where we felt we were headed: We had a love of adventure, many had had more than one career, most of us had travelled or lived in a variety of places, and, most importantly, we all wanted to make a difference in Washington. We had a strong sense that we had something important we could contribute to the policy arena.

Our first 3 weeks of the Fellowship consisted of a whirlwind of briefings provided through AAAS, which was an incredibly valuable educational experience in itself. In addition to the educational value, however, the 3 weeks gave us the opportunity to become acquainted with our colleagues, so that when we finally became part of legislative offices, we would already have contacts on Capitol Hill. Briefings covered "everything you ever wanted to know about Washington, but didn't know who to ask"—from staff of the Congressional Research Service through lobbying activities, international affairs, the Congressional Budget Office, and various congressional committees.

During our 3-week orientation, collaborations began among fellows, which, for some of us, would continue for years afterward, just as was intended by those designing the program. Our own collaboration began in just this way. During orientation, Fellows often rushed from one event to another around the Hill, from the Library of Congress over to a House hearing room, even to the Supreme Court (where we heard about judicial fellowships). On one jaunt over the Hill, the two of us, following two of our fellow colleagues who were male, became so engrossed in conversation about mutual policy interests that we suddenly looked up to discover we'd been following the wrong two sets of male suits, which are so prevalent on the Hill. When we recovered from our laughter, we found our way to the next briefing, continuing our animated discussion of child and family policy along the way. Our collaborative efforts blossomed over the fellowship year and have continued since that time, as we described in the preceding chapters.

One of our colleagues, a particularly creative thinker in a group of exceptionally creative Fellows, wrote a poem at the beginning of our fellowship year, which captures the feelings of camaraderie, the recognition of differences and the common bond among Fellows. James O. Denney, who worked tirelessly for Rep. George Brown during his fellowship year, became seriously ill and died suddenly, shortly after our fellowship year was completed, making his poem particularly poignant in retrospect. We would like to share Jim Denney's poem with our readers, for Jim Denney made a difference, not only on the Hill, but also, through his wit and creativity, with his fellow Fellows:

The Hydrogen Bond
We come
    from different places
    from distinct disciplines
To this wrinkle
    in the fabric of
    time and space
To share
    our knowledge
    our efforts
    ourselves
As scientists and professionals
    we pledge
    integrity
    intensity
    introspection
    circumspection
    love of country
    global consciousness
As colleagues and associates
    we affirm that
    our friendship
    is as eternal as
    the universal continuum
    of matter and energy
As humans and creatures of
    this jade and sapphire planet
    we acknowledge that
    our year together
    is as fleeting and fragile as
    the hydrogen bond,
    the bond of life itself.
                    —James O. Denney, September 1992

After the 3-week orientation, we were provided a small office in the basement of the Capitol with a telephone and a fax machine, where Congressional Fellows congregated while attempting to get interviews with legislative offices. This was no small task. Because of the 1992 impending presidential election, Congress was attempting to adjourn early to go on the campaign trail, so staffers, under intense deadline pressures, had less time than usual to talk to Fellows about potential placements. When Congress did adjourn, many staffers, particularly staff directors, took leave to go on the campaign trail, creating still more difficulty for Fellows hoping to get commitments for positions.

Fellows often believe that legislative offices will jump at the chance to get such well-trained scientists and engineers for free for a year; however, this is not the case. Space is at a premium in most offices, so that even if legislators have plenty of work on issues relevant to a Fellows' expertise, in reality there may be literally no desk, no phone, no computer, and no work space for an extra body. Both of us, however, were fortunate to be accepted into offices we had targeted as significant opportunities for the work we wished to accomplish. We were given meaningful work on issues relevant to our interests. We were given a reasonable amount of respect for our expertise and, in general, treated fairly.

The Highest Highs, the Lowest Lows

Few people who have not been there realize just how demanding, fast-paced, and stressful life on the Hill can be. The hours are long, the workloads infinite, and the politics emotionally draining. When one of us (EB) went on the floor of the Senate for the first time to staff the debate on the National Service Act, we learned that once on the floor, we were there for the duration: Staff presence is limited, so that if the debate heats up, and the staff seats are full, no other staffers can get on the floor, so one does not dare give up a seat. Lack of food, need of respite or facilities, all must be ignored, as work is paramount to comfort in this arena. As it happened that day, a minor resolution by a southern senator, which involved display of the Confederate flag, became the object of a rousing debate over the history of slavery and racism and its meaning for citizens of the United States today, eloquently and movingly argued by Senator Carol Moseley Braun. The opportunity to be present for such momentous events in our history is one of the many attractions of the fellowship program.

Many who come to the Hill from academia, where publishing is so important, found writing documents and talks for which others took credit a daunting experience. As the saying goes, "no one in Washington signs what they write nor writes what they sign." Further disappointment may loom when you realize that, unless you're a senator or representative, no one will be impressed by your credentials. You may be the top in your field, an internationally known expert, or even a nominee for the Nobel prize; no one will care. Most Fellows found they had to prove their worth—as a team player, as a writer, as a willing worker—regardless of from whence they came.

In this book we have described our individual experiences and impressions of the fellowship program. We came together around common interests in children and families, in prevention, in the belief that psychology had much to offer to policy makers, and in the hope that the new president, reported to be favorably disposed toward children's issues, would set a new course for the country. We saw compromises at every turn. Yet, in the end, we came to feel that the system does work, more often than it fails. We met inspiring individuals, on and off the Hill, who had dedicated their lives to the betterment of humankind. Despite the common beliefs of widespread cynicism among legislators and their staff, many surprised us with their idealism, their commitment, and their sense of meaning and purpose.

In particular, we were struck by the difference that could be made by committed individuals. From our vantage point in the Capitol, we had the opportunity to meet and talk with individuals from around the country who were intervening with children and families to improve their lives, one at a time. We noted that legislators do care what constituents think, and that letter-writing and telephoning by concerned citizens can (and must) make a difference.

Our Individual Experiences

Annette Rickel. As an APA Congressional Fellow, I had the good fortune to be in Washington, DC at a most exciting time in U.S. history. Because I worked on health policy for Senator Donald W. Riegle, Jr. (D–Michigan), who chaired the Senate Finance Subcommittee on Health for Families and the Uninsured, I was designated to serve on the President's Task Force for National Health Care Reform, chaired by Hillary Rodham Clinton. This opportunity to work with Senator Riegle, a most able statesman, and to serve on the President's Task Force, was a dream come true for a professor of psychology from Michigan—the chance to integrate practical experience with public policy.

President Clinton was to present a proposal for comprehensive health care reform in the United States. His plan would have fundamentally overhauled the current system and protected and expanded quality of care. Mental health care was also part of his solution.

Working with health care experts, officials from various agencies, congressional staff and White House personnel, I was involved in the drafting of a comprehensive plan for delivery of mental health services as part of national health care reform. Specifically, I participated in the Mental Health Working Group for Children and Adolescent Services, one of the clusters established to design a benefit structure in this health policy area. Tipper Gore, who chaired our work group and spearheaded the mental health initiative, had been advocating to ensure that children and adolescents with mental disorders receive equitable treatment under the new health care reform plan. In the past decade, research has demonstrated that a comprehensive array of services, managed in an organized system of care, is the most effective and efficient approach to serving children and adolescents with emotional and substance abuse problems. Therefore, the benefit plan that was proposed recognized the viability of alternative home- and community-based services, the importance of involving families as partners in the treatment of children's disorders, and the necessity of outreach efforts to identify children at risk.

The policy development and evaluation effort of the Task Force was based on the "Tollgate" system. Under this process, the working groups that were divided into health policy subject areas, such as malpractice and tort reform, financing, and workforce development, were guided in their research and proposal development through a series of tests, or *tollgates*. During the first series of tollgates—the broadening phase—each working group was asked to put all options "on the table" to guarantee that all issues were considered and correct mechanisms applied. This phase concluded with a presentation of options to the president and other Task Force Members as a final check to be sure that sufficient breadth had been achieved.

In the next phase, the broad group of options was narrowed and recommendations drafted that made explicit the analyses and assumptions that supported the conclusions. Subsequently, we presented a comprehensive set of proposals that sought decisions on key issues by the president and other members of the Task Force in order that legislation could be drafted when numbers, legal and political audits, were complete. Just like the tollgate on an expressway, these stopping points interrupted the flow of work, so that courses of action could be checked at various points along the way. Task Force members worked late into the night and on weekends to meet the deadlines imposed by the process. In our case we started work in mid-January and completed our proposal at the end of April.

Along with my obligations on the Task Force, I had several areas of responsibility in Senator Riegle's office. I helped craft bills for Medicare outpatient prescription drug benefits, and childhood immunizations as well as contributed to higher education issues. My experience in university administration provided a background and perspective for involvement in the 1993 National and Community Service Trust Act and the 1993 Direct Student Loan Program, which Senator Riegle co-sponsored. I also provided briefings on systemic educational reform that is taking place in many of our elementary and secondary schools as a result of *Goals 2000* legislation.

Support for fundamental change must be built from the grass roots up not the top down. Whether we are mental health professionals or social science researchers we can contribute to the formulation of public policy. My experience in Washington has taught me that we each have a responsibility to make our knowledge and expertise available to policy makers as often as possible. If they are ignorant of our areas of expertise, we have only ourselves to blame.

Evvie Becker. Prior to graduate school in clinical psychology, I had a former career as a Public Information Officer for the National Aeronautics and Space Administration (NASA), handling press relations for NASA's Life Sciences program. In that capacity, I had experience in the federal government handling controversial and sensitive issues, managing public affairs activities at the national level, preparing background materials and conducting briefings for the national science press, and writing speeches for NASA management.

Leaving this career at mid-life to pursue an interest in the "helping professions," I found in my clinical training a strong interest in the needs of children and families. In my doctoral and postdoctoral training, I worked primarily with low-income families, those who were working and those who were on public support, most of whom lacked sufficient social supports to meet the demands of family life.

When I learned of the Congressional Fellows' program, I began to believe that I could combine the skills I had used in my former career with my psychology training to advocate for children and families within the legislative arena. From my years in Connecticut, I knew that Senator Christopher Dodd (D–Connecticut) had a strong commitment to children and families. As chairman of the Senate Labor Subcommittee on Children, Senator Dodd had sponsored many of the key bills related to child and family issues. Fortunately, I was successful in obtaining a placement for my fellowship year with the staff of the Children's Subcommittee, working for Senator Dodd.

My major policy responsibility in the beginning was youth and violence, and I was actively involved in the Senator's work in this area throughout my fellowship year. I worked with the Senator to prepare a hearing on youth violence, to support his efforts in the spring of 1993 to make regular Senate floor statements deploring the level of violence in the country, to assist him in writing three pieces of legislation in this area, and to otherwise staff all activities for the Senator related to violence.

Because of the new Administration in the White House, our fellowship year was marked by massive turnovers in congressional staff, as many of them exited the Hill to head for the White House or Executive Branch appointments. With all this upheaval, the Subcommittee staff in the spring was down to two regular staff and myself. As one of the regular staff was providing full-time support for health care reform, that left only two of us to cover the rest of the child and family issues. So it was that by April 1993, the official list of issues I covered for the subcommittee had expanded beyond violence issues to include substance abuse, child protection, adoption/foster care and child welfare reform.

The Family and Medical Leave Act was the first real piece of legislation on which I was privileged to work. Passing Congress for the third time in seven years, the Leave Act was the first bill signed into law by President Clinton in January 1993. Senator Dodd had fought hard for this legislation, which he introduced throughout all the years it had been debated in Congress. Senator Dodd is a gifted speaker, one who can eloquently articulate the most complex issues so that they can be understood by everyone. When someone raised concerns about support for a key effort, he would say calmly, "We have to make a case for it"—as if to say that this making a case, after all, is the essence of politics.

I think of that phrase often—*making a case for it*. Here in these pages we have attempted to make a case for prevention, for community involvement, for applied research that has the potential to contribute to the public good, and for all of us doing our part, one child or family at a time where necessary, to build a better life for all.

The support of the American Psychological Association for our fellowships and the encouragement of Patrick DeLeon, a seasoned veteran of the Hill, enabled us to see the importance of this project. DeLeon, the Administrative Assistant to Senator Daniel K. Inouye, and a psychologist actively involved in APA governance, has been a long standing, strong supporter of the Congressional Fellowship Program.

We are also indebted to former Senator Donald W. Riegle and Senator Christopher J. Dodd and their respective staffs who treated us as "regular" staff members. From the Senators, we learned the value of compromise, and what a difference one can make by listening to the "other side," by taking their concerns into account, and by building coalitions of diverse groups.

In addition, we thank the staff of the American Association for the Advancement of Science for their advice and assistance during our fellowship year and our fellow Fellows for their support and camaraderie.

Annette U. Rickel
Evvie Becker

References

Abbott, B., Jordan, P., & Murtaza, N. (1995). Interagency collaboration for children's mental health services: The San Mateo County model for managed care. *Administration and Policy in Mental Health, 22,* 301–313.

Achenbach, T. M., & Edelbrock, C. (1986). *Manual for the Teacher's Report Form and Teacher Version of the Child Behavior Profile.* Burlington: University of Vermont.

Acts of Principle. (1996, September 13). *New York Times,* p. A34.

Adler, A. (1929). *Problems of neurosis.* New York: Harper & Row.

Adler, N. (1994). *Adolescent sexual behavior looks irrational—but looks are deceiving.* Washington, DC: Federation of Behavioral, Psychological and Cognitive Sciences.

Alan Guttmacher Institute. (1986). *Teenage pregnancy in industrialized countries: A study.* New Haven, CT: Yale University Press.

Albee, G. W. (1959). *Mental health manpower trends.* New York: Basic Books.

Allen, B. (1995). Personal communication.

Allers, C. T., & Benjack, K. J. (1991). Connections between childhood abuse and HIV infection. *Journal of Counseling and Development, 70,* 309–313.

Alloy, L. B., & Abramson, L. Y. (1979). Judgment of contingency in depressed and nondepressed students: Sadder but wiser? *Journal of Experimental Psychology: General, 108,* 441–485.

Amato, P. R., Loomis, L. S., & Booth, A. (1995). Parental divorce, marital conflict, and offspring well-being during early adulthood. *Social Forces, 73,* 895–915.

Amato, P. R., & Rezac, S. J. (1994). Contact with nonresidential parents, interparental conflict, and children's behavior. *Journal of Family Issues, 15*(2), 191–207.

American Bar Association. (1993). *America's children at risk: A national agenda for legal action.* Report of the American Bar Association Presidential Working Group on the Unmet Legal Needs of Children and Their Families. Chicago: Author.

American Psychological Association. (1996). *Violence and the family.* Report of the APA Presidential Task Force on Violence and the Family. Washington, DC: Author.

American Psychological Association Commission on Violence and Youth. (1993). *Violence and youth: Psychology's response.* Washington, DC: American Psychological Association.

Ammerman, R. T. (1991). The role of the child in physical abuse: A reappraisal. *Violence and Victims, 6,* 87–101.

Anderson, J. E., Kann, L., Holtzman, D., Arday, S., Truman, B., & Kolbe, L. (1990). HIV/AIDS knowledge and sexual behavior among high school students. *Family Planning Perspectives, 22*(6), 252–255.

Anthony, E. J., & Cohler, B. J. (1987). *The invulnerable child.* New York: Guilford Press.

Armsworth, M. W., & Holaday, M. (1993). The effects of psychological trauma on children and adolescents. *Journal of Counseling and Development, 72,* 49–56.

Arnold, E. H., O'Leary, S., & Edwards, G. H. (1997). Father involvement and self-reported parenting of children with attention-deficit/hyperactivity disorder. *Journal of Consulting and Clinical Psychology, 65,* 337–342.

Ashby, L. (1984). *Saving the waifs: Reformers and dependent children, 1890–1917.* Philadelphia: Temple University Press.

Astone, N. M., & McLanahan, S. S. (1991). Family structure, parental practices and high school completion. *American Sociological Review, 56,* 309–320.

Atkinson, A. K., & Rickel, A. U. (1984). Postpartum depression in primiparous parents. *Journal of Abnormal Psychology, 93,* 115–119.

Atlas, J., & Rickel, A. U. (1988). Maternal coping styles and adjustment in children. *Journal of Primary Prevention, 10,* 195–206.

Azar, S. T., Robinson, D. R., Hekimian, E., & Twentyman, C. T. (1984). Unrealistic expectations and problem solving ability in maltreating and comparison mothers. *Journal of Consulting and Clinical Psychology, 52,* 687–691.

Azar, S. T., & Rohrbeck, C. A. (1986). Child abuse and unrealistic expectations: Further validation of the Parent Opinion Questionnaire. *Journal of Consulting and Clinical Psychology, 54,* 867–868.

Babor, T. F., DelBoca, F. K., McLaney, M. A., Jacobi, B., Higgins-Biddle, J., & Hass, W. (1991). Just say Y.E.S.: Matching adolescents to appropriate interventions for alcohol and other drug-related problems. *Alcohol Health & Research World, 15*(1), 77–86.

Barnett, W. S. (1993). Benefit–cost analysis of preschool education: Findings from a 25-year follow-up. *American Journal of Orthopsychiatry, 63,* 500–508.

Barth, J. M., & Parke, R. D. (1993). Parent–child relationship influences on children's transition to school. *Merrill-Palmer Quarterly, 39*(2), 173–195.

Barth, R. P., Schinke, S. P., & Maxwell, J. S. (1983). Psychological correlates of teenage motherhood. *Journal of Youth and Adolescence, 12,* 471–487.

Baumrind, D. (1971). Current patterns of parental authority. *Developmental Psychology Monograph, 4*(1, Pt. 2).

Baumrind, D. (1978). Parental disciplinary patterns and social competence in children. *Youth & Society, 9,* 239–276.

Bayley, N. (1993). *Bayley Scales of Infant Development Manual* (2nd ed.). New York: Psychological Corporation.

Beck, A. T. (1972). *Depression: Causes and treatment.* Philadelphia: University of Pennsylvania Press.

Becker-Lausen, E., Barkan, S., & Newberger, E. M. (1994, May). *Physician ignorance of family violence: Implications for women's health.* Paper presented at the American Psychological Association Conference "Psychosocial and Behavioral Factors in Women's Health: Creating an Agenda for the Twenty-First Century," Washington, DC.

Becker-Lausen, E., & Gleeson, M. K. (1996, May). *Child maltreatment and high-risk sexual behavior: Data from two diverse populations.* Paper presented at the 73rd Annual Meeting of the American Orthopsychiatric Association, Boston.

Becker-Lausen, E., & Mallon-Kraft, S. (1995, July). *Pandemic outcomes: The intimacy variable.* Paper presented at the 4th International Family Violence Research Conference, Durham, NH.

Becker-Lausen, E., & Rickel, A. U. (1995). Integration of teen pregnancy and child abuse research: Identifying mediator variables for pregnancy outcome. *Journal of Primary Prevention, 16*(1), 35–49.

Becker-Lausen, E., & Rickel, A. U. (1997). Chi-squares versus green eye shades. Psychology and the press. *Journal of Community Psychology, 25*(2), 111–123.

Becker-Lausen, E., & Rickel, A. U. (in press). Incarcerated juvenile offenders: Integrating trauma-oriented treatment with state-of-the-art delinquency interventions. In T. P. Gullotta (Ed.), *Delinquency, juvenile justice and adolescence.* Thousand Oaks, CA: Sage.

Becker-Lausen, E., Sanders, B., & Chinsky, J. M. (1995). Mediation of abusive childhood experiences: Depression, dissociation, and negative life outcomes. *American Journal of Orthopsychiatry, 65,* 560–573.

Behind closed doors: Family violence in the home: Testimony before the Subcommittee on Children, Family, Drugs and Alcoholism of the Committee on Labor and Human Resources, United States Senate, 102d Cong., 1st Sess. 13 (1991) (testimony of A. Browne).

Beitchman, J. H., Zucker, K. J., Hood, J. E., DaCosta, G. A., & Akman, D. (1991). A review of the short-term effects of child sexual abuse. *Child Abuse and Neglect, 15,* 537–556.

Bell, D., Feraios, A., & Bryan, T. (1990). Adolescent males' knowledge and attitudes about AIDS in the context of their social world [Monograph]. *Journal of Applied Social Psychology, 20,* 424–448.

Berkowitz, B., & Graziano, A. (1972). Training parents as behavior therapists: A review. *Behavior Research and Therapy, 10,* 297–317.

Berliner, L. (1993). Commentary: Sexual abuse effects or not? *Journal of Interpersonal Violence, 8,* 428–429.

Bhavnagri, N. P., & Parke, R. D. (1991). Parents as direct facilitators of children's peer relationships: Effects of age of child and sex of parent. *Journal of Social and Personal Relationships, 8,* 423–440.

Biglan, A., Metzler, C. W., Wirt, R., Ary, D. V., Noell, J., Ochs, L., French, C., & Hood, D. (1990). Social and behavioral factors associated with high-risk sexual behavior among adolescents. *Journal of Behavioral Medicine, 13,* 245–261.

Birch, H., & Gussow, G. D. (1970). *Disadvantaged children*. New York: Grune & Stratton.

Block, J. (1965). *The child rearing practices report*. Berkeley: University of California, Institute of Human Development.

Block, J. H., Block, J., & Gjerde, P. F. (1986). The personality of children prior to divorce: A prospective study. *Child Development, 57*, 827–830.

Bowlby, J. (1980). *Loss: Sadness and depression* (Vol. 3). New York: Basic Books.

Bradburn, I. S. (1991). After the earth shook: Children's stress symptoms 6–8 months after a disaster. *Advances in Behaviour Research and Therapy, 13*(3), 173–179.

Brassard, M. R., Germain, R., & Hart, S. N. (1987). *Psychological maltreatment of children and youth*. New York: Pergamon Press.

Briere, J. N. (1992). *Child abuse trauma: Theory and treatment of the lasting effects*. Newbury Park, CA: Sage.

Briere, J. N., & Runtz, M. (1988a). Multivariate correlates of childhood psychological and physical maltreatment among university women. *Child Abuse and Neglect, 12*, 331–341.

Briere, J. N., & Runtz, M. (1988b). Symptomatology associated with childhood sexual victimization in a nonclinical adult sample. *Child Abuse and Neglect, 12*, 51–59.

Briere, J. N., & Runtz, M. (1993). Childhood sexual abuse: Long-term sequelae and implications for psychological assessment. *Journal of Interpersonal Violence, 8*, 312–330.

Broussard, E. R. (1982). Primary prevention of psychosocial disorders: Assessment of outcome. In L. A. Bond & J. M. Joffe (Eds.), *Facilitating infant and early childhood development* (pp. 180–196). Hanover, NH: University Press of New England.

Brown, L. K., Fritz, G. K., & Barone, V. J. (1989). The impact of AIDS education on junior and senior high school students: A pilot study. *Journal of Adolescent Health Care, 10*, 386–392.

Brown v. Board of Educ., 347 U.S. 483 (1954).

Browne, A. (1987). *When battered women kill*. New York: Macmillan Free Press.

Browne, A., & Finkelhor, D. (1986). Impact of child sexual abuse: A review of the research. *Psychological Bulletin, 99*, 66–77.

Bruce, K. E., Shrum, J. C., Trefethen, C., & Slovik, L. F. (1990). Students' attitudes about AIDS, homosexuality, and condoms. *AIDS Education & Prevention, 2*(3), 220–234.

Bruhn, J. G. (1990). A community model for AIDS prevention. *Family and Community Health, 13*(2), 65–77.

Bruner, J. (1961). *The process of education*. Cambridge, MA: Harvard University Press.

Bry, B. H. (1996). Psychological approaches to prevention. In W. K. Bickel & R. J. DeGrandpre (Eds.), *Drug policy and human nature: Psychological perspectives on the prevention, management, and treatment of illicit drug abuse* (pp. 55–76). New York: Plenum Press.

Buchanan, C. M., Maccoby, E. E., & Dornbusch, S. M. (1991). Caught between parents: Adolescents' experience in divorced homes. *Child Development, 62,* 1008–1029.

Burnham, J. C. (1993). *Bad habits.* New York: New York University Press.

Burton, L. M. (1992). Black grandparents rearing children of drug-addicted parents; Stressors, outcomes, and social service needs. *Gerontologist, 32,* 744–751.

Butler, C., Rickel, A. U., Thomas, E., & Hendren, M. (1993). An intervention program to build competencies in adolescent parents. *Journal of Primary Prevention, 13,* 183–198.

Campbell, D. T., & Erlebacher, A. (1970). How regression artifacts in quasi-experimental evaluations can mistakenly make compensatory education look harmful. In J. Hellmuth (Ed.), *Compensatory education: A national debate. (Vol. III)* New York: Brunner/Mazel, 185–210.

Campbell, S. B., & Cohen, J. F. (1991). Prevalence and correlates of postpartum depression in first-time mothers. *Journal of Abnormal Psychology, 100,* 594–599.

Caplan, G. (1964). *Principles of preventive psychiatry.* New York: Basic Books.

Carnegie Council on Adolescent Development. (1995). *Great transitions: Preparing adolescents for a new century.* Concluding report of the Carnegie Council on Adolescent Development. Woodlawn, MD: Graphtec, Inc.

Carr, R. (1981). *Theory and practice of peer counseling* [Monograph]. Ottawa, Canada: Employment and Immigration Commission.

Carrillo, J. E., & de la Cancela, V. (1992). The Cambridge Hospital Latino Health Clinic. A model for interagency integration of health services for Latinos at the provider level. *Journal of the National Medical Association, 84,* 513–519.

Center for the Study of Social Policy. (1993). *Kids count.* Washington, DC: The Annie E. Casey Foundation.

Centers for Disease Control. (1991, January). *HIV/AIDS Surveillance Report,* 1–22. Atlanta: U.S. Department of Health and Human Services, Public Health Service.

Centers for Disease Control. (1992). *Morbidity and mortality weekly report* (Vol. 41, no. 34). Atlanta: U.S. Department of Health and Human Services, Public Health Service.

Chase-Lansdale, P. L., Cherlin, A. J., & Kiernan, K. E. (1995). The long-term effects of parental divorce on the mental health of young adults: A developmental perspective. *Child Development, 66,* 1614–1634.

Children of war: Violence and America's youth. Hearing before the Subcommittee on Children, Family, Drugs and Alcoholism, Senate Committee on Labor and Human Resources, 102d Cong., 2nd Sess. (1992) (testimony of J. Garbarino).

Children's Defense Fund. (1996). *The state of America's children yearbook, 1996*. Washington, DC: Author.

Chilman, C. (1986). Some psychosocial aspects of adolescent sexual and contraceptive behaviors in a changing American society. In J. Lancaster & B. Hamburg (Eds.), *School age pregnancy and parenthood* (pp. 191–217). New York: Adine DeGruyter.

Chu, J. A., & Dill, K. I. (1990). Dissociative symptoms in relation to childhood physical and sexual abuse. *American Journal of Psychiatry, 147,* 887–892.

Cicchetti, D., & Carlson, V. (Eds.). (1989). *Child maltreatment: Theory and research on the causes and consequences of child abuse and neglect.* New York: Cambridge University Press.

Claussen, A. I. E., & Crittenden, P. M. (1991). Physical and psychological maltreatment: Relations among types of maltreatment. *Child Abuse and Neglect, 15,* 5–18.

Clinton, H. R. (1996). *It takes a village and other lessons children teach us.* New York: Simon & Schuster.

Cloninger, C. R., Dinwiddie, S. H., & Reich, T. (1989). Epidemiology and genetics of alcoholism. *Annual Review of Psychiatry, 8,* 331–346.

Coates, T. J. (1990). Strategies for modifying sexual behavior for primary and secondary prevention of HIV infection. *Journal of Consulting and Clinical Psychology, 58,* 57–69.

Cohen, A. J. (1996). A brief history of federal financing for child care in the United States. *The Future of Children, 6,* (2), 26–40.

Cole, E. S. (1995). Becoming family centered: Child welfare's challenge. *Families in Society: The Journal of Contemporary Human Services, 76,* 163–172.

Conger, K. J., & Conger, R. D. (1994). Differential parenting and change in sibling differences in delinquency. *Journal of Family Psychology, 8,* 287–302.

Conger, R. D., Conger, K. J., Elder, G. H., Lorenz, F. O., Simons, R. L., & Whitbeck, L. B. (1992). A family process model of economic hardship and adjustment of early adolescent boys. *Child Development, 63,* 526–541.

Conger, R. D., Conger, K. J., Elder, G. H., Lorenz, F. O., Simons, R. L., & Whitbeck, L. B. (1993). Family economic stress and adjustment of early adolescent girls. *Developmental Psychology, 29,* 206–219.

Conger, R. D., Ge, X., Elder, G. H., Lorenz, F. O., & Simons, R. L. (1994). Economic stress, coercive family process, and developmental problems of adolescents. *Child Development, 65,* 541–561.

Conger, R. D., Patterson, G. R., & Ge, X. (1995). It takes two to replicate: A mediational model for the impact of parents' stress on adolescent adjustment. *Child Development, 66,* 80–97.

Cooley, W. C. (1994). Commentary: The ecology of support for caregiving families. *Developmental and Behavioral Pediatrics, 15,* 117–119.

Coons, P. M., & Milstein, V. (1986). Psychosexual disturbances in multiple personality: Characteristics, etiology, and treatment. *Journal of Clinical Psychiatry, 47,* 106–110.

Courtois, C. A. (1988). *Healing the incest wound: Adult survivors in therapy.* New York: Norton.

Cowen, E. L., Hightower, A. D., Pedro-Carroll, J. L., Work, W. C., Whyman, P. A., & Haffey, W. G. (1996). *School-based prevention for children at risk.* Washington, DC: American Psychological Association.

Cowen, E. L., Lotyczewski, B. S., & Weissberg, R. P. (1984). Risk and resource indicators and their relationship to young children's school adjustment. *American Journal of Community Psychology, 12,* 353–367.

Cowen, E. L., Trost, M. A., Izzo, L. D., Lorian, R. P., Dorr, D., & Isaacson, R. V. (1975). *New ways in school mental health: Early detection and prevention of school maladaptation.* New York: Human Sciences.

Cunningham, R. M., Stiffman, A. R., Dore, P., & Earls, F. (1994). The association of physical and sexual abuse with HIV risk behaviors in adolescence and young adulthood: Implications for public health. *Child Abuse and Neglect, 18,* 233–245.

Darlington, R. B., Royce, J. M., Snipper, A. S., Murray, H. W., & Lazar, I. (1980). Preschool programs and later school competence of children from low-income families. *Science, 208*(4440), 202–204.

Dekovic, M., Janssens, J. M., & Gerris, J. R. (1991). Factor structure and construct validity of the Block Child Rearing Practices Report (CRPR). *Psychological Assessment, 3,* 182–187.

DeLange, C. (1988, April). *A study of the victimization of children of battered women.* Paper presented at the National Symposium on Child Victimization, Anaheim, CA.

DeLeon, G. (1984). *The therapeutic community: Study of effectiveness* (DHHS Publication No. ADM 84-1286). Rockville, MD: National Institute on Drug Abuse.

Demo, D. H., & Acock, A. C. (1988). The impact of divorce on children. *Journal of Marriage and the Family, 50,* 619–648.

Dickens, C. (1938). *A tale of two cities.* New York: Heritage Club. (Original work published 1859)

Dickstein, S., & Parke, R. D. (1988). Social referencing in infancy: A glance at fathers and marriage. *Child Development, 59,* 506–511.

DiClemente, R. J., Pies, C. A., Stroller, E. J., Straits, C., Olivia, G. E., Haskin, J., & Rutherford, G. W. (1989). Evaluation of school-based AIDS education curricula in San Francisco. *Journal of Sex Research, 26*(2), 188–198.

Dodge, K. A., Bates, J. E., & Pettit, G. S. (1990). Mechanisms in the cycle of violence. *Science, 250,* 1678–1683.

Dollard, J., & Miller, N. E. (1950). *Personality and psychotherapy: An analysis in terms of learning, thinking, and culture.* New York: McGraw-Hill.

Dornbusch, S. M., Ritter, P. L., Leiderman, P. H., Roberts, D. F., & Fraleigh, M. J. (1987). The relation of parenting style to adolescent school performance. *Child Development, 58,* 1244–1257.

Dornbusch, S. M., & Wood, K. (1989). Family processes and educational achievement. In W. J. Weston (Ed.), *Education and the American family: A research synthesis* (pp. 66–95). New York: New York University Press.

Dubik-Unruh, S. (1989). Children of chaos: Planning for the emotional survival of dying children of dying families. *Journal of Palliative Care, 5*(2), 10–15.

Duchnowski, A. J., & Friedman, R. M. (1990). Children's mental health: Challenges for the nineties. *Journal of Mental Health Administration, 17,* 3–12.

Dunst, C. J., Trivette, C. M., & Deal, A. G. (1988). *Enabling and empowering families.* Cambridge, MA: Brookline Books.

Duvall, E. L. (1990). *The relation of marital satisfaction to parental functioning.* Unpublished doctoral dissertation, University of Georgia.

Edsall, T., & Edsall, M. (1991). *Chain reaction: The impact of race, rights, and taxes on American politics.* New York: Norton.

Eiser, C., Eiser, J. R., & Lang, J. (1990). How adolescents compare AIDS with other diseases: Implications for prevention. *Journal of Pediatric Psychology, 15*(1), 97–103.

Elliott, D. M., Briere, J., McNeil, D., Cox, J., & Bauman, D. (1995, July). *Multivariate impacts of sexual molestation, physical abuse and neglect in a forensic sample.* Paper presented at the 4th International Family Violence Research Conference, Durham, NH.

Elliott, D. M., & Gabrielsen, D. L. (1990, August). *Impaired object relations in professional women molested as children.* Paper presented at the 98th Annual Convention of the American Psychological Association, Boston, MA.

Emery, R. E., & Forehand, R. (1994). Parental divorce and children's well being: A focus on resilience. In R. J. Haggerty, M. Rutter, & L. Sherrod (Eds.), *Stress, coping and development: Risk and resilience in children* (pp. 64–99). London: Cambridge University Press.

Epstein, M. H., Cullinan, D., Quinn, K. P., & Cumblad, C. (1994). Characteristics of children with emotional and behavioral disorders in community-based programs designed to prevent placement in residential facilities. *Journal of Emotional and Behavioral Disorders, 2*(1), 51–57.

Espe-Sherwindt, M. (1991). The IFSP and parents with special needs/mental retardation. *Topics in Early Childhood Special Education, 11*(3), 107–120.

Eth, S., & Pynoos, R. (1985). *Posttraumatic stress disorder in children.* Washington, DC: American Psychiatric Press.

Evans, L. (1990). An attempt to categorize the main determinants of traffic safety. *Health Education Research, 5*(2), 111–124.

Farber, E. A., & Egeland, B. (1987). Invulnerability among abused and neglected children. In E. J. Anthony & B. J. Cohler (Eds.), *The invulnerable child* (pp. 253–288). New York: Guilford Press.

Felsman, J. K., & Vaillant, G. E. (1987). Resilient children as adults: A 40-year study. In E. J. Anthony & B. J. Cohler (Eds.), *The invulnerable child* (pp. 289–314). New York: Guilford Press.

Fichman, L., Koestner, R., & Zuroff, D. C. (1994). Depressive styles in adolescence: Assessment, relation to social functioning, and developmental trends. *Journal of Youth and Adolescence, 23*(3), 315–330.

Field, T. (1981). Early development of the pre-term offspring of teenage mothers. In K. Scott, T. Field, & E. G. Robertson (Eds.), *Teenage parents and their offspring*. New York: Grune & Stratton.

Field, T. M. (1982). Infants born at risk: Early compensatory experiences. In L. A. Bond & J. M. Joffe (Eds.), *Facilitating infant and early childhood development* (pp. 309–342). Hanover, NH: University Press of New England.

Field, T. M. (1990). *Infancy*. Cambridge, MA: Harvard University Press.

Field, T. M., Schanberg, S. M., Scafidi, F., Bauer, C. R., Vega-Lahr, N., Garcia, R., Nystrom, J., & Kuhn, C. M. (1986). Tactile/kinesthetic stimulation effects on preterm neonates. *Pediatrics, 77*(5), 654–658.

Finkelhor, D. (1995). The victimization of children: A developmental perspective. *American Journal of Orthopsychiatry, 65*(2), 177–193.

Finkelhor, D., & Browne, A. (1985). The traumatic impact of child sexual abuse: A conceptualization. *American Journal of Orthopsychiatry, 55*(4), 530–541.

Finkelhor, D., & Dziuba-Leatherman, J. (1994). Victimization of children. *American Psychologist, 49*, 173–183.

Finkelhor, D., Hotaling, G. T., Lewis, I. A., & Smith, C. (1989). Sexual abuse and its relationship to later sexual satisfaction, marital status, religion, and attitudes. *Journal of Interpersonal Violence, 4*(4), 379–399.

Fisher, J. D., & Fisher, W. A. (1992). Changing AIDS risk behavior. *Psychological Bulletin, 111*, 455–474.

Fisher, J. D., & Misovich, W. A. (1992). Evaluation of college students' AIDS-related behavioral responses, attitudes, knowledge, and fear. *AIDS Education and Prevention, 2*, 322–337.

Forehand, R., Armistead, L., & Klein, K. (1995). Children's school performance: The roles of interparental conflict and divorce. In B. A. Ryan, G. R. Adams, T. P. Gullotta, R. P. Weissberg, & R. L. Hampton (Eds.), *The family school connection* (pp. 250–269). Thousand Oaks, CA: Sage.

Forehand, R., & Thomas, A. M. (1992). Conflict in the home environment of adolescents from divorced families: A longitudinal analysis. *Journal of Family Violence, 7*(2), 73–84.

Forst, M., Moore, M., & Jang, M. (1990). Issues in the evaluation of AIDS education programs: The case of California. *Evaluation and the Health Professions, 13*(2), 147–167.

Fox, G. L. (1979, May/June). The family's influence in adolescent sexual behavior. *Children Today*, 21–36.

Freedman, J. (1993). *From cradle to grave: The human face of poverty in America*. New York: Atheneum.

Freud, S. (1957). Mourning and melancholia. In J. Strachey (Ed. and Trans.), *The standard edition of the complete psychological works of Sigmund Freud* (Vol. 14, pp. 243–258). London: Hogarth Press. (Original work published 1917)

Fulghum, R. (1993). *All I really need to know I learned in kindergarten: Uncommon thoughts on common things.* New York: Fawcett.

Garbarino, J., & Vondra, J. (1987). Psychological maltreatment: Issues and perspectives. In M. R. Brasard, R. Germain, & S. N. Hart (Eds.), *Psychological maltreatment of children and youth* (pp. 24–44). New York: Pergamon Press.

Garfinkel, I., & McLanahan, S. (1986). *Single mothers and their children.* Washington, DC: Urban Institute Press.

Garralda, M. E. (1994). Chronic physical illness and emotional disorders in childhood: Where the brain's not involved, there may still be problems. *British Journal of Psychiatry, 164,* 8–10.

Garrison, E. G. (1987). Psychological maltreatment of children: An emerging focus for inquiry and concern. *American Psychologist, 42,* 157–159.

Ge, X., Conger, R. D., Lorenz, F. O., Shanahan, M., & Elder, G. H. (1995). Mutual influences in parent and adolescent psychological distress. *Developmental Psychology, 31,* 406–419.

Gelles, R. J. (1987). The family and its role in the abuse of children. *Psychiatric Annals, 17,* 229–232.

Gibbs, M. (1989). Factors in the victim that mediate between disaster and psychopathology: A review. *Journal of Traumatic Stress, 2,* 489–514.

Gilchrist, L. D. (1990). The role of schools in community-based approaches to prevention of AIDS and intravenous drug use. *National Institute on Drug Abuse: Research Monograph Series, 93,* 150–166.

Gleaves, D. H. (1996). The socio-cognitive model of dissociative identity disorder: A reexamination of the evidence. *Psychological Bulletin, 120,* 42–59.

Gleeson, M. K. (1996). *High-risk sexual behavior in college students: An examination of antecedents from childhood maltreatment.* Unpublished doctoral dissertation, University of Connecticut, Storrs.

Glenn, N. D., & McLanahan, S. (1982). Children and marital happiness: A further specification of the relationship. *Journal of Marriage and Family, 44*(1), 63–72.

Glogower, F., & Sloop, E. W. (1976). Two strategies of group training of parents as effective behavioral modifiers. *Behavior Therapy, 7,* 177–184.

Goddard, C. R., & Stanley, J. R. (1994). Viewing the abusive parent and the abused child as captor and hostage: The application of hostage theory to the effects of child abuse. *Journal of Interpersonal Violence, 9,* 258–269.

Gold, S. R., Milan, L. D., Mayall, A., & Johnson, A. E. (1994). A cross-validation study of the Trauma Symptom Checklist: The role of mediating variables. *Journal of Interpersonal Violence, 9,* 12–26.

Goldston, S. E. (1991). A survey of prevention activities in state mental health authorities. *Professional Psychology: Research and Practice, 22,* 315–321.

Gordon, E. W. (1995, March). Putting them in their place. Review of *The Bell Curve*: Intelligence and class structure in American life. *Readings: A Journal of Reviews and Commentary in Mental Health, 10*(1), 8–14.

Grace, M. C., Green, B. L., Lindy, J. D., & Leonard, A. C. (1993). The Buffalo Creek Disaster: A 14-year follow-up. In J. P. Wilson & B. Raphael (Eds.), *International handbook of traumatic stress syndromes* (pp. 441–449). New York: Plenum Press.

Gyulay, J. E. (1989). Home care for the dying child. *Issues in Comprehensive Pediatric Nursing, 12*(1), 33–69.

Hanson, R. F., Lipovsky, J. A., & Saunders, B. E. (1994). Characteristics of fathers in incest families. *Journal of Interpersonal Violence, 9,* 155–169.

Hart, S. N., & Brassard, M. R. (1987). A major threat to children's mental health: Psychological maltreatment. *American Psychologist, 42,* 160–165.

Hartman, A. E., Radin, M. B., & McConnell, B. (1992). Parent-to-parent support: A critical component of health care services for families. *Issues in Comprehensive Pediatric Nursing, 15,* 55–67.

Health Care and Family Violence Field Project. (1992, June 4). *Family violence and the health care system: Lessons from five communities* (RWJ Contract No. PC234). Princeton, NJ: Robert Wood Johnson Foundation.

Heider, F. (1958). *The psychology of interpersonal relations.* New York: Wiley.

Heilman, M. E., & Stopeck, M. H. (1985). Attractiveness and corporate success: Different causal attributions for males and females. *Journal of Applied Psychology, 70,* 379–388.

Helburn, S. W., & Howes, C. (1996). Child care cost and quality. *The Future of Children, 6*(2), 62–82.

Herman, J. (1992). *Trauma and recovery.* New York: Basic Books.

Herrnstein, R. J., & Murray, C. (1994). *The bell curve: Intelligence and class structure in American life.* New York: Free Press.

Hess, R. D., & Shipman, V. C. (1967). Cognitive elements in maternal behavior. In J. Hill (Ed.), *Minnesota Symposia on Child Psychology* (Vol. 1, pp. 57–81). Minneapolis: University of Minnesota Press.

Hetherington, E. M., Cox, M., & Cox, R. (1982). Effects of divorce on parents and children. In M. Lamb (Ed.), *Nontraditional families* (pp. 233–288). Hillsdale, NJ: Erlbaum.

Hilbers, S. M., Graham, R. S., Wilson, D. E., O'Connor, R. M., & Duck, R. J. (1996, June). *An attributional analysis on perceptions of poverty: Weiner's theory of social conduct applied to perceptions of welfare recipients.* Paper presented at the 60th Anniversary Convention of the Society for the Psychological Study of Social Issues, Ann Arbor, MI.

Hofferth, S. L. (1996). Child care in the United States today. *The Future of Children, 6*(2), 41–61.

Holden, G. W., & Zambarno, R. J. (1992). Passing the rod: Similarities between parents and their young children in orientations toward physical punishment. In I. E. Sigel, A. V. McGillicuddy-Delisi, & J. J. Goodnow (Eds.), *Parental belief systems: The psychological consequences for children* (pp. 143–172). Hillsdale, NJ: Erlbaum.

Hotaling, G., & Sugarman, D. (1986). An analysis of risk markers in husband to wife violence: The current state of knowledge. *Violence and Victims, 1*(2), 101–124.

Hugo, V. (1967). *Les miserables.* Paris: Garnier-Flammarion. (Original work published 1862)

Hunter, J. A. (1991). A comparison of the psychosocial maladjustment of adult males and females sexually molested as children. *Journal of Interpersonal Violence, 6,* 205–217.

Hyman, I. A. (1994, August). *Is spanking child abuse? Conceptualizations, research and policy implications.* Paper presented at the 102nd Annual Convention of the American Psychological Association, Los Angeles, CA.

Illback, R. J., Cobb, C. T., & Joseph, H. M., Jr. (in press). Integrated services for children and families: Opportunities for psychological practice. Washington, DC: American Psychological Association.

Ingraham v. Wright, 525 F. 2d 909 (1976).

Institute of Medicine. (1994). *Reducing risks for mental disorders.* Washington, DC: National Academy Press.

Iscoe, I., & Spielberger, C. D. (Eds.). (1970). *Community psychology: Perspectives in training and research.* New York: Appleton-Century-Crofts.

Jessor, S., & Jessor, R. (1975). Transition from virginity to nonvirginity among youth: A social–psychological study over time. *Developmental Psychology, 11,* 473–484.

Johnson, C. A., & Katz, R. C. (1973). Using parents as change agents for their children: A review. *Journal of Child Psychology and Psychiatry, 14,* 181–200.

Johnson, K. (1989). *Trauma in the lives of children.* Claremont, CA: Hunter House.

Johnson, S. (1993, January 3). Killing our children. *Chicago Tribune,* pp. 1, 16–17.

Johnston, L. D., O'Malley, P. M., & Bachman, J. G. (1991). *Drug use among American high school seniors, college students, and young adults, 1975–1990: Vol. 1. High school seniors.* Washington, DC: Department of Health and Human Services.

Jones, D. C., Rickel, A. U., & Smith, R. L. (1980). Maternal childrearing practices and social problem solving strategies among preschoolers. *Developmental Psychology, 16,* 241–242.

Jones, E. E., Farina, A., Hastorf, A. H., Marcus, H., Miller, D. T., & Scott, R. A. (1984). *Social stigma: The psychology of marked relationships.* New York: W. H. Freeman.

Kamerman, S. B., & Kahn, A. J. (1995). Innovations in toddler day care and family support services: An international overview. *Child Welfare, 74*, 1281–1300.

Kantrowitz, B. (1993, August 2). Wild in the streets. *Newsweek*, pp. 40–46.

Kaufman, J., & Zigler, E. (1987). Do abused children become abusive parents? *American Journal of Orthopsychiatry, 57*, 186–192.

Keeping every child safe: Curbing the epidemic of violence. Hearing before the Subcommittee on Children, Family, Drugs and Alcoholism of the Senate Committee on Labor and Human Resources, 103d Cong., 1st Sess. (1993) (testimonies of L. Arroyo, B. Phillips-Taylor, and D. Prothrow-Stith).

Kelder, L. R., McNamara, J. R., Carlson, B., & Lynn, S. J. (1991). Perceptions of physical punishment: The relation to childhood and adolescent experiences. *Journal of Interpersonal Violence, 6*, 432–445.

Kendler, K. S., Neale, M. C., Kessler, R. C., Heath, A. C., & Eaves, L. J. (1992). Childhood parental loss and adult psychopathology in women: A twin study perspective. *Archives of General Psychiatry, 49*, 109–116.

Kessler, R. C., & Cleary, P. D. (1980). Social class and psychological distress. *American Sociological Review, 45*, 463–477.

Kitzmann, K. M., & Emery, R. B. (1994). Child and family coping one year after mediated and litigated child custody disputes. *Journal of Family Psychology, 8*(2), 150–159.

Klein, D. C., & Goldston, S. (1977). *Primary prevention: An idea whose time has come*. Washington, DC: Government Printing Office.

Klitzner, M., Fisher, D., Stewart, K., & Gilbert, S. (1993). *Substance abuse: Early intervention for adolescents*. Princeton, NJ: Robert Wood Johnson Foundation.

Kluft, R. P. (Ed.). (1985). *Childhood antecedents of multiple personality*. Washington, DC: American Psychiatric Press.

Knitzer, J., & Aber, J. L. (1995). Young children in poverty: Facing the facts. *American Journal of Orthopsychiatry, 65*, 174–176.

Kolko, D. J. (1992). Characteristics of child victims of physical violence: Research findings and clinical implications. *Journal of Interpersonal Violence, 7*, 244–276.

Kolko, D. J., Kazdin, A. E., Thomas, A. M., & Day, B. (1993). Heightened child physical abuse potential: Child, parent, and family dysfunction. *Journal of Interpersonal Violence, 8*, 169–192.

Koss, M., Goodman, L., Fitzgerald, L., Russo, N. F., Keita, G. P., & Browne, A. (1994). *No safe haven: Male violence against women at home, at work, and in the community*. Washington, DC: American Psychological Association.

Kupers, T. A. (1996). Trauma and its sequelae in male prisoners: Effects of confinement, overcrowding, and diminished services. *American Journal of Orthopsychiatry, 66*, 189–196.

Kutash, K., & Rivera, V. R. (1995). Effectiveness of children's mental health services: A review of the literature. *Education and Treatment of Children, 18*, 443–477.

Lachar, D. (1974). *The MMPI: Clinical asessment and automated interpretation.* Los Angeles: Western Psychological Services.

Ladame, F., & Jeanneret, O. (1982). Suicide in adolescence: Some comments on epidemiology and prevention. *Journal of Adolescence, 5,* 355–366.

Lamb, M. E. (1986). The changing roles of fathers. In M.E. Lamb (Ed.), *The father's role: Applied perspectives* (pp. 3–27). New York: Wiley.

Landerman, R., George, L. K., & Blazer, D. G. (1991). Adult vulnerability for psychiatric disorders: Interactive effects of negative childhood experiences and recent stress. *The Journal of Nervous and Mental Disease, 179,* 656–663.

Larry P. v. Riles, 343 F. Supp. 1306 (N.D. Calif, 1972).

Layne, C. (1983). Painful truths about depressives' cognitions. *Journal of Clinical Psychology, 39,* 848–853.

Lewinsohn, P. M., Rohde, P., and Seeley, J. R. (1996). Adolescent suicidal ideation and attempts: Prevalence, risk factors, and clinical implications. *Clinical Psychology: Science and Practice, 3,* 25–46.

Limber, S. B., & Wilcox, B. L. (1996). Application of the U.N. Convention on the Rights of the Child to the United States. *American Psychologist, 51,* 1246–1250.

Loeb, R. C., Horst, I., & Horton, P. J. (1980). Family interaction patterns associated with self-esteem in preadolescent girls and boys. *Merrill Palmer Quarterly, 26,* 203–217.

Loose, C. (1996, June 2). On behalf of sons and daughters. *The Washington Post,* pp. 1, 22.

Lorian, R. P., Iscoe, I., DeLeon, P. H., & VandenBos, G. R. (Eds.). (1996). *Psychology and public policy: Balancing public service and professional need.* Washington, DC: American Psychological Association.

Luthar, S. S., & Zigler, E. (1991). Vulnerability and competence: A review of the research on resilience in childhood. *American Journal of Orthopsychiatry, 61,* 6–22.

MacFarquhar, K. W., Dowrick, P. W., & Risley, T. R. (1993). Individualizing services for seriously emotionally disturbed youth: A nationwide survey. *Administration and Policy in Mental Health, 20*(3), 165–174.

Magidson, J. (1977). *Toward a causal model approach for adjusting for pre-existing differences in the non-equivalent control group situation: A general alternative to ANCOVA.* New York: Abt Associates.

Mallon-Kraft, S. (1996). *Child maltreatment, parental child-rearing practices, and intimate relationships of college students.* Master's thesis in preparation, University of Connecticut, Storrs.

Marshall, W. L. (1989). Intimacy, loneliness, and sexual offenders. *Behavioral Research and Therapy, 27*(5), 491–503.

Mayer, S., & Jencks, C. (1995, November 9). War on poverty: No apologies, please. *The New York Times,* p. A29.

McCord, J. (1988). Alcoholism: Toward understanding genetic and social factors. *Psychiatry, 51,* 131–141.

McCoy, C. B., Chitwood, D. D., Khoury, E. L., & Miles, C. E. (1990). The implementation of an experimental research design in the evaluation of an intervention to prevent AIDS among IV drug users. *Journal of Drug Issues, 20,* 215–222.

McCurdy, K., & Daro, D. (1993). *Current trends in child abuse reporting and fatalities: The results of the 1992 annual fifty state survey.* Chicago: National Committee for Prevention of Child Abuse.

McDonald, B. A., Boyd, L. A., Clark, H. B., & Stewart, E. S. (1995). Recommended individualized wraparound strategies for foster children with emotional/behavioral disturbances and their families. *Community Alternatives International Journal of Family Care, 7*(2), 63–82.

McDowell, E. E. & Stillian, J. M. (1994). Suicide across the phases of life. In G. G. Noam & S. Borst (Eds.), *Children, Youth and Suicide: Developmental Perspectives.* San Francisco: Jossey-Bass.

McIntyre, D., Thomas, G., & Borgen, W. (1982). A peer counseling model for use in secondary schools. *Canadian Counselor, 17,* 29–36.

McKenzie, J. (1993, Spring). Adoption of children with special needs. *The Future of Children, 3*(1), 62–76. Los Altos, CA: The David and Lucille Packard Foundation.

McLanahan, S., & Adams, J. (1987). Parenthood and psychological well-being. *Annual Review of Sociology, 13,* 237–257.

McLanahan, S., & Adams, J. (1989). The effects of children on adults' psychological well-being: 1957–1976. *Social Forces, 68*(1), 124–146.

McLanahan, S., & Bumpass, L. (1988). Intergenerational consequences of family disruption. *American Journal of Sociology, 94*(1), 130–152.

McLanahan, S. & Sandefur, G. (1994). *Growing up with a single parent.* Cambridge, MA: Harvard University Press.

McLanahan, S., Sorensen, A., & Watson, D. (1989). Sex differences in poverty, 1950–1980. *Signs, 15*(1), 102–122.

McMahon, C., & Johnson, S. (1993, July 9). Portrait of a city's tragedy. *Chicago Tribune,* pp. 1, 16.

McNally, R. J. (1993). Stressors that produce post traumatic stress disorder in children. In J. R. T. Davidson & E. B. Foa (Eds.), *Posttraumatic stress disorder: DSM–IV and beyond* (pp. 207–221). Washington, DC: American Psychiatric Press.

McReynolds, P. (1996). Lightner Witmer: A centennial tribute. *American Psychologist, 51,* 237–240.

Meredith, W. H., Abbott, D. A., & Adams, S. L. (1986). Family violence: Its relation to marital and parental satisfaction and family strengths. *Journal of Family Violence, 1,* 299–305.

Mesibov, G. B., & Johnson, M. R. (1982). Intervention techniques in pediatric psychology. In J. M. Tuma (Ed.), *Handbook for the practice of pediatric psychology* (pp. 110–164). New York: Wiley.

Midence, K. (1994). The effects of chronic illness on children and their families: An overview. *Genetic, Social and General Psychology Monographs, 120*(3), 309–326.

Miller, O. T., & Ross, M. (1975). Self-serving biases in attribution of causality: Fact or fiction? *Psychological Bulletin, 82,* 213–225.

Mills v. Board of Education, 348 F. Supp. 866 (D.D.C. 1972).

Millstein, S. G. (1993). A view of health from the adolescent's perspective. In S. G. Millstein, A. C. Petersen, & E. O. Nightengale (Eds.), *Promoting the health of adolescents: New directions for the twenty-first century* (pp. 97–118). New York: Oxford University Press.

Mireault, G. C., & Bond, L. A. (1992). Parental death in childhood: Perceived vulnerability, and adult depression and anxiety. *American Journal of Orthopsychiatry, 62,* 517–524.

Mordock, J. B. (1990). Funding children's mental health services in an underfunded climate: Collaborative efforts. *Journal of Mental Health Administration, 17,* 108–114.

Morgan, H. (1995). Drug use in high school: Race and gender issues. *Journal of Educational Research, 88,* 301–308.

Morin, R. (1995, October 8). A distorted image of minorities: Poll suggests that what whites think they see may affect beliefs. *The Washington Post,* p. A1.

Moynihan, D. P. (1996, Jan. 11). Congress builds a coffin. *New York Review of Books, 43*(1), 33–36.

Mundy, P., Robertson, J., Greenblatt, M., & Robertson, M. (1989). Residential instability in adolescent inpatients. *Journal of the American Academy of Child and Adolescent Psychiatry, 28,* 176–181.

Mundy, P., Robertson, M., Robertson, J., & Greenblatt, M. (1990). The prevalence of psychotic symptoms in homeless adolescents. *Journal of the American Academy of Child and Adolescent Psychiatry, 29,* 724–731.

National Institute on Drug Abuse. (1991). *Drug use among youth: Findings from the 1988 National Household Survey on Drug Abuse* (DHHS Publication No. ADM 91-1765). Rockville, MD: U.S. Department of Health and Human Services.

National Institute of Justice. (1993, May). *Drug use forecasting quarterly report (Third quarter, 1992).* Washington, DC: U.S. Department of Justice.

National Research Council, Panel on High Risk Youth. (1993). *Losing generations: Adolescents in high-risk settings.* Washington, DC: National Academy Press.

Navarro, M. (1996, May 19). Teen-age mothers viewed as abused prey of older men. *The New York Times,* p. 1.

Neighbors, H. W., Jackson, J. S., Bowman, P. J., & Gurin, G. (1983). Stress, coping, and Black mental health: Preliminary findings from a national study. *Prevention in Human Services, 2*(3), 5–29.

Neisser, U., Boodoo, G., Bouchard, T. J., Jr., Boykin, A. W., Brody, N., Ceci, S. J., Halpern, D. F., Loehlin, J. C., Perloff, R., Sternberg, R. J., & Urbina, S. (1996). Intelligence: Knowns and unknowns. *American Psychologist, 51,* 77–101.

New Challenges for Head Start: Hearing before the Subcommittee on Children, Family, Drugs and Alcoholism of the Senate Committee on Labor and

Human Resources, 103d Cong., 1st Sess. 16–19 (1993) (testimony of Delores Baynes).

Newberger, C. M., & DeVos, E. (1988). Abuse and victimization: A lifespan developmental perspective. *American Journal of Orthopsychiatry, 58,* 505–511.

Norman, E. (1994). Personal factors related to substance misuse: Risk abatement and/or resiliency enhancement? In T. P. Gullotta, G. R. Adams, & R. Montemayor (Eds.), *Substance misuse in adolescence* (pp. 15–35). Thousand Oaks, CA: Sage.

Norris, F. H. (1992). Epidemiology of trauma: Frequency and impact of different potentially traumatic events on different demographic groups. *Journal of Consulting and Clinical Psychology, 60,* 409–418.

Novello, A. (1992). From the Surgeon General, U.S. Public Health Service. *Journal of the American Medical Association, 267,* 3007.

O'Dell, S. (1974). Training parents in behavior modification: A review. *Psychological Bulletin, 81,* 418–433.

Office of the Inspector General. (1991). *Youth and alcohol: A national survey* (Document No. OEI-09-00652). Washington, DC: U.S. Department of Health and Human Services.

Office of Substance Abuse Prevention. (1991, May). *OSAP Bulletin: Take a look at college drinking.* Washington, DC: U.S. Department of Health and Human Services.

Osofsky, J. D. (1995). The effects of exposure to violence on young children. *American Psychologist, 50,* 782–788.

Packer, A. J. (1992). *Differences in self-reported child rearing practices and family functioning between pre-recovering alcoholic fathers and recovering alcoholic fathers.* Unpublished doctoral dissertation, Boston College.

Pandiant, J. A., & Maynard, A. G. (1993). Vermont's local interagency teams: An evaluation of service coordination and system change. *Community Alternatives International Journal of Family Care, 5*(1), 85–97.

Parke, R. D., & Kellam, S. G. (Eds.). (1994). *Exploring family relationships with other social contexts.* Hillsdale, NJ: Erlbaum.

Partington, A. (Ed.) (1996). *The Oxford Dictionary of Quotations.* Revised Fourth Edition. New York: Oxford University Press.

Pasamanick, B., & Knobloch, H. (1961). Epidemiologic studies on the complications of pregnancy and the birth process. In G. Caplan (Ed.), *Prevention of mental disorders in children* (pp. 74–94). New York: Basic Books.

Patterson, G. R. (1980). Mothers: The unacknowledged victims. *Monographs of the Society for Research in Child Development, 45,* 1–64.

Payne, M. A., & Furnham, A. (1992). Parents' self-reports of child rearing practices in the Caribbean. *Journal of Black Psychology, 18,* 19–36.

Peck, J. S., Sheinberg, M., & Akamatsu, N. N. (1995). Forming a consortium: A design for interagency collaboration in the delivery of service following the disclosure of incest. *Family Process, 34,* 287–302.

Pellow, K. A., & Jengeleski, J. L. (1991). A survey of current research studies on drug education programs in America. *Journal of Drug Education,* *21,* 203–210.

Pennsylvania Association for Retarded Children v. Commonwealth of PA, 343 F. Supp. 279 (E.D. Penn. 1972).

Peterson, M. S., & Urquiza, A. J. (1993). *The role of mental health professionals in the prevention and treatment of child abuse and neglect.* Washington, DC: U.S. Department of Health and Human Services, National Center on Child Abuse and Neglect.

Pettle, S. A., & Britten, C. M. (1995). Talking with children about death and dying. *Child Care, Health and Development, 21,* 395–404.

Phares, V. (1992). Where's Poppa? The relative lack of attention to the role of fathers in child and adolescent psychopathology. *American Psychologist, 47,* 656–664.

Piaget, J. (1950). *The psychology of intelligence* (M. Percy & D. E. Berlyne, Trans.). London: Routledge and Kegan Paul.

Pianta, R., Egeland, B., & Erickson, M. F. (1989). The antecedents of maltreatment: Results of the Mother–Child Interaction Project. In D. Cicchetti & V. Carlson (Eds.), *Child maltreatment: Theory and research on the causes and consequences of child abuse and neglect* (pp. 203–253). New York: Cambridge University Press.

Pless, I. B., Cripps, H. A., Davies, J. M. C., & Wadsworth, M. E. J. (1989). Chronic physical illness in childhood: Psychological and social effects in adolescence and adult life. *Developmental Medicine and Child Neurology, 31,* 746–755.

Price, R., & Smith, S. S. (1985). *A guide to evaluating prevention programs in mental health.* Washington, DC: Government Printing Office.

Prinos, M. J. (1996). *Intergenerational patterns of psychological maltreatment, child rearing practices, and trauma-related symptomatology in a clinical population.* Unpublished doctoral dissertation, University of Connecticut, Storrs.

Putnam, F. W., Guroff, J. J., Silberman, E. K., Barban, I., & Post, R. M. (1986). The clinical phenomenology of multiple personality disorder: A review of 100 recent cases. *Journal of Clinical Psychiatry, 47,* 285–293.

Pynoos, R. S., Steinberg, A. M., & Goenjian, A. (1996). Traumatic stress in childhood and adolescence: Recent developments and current controversies. In B. A. van der Kolk, A. C. McFarland, & L. Weisaeth (Eds.), *Traumatic stress: The effects of overwhelming experience on mind, body, and society* (pp. 331–358). New York: Guilford Press.

Random House Webster's College Dictionary. (1992). New York: Random House.

Reisinger, J. J., & Lavigne, J. V. (1980). An early intervention model for pediatric settings. *Professional Psychology, 11,* 582–590.

Rickel, A. U. (1979). *Preschool Mental Health Project: Training Manual.* Lansing: State of Michigan, Department of Mental Health.

Rickel, A. U. (1986). Prescriptions for a new generation: Early life interventions. *American Journal of Community Psychology, 14,* 1–15.

Rickel, A. U. (1989). *Teen pregnancy and parenting*. New York: Hemisphere/ Taylor and Francis.

Rickel, A. U., & Allen, L. (1987). *Preventing maladjustment from infancy through adolescence*. Beverly Hills, CA: Sage.

Rickel, A. U., & Becker-Lausen, E. (1994). Treating the adolescent drug misuser. In T. P. Gullotta, G. R. Adams, & R. Montemayor (Eds.), *Substance misuse in adolescence* (pp. 175–200). Beverly Hills, CA: Sage.

Rickel, A. U., & Becker-Lausen, E. (1995). Intergenerational influences on child outcomes: Implications for prevention and intervention. In B. Ryan & G. R. Adams (Eds.), *The family–school connection* (pp. 315–340). Beverly Hills, CA: Sage.

Rickel, A. U., & Biasetti, L. L. (1982). Modification of the Block Child Rearing Practices Report. *Journal of Clinical Psychology, 38*(1), 129–134.

Rickel, A. U., & Dudley, G. (1983). A parent training group in a preschool mental health project. In R. Rosenbaum (Ed.), *Varieties of short-term therapy groups: A handbook for mental health professionals* (pp. 39–57). New York: McGraw-Hill.

Rickel, A. U., Dudley, G., & Berman, S. (1980). An evaluation of parent training. *Evaluation Review, 4*, 389–403.

Rickel, A. U., & Lampi, L. A. (1981). A two-year follow-up study of a preventive mental health program for preschoolers. *Journal of Abnormal Child Psychology, 9*, 455–464.

Rickel, A. U., & Langner, T. S. (1985). Short- and long-term effects of marital disruption on children. *American Journal of Community Psychology, 13*, 599–611.

Rickel, A. U., & Smith, R. L. (1979). Maladapting preschool children: Identification, diagnosis, and remediation. *American Journal of Community Psychology, 7*, 197–208.

Rickel, A. U., Smith, R. L., & Sharp, K. C. (1979). Description and evaluation of a preventive mental health program for preschoolers. *Journal of Abnormal Child Psychology, 7*, 101–112.

Rickel, A. U., Williams, D. L., & Loigman, G. A. (1988). Predictors of maternal child rearing practices: Implications for intervention. *Journal of Community Psychology, 16*, 32–40.

Roscoe, B., & Kruger, T. L. (1990). AIDS: Late adolescents' knowledge and its influence on sexual behavior. *Adolescence, 25*(97), 39–48.

Rose, S. A., Feldman, J. F., Rose, S. L., Wallace, I. F., & McCarton, C. (1992). Behavior problems at 3 and 6 years: Prevalence and continuity in full-terms and preterms. *Development and Psychopathology, 4*, 361–374.

Rosen, M., Clark, G. R., & Kivitz, M. S. (Eds.). (1976). *The history of mental retardation: Collected papers* (Vol. 1). Baltimore: University Park Press.

Rosenberg, M. S. (1987). New directions for research on the psychological maltreatment of children. *American Psychologist, 42*, 166–171.

Ross, A. O. (1959). *The practice of clinical child psychology*. New York: Grune & Stratton.

Ross, L. (1977). The intuitive psychologist and his shortcomings: Distortions in the attribution process. In L. Berkowitz (Ed.), *Advances in experimental social psychology* (Vol. 10, pp. 173–220). New York: Academic Press.

Rossner, J. (1975). *Looking for Mr. Goodbar.* New York: Simon and Schuster.

Roth, J., Siegel, R., & Black, S. (1994). Identifying the mental health needs of children living in families with AIDS or HIV infection. *Community Mental Health Journal, 30,* 581–593.

Roth, R., & Constantine, L. M. (1995, April). Psychological intervention may prevent retardation. *APA Monitor,* p. 46.

Rous, B., Hemmeter, M. L., & Schuster, J. (1994). Sequenced transition to education in the public schools: A systems approach to transition planning. *Topics in Early Childhood Special Education, 14,* 374–393.

Routh, D. K. (1996). Lightner Witmer and the first 100 years of clinical psychology. *American Psychologist, 51,* 244–247.

Rubin, L. (1976). *Worlds of pain.* New York: Basic Books.

Rubin, L. B. (1994). *Families on the faultline: America's working class speaks about the family, the economy, race, and ethnicity.* New York: Harper-Collins.

Ruder, A. M., Flam, R., Flatto, D., & Furran, A. S. (1990). AIDS education: Evaluation of school and worksite based presentations. *New York State Journal of Medicine, 90,* 129–133.

Rueter, M. A., & Conger, R. D. (1995). Interaction style, problem-solving behavior, and family problem-solving effectiveness. *Child Development, 66,* 98–115.

Saler, L., & Skolnick, N. (1992). Childhood parental death and depression in adulthood: Roles of surviving parent and family environment. *American Journal of Orthopsychiatry, 62,* 504–516.

Sameroff, A. J., & Chandler, M. J. (1975). Reproductive risk and the continuum of caretaking casualty. In F. D. Horowitz, M. Hetherington, & S. Scarr-Salopatek (Eds.), *Review of child development research* (Vol. 4, pp. 187–244). Chicago: University of Chicago Press.

Samuels, C. A., & Ewy, R. (1985). Aesthetic perception of faces during infancy. *British Journal of Developmental Psychology, 3,* 221–228.

Sandefur, G. D., McLanahan, S., & Wojtkiewicz, R. A. (1992). The effects of parental marital status during adolescence on high school graduation. *Social Forces, 71*(1), 103–121.

Sanders, B., & Becker-Lausen, E. (1995). The measurement of psychological maltreatment: Early data on the Child Abuse and Trauma Scale. *Child Abuse and Neglect, 19*(3), 315–323.

Sanders, B., & Becker-Lausen, E. (in press). Dissociation, trauma and memory. In A. Tishelman, E. H. Newberger, & C. M. Newberger (Eds.), *Trauma and memory.* Cambridge, MA: Harvard University Press.

Sanders, B., & Giolas, M. (1991). Dissociation and childhood trauma in psychologically disturbed adolescents. *American Journal of Psychiatry, 148,* 50–53.

Sanders, B., McRoberts, G., & Tollefson, C. (1989). Childhood stress and dissociation in a college population. *Dissociation, 2*(1), 17–23.

Sandler, I. N., Reynolds, K. D., Kliewer, W., & Ramirez, R. (1992). Specificity of the relation between life events and psychological symptomatology. *Journal of Clinical Child Psychology, 21,* 240–248.

Santrock, J. W., & Sitterle, K. A. (1987). Parent–child relations in stepmother families. In K. Pasley & M. Ihinger-Tallman (Eds.), *Remarriage and stepparenting: Current research and theory* (pp. 273–299). New York: Guilford Press.

Schechter, S., & Mihaly, L. K. (1992). *Ending violence against women and children in Massachusetts families: Critical steps for the next five years.* Boston: Massachusetts Coalition of Battered Women Service Groups.

Scherling, D. (1994). Prenatal cocaine exposure and childhood psychopathology: A developmental analysis. *American Journal of Orthopsychiatry, 64,* 9–19.

Schonberg, S. K. (1993). *Treatment of alcohol-and-other-drug (AOD)-abusing adolescents* (SAMHSA Contract No. ADM 270-91-0007). Rockville, MD: Substance Abuse and Mental Health Services Administration, Center for Substance Abuse Treatment.

Schuckit, M. A. (1994). A clinical model of genetic influences in alcohol dependence. *Journal of Studies on Alcohol, 5,* 5–17.

Schwartz, I. (1993, July). Staff briefing, United States Congress, Washington, DC.

Schweinhart, L. J., Barnes, H. V., & Weikart, D. P. (1993). *Significant benefits: The High/Scope Perry Preschool Study Through Age 27.* Monographs of the High/Scope Educational Research Foundation, no. 10. Ypsilanti, MI: High/Scope Press.

Seligman, M. E. P. (1975). *Helplessness.* San Francisco: W. H. Freeman.

Seligman, M. E. P., & Rosenhan, D. L. (1984). *Abnormal Psychology.* New York: Norton.

Selye, H. (1956). *The stress of life.* New York: McGraw-Hill.

Shannon, M. P., Lonigan, C. J., Finch, A. J., & Taylor, C. W. (1994). Children exposed to disaster: I. Epidemiology of post-traumatic symptoms and symptom profiles. *Journal of the American Academy of Child and Adolescent Psychiatry, 33*(1), 80–93.

Shedler, J., & Block, J. (1990). Adolescent drug use and psychological health, a longitudinal inquiry. *American Psychologist, 45,* 612–630.

Short, R. J., & Shapiro, S. K. (1993). Conduct disorders: A framework for understanding and intervention in schools and communities. *School Psychologist Review, 22,* 362–375.

Sidel, R. (1994, September). Poor relations. *Readings: A Journal of Reviews and Commentary in Mental Health, 9*(3), 22–25.

Sidel, R. (1996). *Keeping women and children last: America's war on the poor.* New York: Penguin Books.

Siegel, K., & Gorey, E. (1994). Childhood bereavement due to parental death from acquired immunodeficiency syndrome. *Journal of Developmental and Behavioral Pediatrics, 15*(3,Suppl.), S66–S70.

Silverman, I. W., & Dubow, E. F. (1991). Looking ahead to parenthood: Nonparents' expectations of themselves and their future children. *Merrill-Palmer Quarterly, 37,* 231–251.

Simons, R. L., Lorenz, F. O., Conger, R. D., & Wu, C. (1992). Support from spouse as mediator and moderators of the disruptive influence of economic strain on parenting. *Child Development, 63,* 1282–1301.

Simons, R. L., Lorenz, F. O., Wu, C., & Conger, R. D. (1993). Social network and marital support as mediators and moderators of the impact of stress and depression on parental behavior. *Developmental Psychology, 29,* 368–381.

Simons, R. L., Whitbeck, L. B., Conger, R. D., & Wu, C. (1991). Intergenerational transmission of harsh parenting. *Developmental Psychology, 27,* 159–171.

Smith, H. (1988). *The power game.* New York: Ballantine Books.

Smith, M. S., & Bissell, J. S. (1970). Report analysis: The impact of Head Start. *Harvard Educational Review, 40,* 51–104.

Sobey, F. (1970). *The nonprofessional revolution in mental health.* New York: Columbia University Press.

Speece, M. W., & Brent, S. B. (1992). The acquisition of a mature understanding of three components of death. *Death Studies, 16,* 211–229.

Spirito, A., Stark, L. J., & Tye, V. L. (1994). Stressors and coping strategies described during hospitalization by chronically ill children. *Journal of Clinical Child Psychology, 23,* 314–322.

Stark, E., & Flitcraft, A. (1988). Violence among intimates: An epidemiological review. In V. B. Van Hasselt, R. L. Morrison, A. S. Bellack, & M. Hersen (Eds.), *Handbook of family violence* (pp. 293–317). New York: Plenum Press.

Stein, D., & Polyson, J. (1984). The primary health project reconsidered. *Journal of Consulting and Clinical Psychology, 52,* 940–945.

Steinberg, L., Dornbusch, S. M., & Brown, B. B. (1992). Ethnic differences in adolescent achievement. *American Psychologist, 47,* 723–729.

Stine, J. K. (1994). *Twenty years of science in the public interest: A history of the Congressional Science and Engineering Fellowship Program.* Washington, DC: American Association for the Advancement of Science.

Strasburger, V. C. (1995). *Adolescents and the media: Medical and psychological implications.* Newbury Park, CA: Sage.

Straus, M., Gelles, R., & Steinmetz, S. (1980). *Behind closed doors: Violence in the American family.* New York: Anchor Press.

Sugg, N. K., & Inui, T. (1992). Primary care physicians' response to domestic violence: Opening Pandora's box. *Journal of the American Medical Association, 267,* 3157–3160.

Summit, R. C. (1983). The child sexual abuse accommodation syndrome. *Child Abuse and Neglect, 7,* 177–193.

Sweeney, P. D., Anderson, R., & Bailey, S. (1986). Attributional style in depression: A meta-analytic review. *Journal of Personality and Social Psychology, 50,* 974–991.

Szatmari, P., & Nagy, J. (1990). Children of schizophrenic parents: A critical review of issues in prevention. *Journal of Preventive Psychiatry and Allied Disciplines, 4,* 311–327.

Tasker, F. L., & Richards, M. P. M. (1994). Adolescents' attitudes toward marriage and marital prospects after parents' divorce: A review. *Journal of Adolescent Research, 9,* 340–362.

Terr, L. C. (1991). Childhood traumas: An outline and overview. *American Journal of Psychiatry, 148,* 10–20.

Thomas, E. A., & Rickel, A. U. (1995). Teen pregnancy and maladjustment: A study of base rates. *Journal of Community Psychology, 23,* 200–215.

Thomas, E., Rickel, A. U., Butler, C., & Montgomery, E. (1990). Adolescent pregnancy and parenting. *Journal of Primary Prevention, 10*(3), 195–205.

Thomson, E., Hanson, T. L., & McLanahan, S. S. (1994). Family structure and child well-being: Economic resources vs. parental behaviors. *Social Forces, 73*(1), 221–242.

Tinker v. Des Moines Independent School District, 393 U.S. 503 (1969).

Tomes, H., & Rickel, A. U. (1996). Reflections by policy makers on the policy process. In R. P. Lorian, I. Iscoe, P. H. DeLeon, & G. R. Vandenbos (Eds.), *Psychology and public policy* (pp. 325–330). Washington, DC: American Psychological Association.

Trute, B., Sarsfield, P., & Mackenzie, D. A. (1988). Medical response to wife abuse: A survey of physicians' attitudes and practices. *Canadian Journal of Community Mental Health, 7*(2), 61–71.

U.S. Advisory Board on Child Abuse and Neglect. (1995). *A nation's shame: Fatal child abuse and neglect in the United States.* A report of the U.S. Advisory Board on Child Abuse and Neglect. Washington, DC: U.S. Department of Health and Human Services.

U.S. Bureau of the Census. (1994). *Statistical abstract of the United States, 1994* (114th ed.). Washington, DC: Author.

U.S. Bureau of the Census. (1995). *Statistical abstract of the United States, 1995* (115th ed.). Washington, DC: Author.

U.S. Department of Health and Human Services. (1991). *Prevention profile.* Washington, DC: Author.

U.S. Public Health Service. (1993, Febuary/March). *Prevention report.* Washington, DC: U.S. Department of Health and Human Services.

Vanderbilt, G. (1996). *A mother's story.* New York: Knopf.

Van der Kolk, B. A. (Ed.). (1987). *Psychological trauma.* Washington, DC: American Psychiatric Press.

Vandeven, A. M., & Newberger, E. H. (1994). Child abuse. *Annual Review of Public Health, 15,* 367–379.

Vissing, Y. M., Straus, M. A., Gelles, R. J., & Harrop, J. W. (1991). Verbal aggression by parents and psychosocial problems of children. *Child Abuse and Neglect, 15*(3), 223–238.

Walker, J. R. (1996). Funding child rearing: Child allowance and parental leave. *The Future of Children, 6*(2), 122–136.

Walker, L. (1993, Fall). *Symposium on violence against women.* University of Hartford, West Hartford, CT.

Wardlaw, G. (1982). *Political terrorism: Theory, tactics and counter-measures.* Cambridge: Cambridge University Press.

Wattleton, F. (1989, July 24–31). Teenage pregnancy: The case for national action. *The Nation,* pp. 138–141.

Webster-Stratton, C., & Hammond, M. (1988). Maternal depression and its relationship to life stress, perceptions of child behavior problems, parenting behaviors, and child conduct problems. *Journal of Abnormal Child Psychology, 16*(3), 299–315.

Weinberg, R. A. (1979). Early childhood education and intervention: Establishing an American tradition. *American Psychologist, 34,* 912–916.

Weiss, H. (1990). Beyond *parens patriae:* Building policies and programs to care for our own and others children. *Children and Youth Services Review, 12,* 269–284.

Wellman, M. M. (1984). The school counselor's role in the communication of suicidal ideation by adolescents. *School Counselor, 32,* 104–109.

Werner, E. E. (1988). Individual differences, universal needs: A thirty-year study of resilient high-risk infants. *Zero to Three, 8,* 1–5.

Werner, E. E., Bierman, J. M., & French, F. E. (1971). *The children of Kauai.* Honolulu: University of Hawaii Press.

Werner, E. E., & Smith, R. S. (1992). *Overcoming the odds: High risk children from birth to adulthood.* Ithaca: Cornell University Press.

Westinghouse Learning Corporation, Ohio University. (1969). *The impact of Head Start: An evaluation of the effects of Head Start on children's cognitive and affective development.* Washington, DC: U.S. Office of Economic Opportunity.

Westman, J. C. (1979). *Child advocacy.* New York: Free Press.

Whitbeck, L. B., Hoyt, D. R., Simons, R. L., Conger, R. D., Elder, G. H., Lorenz, F. O., & Huck, S. (1992). Intergenerational continuity of parental rejection and depressed affect. *Journal of Personality and Social Psychology, 63,* 1036–1045.

Whitbeck, L. B., Simons, R. L., & Conger, R. D. (1991). The effects of early family relationships on contemporary relationships and assistance patterns between adult children and their parents. *Journal of Gerontology, 46,* 330–337.

Whitbeck, L. B., Simons, R. L., Conger, R. D., & Lorenz, F. O. (1989). Value socialization and peer group affiliation among early adolescents. *Journal of Early Adolescents, 9,* 436–453.

Widom, C. S. (1989a). The cycle of violence. *Science, 244,* 160–166.

Widom, C. S. (1989b). Does violence beget violence? A critical examination of the literature. *Psychological Bulletin, 1,* 3–28.

Wiehe, V. R. (1992). Abusive and nonabusive parents: How they were parented. *Journal of Social Services Research, 15,* 81–93.

Wolfe, D. A. (1993). Prevention of child neglect: Emerging issues. *Criminal Justice and Behavior, 20,* 90–111.

Wolff, M., & Stein, A. (1966). *Factors influencing the recruitment of children into the Head Start Program, summer 1965: A case study of six centers in New York City (Study II).* New York: Yeshiva University.

Zahner, G. E., Pawelkiewicz, W., DeFrancesco, J. J., & Adnopoz, J. (1992). Children's mental health service needs and utilization patterns in an urban community: An epidemiological assessment. *Journal of the American Academy of Child and Adolescent Psychiatry, 31,* 951–960.

Zelnik, M., Kantner, J., & Ford, K. (1982). *Adolescent pathways to pregnancy.* Beverly Hills, CA: Sage.

Zierler, S., Feingold, L., Laufer, D., Velentgas, P., Krantrowitz-Gordon, I., & Mayer, K. (1991). Adult survivors of childhood sexual abuse and subsequent risk of HIV infection. *American Journal of Public Health, 81,* 572–575.

Zigler, E. (1994, September). *The status of day care in America.* Lecture given at Bush Center for Child Development and Social Policy, Yale University, New Haven, CT.

Zigler, E., & Finn-Stevenson, M. (1996). Funding child care and public education. *The Future of Children, 6*(2), 104–121.

Zigler, E., & Gordon, E. (1982). *Day care.* Boston: Auburn House.

Zigler, E., & Muenchow, S. (1992). *Head Start: The inside story of America's most successful educational experiment.* New York: Basic Books.

Zonger, C. E. (1977). The self concept of pregnant adolescent girls. *Adolescence, 12*(48), 477–488.

Zucker, G. S., & Weiner, B. (1993). Conservatism and perceptions of poverty: An attributional analysis. *Journal of Applied Social Psychology, 23,* 925–943.

Zuravin, S. J. (1989). *Fertility and contraception among low-income child abusing mothers in Baltimore, MD, 1984–1985.* Archived dataset, National Data Archive on Child Abuse and Neglect, Cornell University, Ithaca, NY.

Zuravin, S. J., & DiBlasio, F. A. (1992). Child-neglecting adolescent mothers: How do they differ from their nonmaltreating counterparts? *Journal of Interpersonal Violence, 7,* 471–489.

Index

About the Authors

Annette U. Rickel, PhD, has been a professor of psychology at Wayne State University in Detroit, Michigan for several years and most recently is a clinical professor of psychiatry at Georgetown University Medical Center. She was an American Psychological Association (APA) Senior Congressional Science Fellow from 1992 to 1994 and worked on health policy for Senator Donald W. Riegle, Jr., as well as served on President Clinton's Task Force for National Health Care Reform. Dr. Rickel received her PhD from the University of Michigan and is a Fellow and past president of the APA's Society for Community Research and Action. In addition, she was an American Council on Education Fellow and was a resident at Princeton and Rutgers Universities. Her research and clinical interests have focused on identification and intervention with high-risk populations. She has authored or coauthored four books and numerous research articles. Dr. Rickel serves on the Board of Directors of Children's Center and the Family Life Education Council and is a consulting editor for several scientific journals.

Evvie Becker, PhD, assistant professor of psychology at the University of Connecticut, was a 1992–1993 Congressional Science Fellow sponsored by the APA, working for Senator Christopher J. Dodd in his capacity as chairman of the Senate Labor Subcommittee on Children. Dr. Becker was also a Fellow at Harvard University and Boston Children's Hospital, funded by a National Research Service Award for family violence research, and a Psychology Fellow in Pediatrics at Harbor-UCLA Medical Center. Dr. Becker serves on the Board of Directors for the Connecticut Children's Law Center, was a member of the APA's ad hoc Committee on Legal and Ethical Issues in the Treatment of Interpersonal Violence, and served on the APA's Committee on Legal Issues from 1994 to 1996. Prior to receiving her doctorate from the University of Connecticut in 1991, she was a Public Information Officer for the National Aeronautics and Space Administration and received a NASA Special Achievement Award in 1985.